Women and Work

Born in Colombo, Ceylon, Sheila Lewenhak has been a world traveller all her life, visiting North, South and Central America, the USSR, Japan and most European countries. She gained her PhD at the London School of Economics in 1971.

As well as lecturing at the Universities of Durham, London and Strathclyde, she has written an outline history, *Women and Trade Unions* (1977) on British women's trade unionism and papers on aspects of women's work and trade unionism for Universities and Labour History Societies, national and international. Earlier she wrote several economic and social history books for children. She is currently doing research on the European Investment Bank's policies on employment of women and men and technological development.

Sheila Lewenhak

WOMEN and WORK

Consultant editor: Heather Gordon Cremonesi

If woman had not been created there would have been no
sun and no moon, no agriculture and no fire.

Arab saying

St. Martin's Press
New York

© Sheila Lewenhak 1980

All rights reserved. For information, write:
St. Martin's Press, Inc., 175 Fifth Avenue, New York, NY 10010
Printed in Great Britain
First published in the United States of America in 1980

ISBN 0–312–88778–7

Library of Congress Cataloging in Publication Data

Lewenhak, Sheila.
Women and work.

Includes bibliographical references.
1. Women—Economic conditions—History.   2. Division of labor—History.   3. Women—Employment—History.   I. Title.
HQ1122.L48   1980   305.4'3   80–16906
ISBN 0–312–88778–7

Contents

List of Tables

Foreword

The historiographical model for this book is a solution to the daunting problems involved in introducing and committing large areas of history to an ignoring collective memory. The model had to be a vehicle to give shape, form and logic to a massive body of information which could force women's history to penetrate and be accepted by a somewhat hesitant 'history' establishment. We still teach and learn a type of traditional history which not only ignores the activities of the female half of humanity (history's heroines excepted) but also disendows half of humanity by precluding even vicarious gender-identification. The historiographical model for the writing of women's history needs to incorporate women into a main body of history and to endow women with an historical and a present identity.

Women have worked, constantly, continuously, always and everywhere, in every type of society in every part of the world since the beginning of human time. Nonetheless the easy availability today of massive evidence to statisticians, sociologists, historians, politicians and paymasters, as well as to the man in the street, television viewer or housewife, persists in failing to dislodge the obviousness of this face, from the oblivion to which social prejudices and concomitant historical omissiveness have relegated it. It is society's collective apperceptiveness which is divided.

Thus, although we accept the obvious fact that women are workers, the human image evoked by the word 'worker' remains stereotypically masculine; the power and prevalence of traditional prejudices can demonstrably so divide a society's collective apperceptiveness. The representation of obvious, objective, commonplace fact and truths has not been the motivating force of traditional historiography (loosely labelled 'history'); historians have avoided stating, valuing and revaluing the historically obvious facts about women.

Traditionally history has been selective about what it represents to suit the values prevailing in the historian's society. The Napoleonic Wars are represented with significant historical differences by French, Russian and English historians and reflect divergent interests and values to each of them. The greater mass of historiography has traditionally held up a polishing, moralizing mirror to current values. Indeed a good deal of new historiography perpetuates this tradition under the guise of radical reform. Black history, proletarian history, Jewish history, US immigrant group history have all performed the admirable task of rescuing minority historical facts from the historical oblivion to which patrician, anti-semitic, WASP, heroic historians had previously relegated them and have indeed endowed these omitted minorities with the social dignity and concomitant economic esteem that only history can induce by its power to mould, remould and condition a society's collective apperception. Yet all minority historiography has been produced by the rise of its subjects to social significance with economic clout. The function it has served is to provide acceptability, respect and permanence by forcing a family tree of historical validity onto a persistently prejudiced, neglectful society's collective apperceptive value scale. It is only after the genuine reforms in society are under way that historiographers feel able to reform history. Once the proletariat had threatened the old order and claimed power, the proletarian historians provided them with a distinguished service record. Now the proletariat is in, and is regarded as an indisputably historical fact.

The same great efforts must be made for women, who are not – obviously – a minority group as they are often called, but constitute half of humanity. The task is therefore not to provide women with acceptability and respect by grafting them onto a pre-existing body of historical fact, as 'minority' history has done. A body of historical fact which rigorously excludes half of humanity must itself be replaced. The historiographical model for women's history required a radical revision of the standards by which historians judge what is historically significant, what is worthy of mention. The model undertakes this more fundamental fusion of women's history as majority history with establishment historiography. It is necessarily multi-disciplinary, more elaborately deductive than traditional historiography, and thematic in its approach to chronology. The tasks ahead are sizeable. Sheila Lewenhak's *Women and Work* is a remarkable stride in the right historical direction.

HEATHER GORDON CREMONESI

Introduction and Acknowledgements

In modern advanced technological societies women's work on a mass scale and their individual expertise are regarded as startlingly new. Yet women's work and skills are old, as old as humankind. The importance of women's work in the Stone Ages has been generally recognized by many of those who have studied the subject. Women's contributions to early technical development have received some acknowledgement in their written works. However, most of the history we read has been written only in the last 6000 years when other technologies and social forms were developing. It therefore reflects the roles of women in these civilizations. It is difficult to grasp that this testimony from so brief a part of the half million or so years of human evolution, stands on its head the history of women's work. Other kinds of evidence seem to indicate that during most of human existence the main responsibility for providing a livelihood for families rested on women, the reverse of the allocation of work roles in most industrialized nations today. By trying to trace developments in women's work and their interaction with women's social status, as technologies and social organization have changed, this short survey attempts to bridge this historical gap and to show that the economic eclipse of women has been relatively short. Their widespread inferiority today is a phase in the changing pattern of technological and economic history.

As might be expected the balance of power between the sexes seems to have see-sawed back and forth; in the last 8000 years it has been changing in favour of men and to the detriment of women. Six thousand years before the birth of Christ seems remote if one counts time by clocks and calendars, but it is much nearer when one calculates by the generation clock. For, counting four or four and a half generations per century, only about eighty-five sets of parents stand between each one of us and the birth of Christ, and only two hundred and four odd between us and the late Stone Age and the dawn of the Iron Age.

Not only are societies of gatherers and hunters much nearer, genealogically and chronologically, to industrial civilization than one might suppose, they still exist in some countries, as do all the intervening stages of civilization between the first and the most recent. The rate of development from one stage to the next varies from place to place. This uneven rate of development means that when we talk of the Stone Age, we are speaking of the distant past for some places but, for others, of the immediate present. When we discuss hoe farmers, we are not just referring to the sixth millennium BC, but to people in living communities in the twentieth century AD. The straightforward chronology of history which applies in a small, defined area cannot be followed when we are looking at world cultures. The confusion that may arise over dates and tenses is smoothed out so long as readers remember that the past for them is also the present for others.

The evidence about human beings' past ways of life, about the structure of their societies and the organization of their work has come from four main sources: the findings of archaeologists; written records of old communities; observations of travellers who came from countries with written languages and who were thus able to record their impressions; and the actual daily lives of people who at this present time, in the late twentieth century, are using tools and artefacts which archaeologists tell us were in use hundreds of thousands of years ago, people whom anthropologists and sociologists have been studying minutely since the mid-nineteenth century. When we find people making and using tools and producing clothes and containers today which are the same as those in use a hundred thousand years ago, and if such people have lived quite undisturbed by outside influences, we can assume, unless there is evidence to the contrary, that their social structures, too, have been altering very slowly.

Early explorers from Europe and North Africa were sometimes simple note-takers who made plain and meticulous records of the practices they found. They came across matriarchal societies in which women were so valuable on account of their knowledge and skills that they were protected and backed by the combined force of their maternal relatives, especially older women. Latter-day historians and even some anthropologists have, however, often ignored these facts and findings, partly because of their own ingrained ideas on the relationship between the sexes, and partly because the compartmentalization of disciplines has rendered some historians apparently unaware of what anthropologists and explorers have discovered. They have written as though men had been the pivots of almost all human societies from time immemorial.

Yet there is no doubt Stone Age women made tools as many observers have seen them doing so. There is no question about their knowledge of chemistry, because in some societies they not only use it, but guard it as a feminine mystery. The only uncertainty at this distance of time is over how far they have been innovators. Assumptions about women as technical originators in prehistory are no less and no more soundly based than those about men. Just because the initiative in invention in the last six or seven thousand years is recorded as having lain largely with men, we cannot say that women did not develop the tools and processes of which they already had a monopoly by that time – in other words, we cannot say that they did not invent pottery, scrapers, some kinds of knives, digging sticks and hoes – any more than we can claim that men did not first develop the use of metals, for the kinds of evidence are the same in both cases. Using the four sources of evidence mentioned we find good reason to believe that women originated some of the technical processes which are the bases of the higher living standards so many people now enjoy. We see again and again in living communities using very early technologies that women have social supremacy based on their economic supremacy. Men's work in many hunter-gatherer and early farming communities seems to be important, but less essential.

Clearly in human history there has not been an unchanging delimitation of work functions on sex lines. In the earliest kinds of societies, travellers, conquerors, settlers, archaeologists and anthropologists have all recorded that the principle of existence was do-it-yourself. With survival as the first aim, every child, girl or boy, was trained to be self-sufficient, to live off a given territory. But the climate changed and food supplies at an existing level of technology were not constant. So people evolved technologies and demarcations of work between women and men and a social organization that best enabled them to live in the given circumstances. What was 'women's work' at one stage of history might be 'men's work' at the next. The evolution of techniques, and work itself, have not been all joyless. Self-expression and enjoyment, too, such as making music and decorations, led to the development of new kinds of work. In Stone Age societies everywhere to this day we have illustrations of the immense creativity, strength and dexterity of women. And even in the most mechanized countries where women are emerging from the depression of the last 5000 years, something of this ancient legacy remains.

Mere work and skill in locating food sources and the means of exploiting them have not been enough in Stone Age peoples' minds to ensure supplies. Ritual supplication to a pantheon of deities was essential. Stone Age women were in many cases the chief custodians of these rituals. Sometimes they shared this responsibility with men; sometimes they performed the rites on their own, entreating goddesses and gods to supply water and make the earth fruitful.

Men were required to take on most but not all of the jobs of defence and fighting when need arose; to take most of the responsibility for long-distance hunting and fishing (although this did not apply everywhere) and fulfil women's sexual needs. In so doing, of course, they fulfilled their own. In these female-dominated societies, they were the suitors who had to plead and work for the right to acceptance in the matriarchy. They had to attract women's favourable attentions, instead of it being the other way round. For much of human existence, the connection between sex and procreation was not understood. In some communities of gatherers and hunters, it is still not understood. Birth was often an entirely feminine mystery and another source of women's high status.

Some modern writers on the history of women bemoan the harshness of women's lives. It is true that biology, that women's role as mothers, does make the life of a woman hard. But men have also endured hardships. They too were slaves and serfs. In wars and in moments of danger like shipwrecks, precisely because they did not bear children, they have been regarded as the more expendable sex. Hence this book is less of a lament about women's undoubted sufferings than a celebration of their skills and creativity and of their fight back against the economic and social inferiority thrust on them.

This book is not a list of different jobs done by women, but attempts to trace the reasons for changes in women's work as well as a description of it. By 'work' we mean all the multifarious processes of getting a livelihood, i.e. of obtaining food, shelter and warmth necessary for human survival.

The terms used have been those in most common use, for example *Eskimo* not *Inuit*, the name these people have for themselves. However, there is one major exception. Instead of the European name *Bushmen*, for one of the most ancient races in the world, I have used the name these South African people give themselves and called them the San people. Also I have employed the old distinctive terms for married and unmarried women, partly because in recent times it has all too often been assumed that married women did no work outside their homes.

Reference has been made to property laws affecting women, but no attempt has been made to go into these in detail, for the subject is so complex that it would require a book on its own to trace the most crucial changes.

Those used to dealing with the statistics of women's employment will be aware of the inadequacy of the available figures. This is particularly the case when one is trying to make some sort of international comparison. For the non-expert it should be pointed out that filling in census forms depends on the level of literacy and social attitudes of individuals. Because of men's greater overall literacy and social superiority in historic times, and sometimes because a woman's workload is greater than that of a man so that she has less time, men have tended to be the fillers-in of forms. In many subsistence economies men tend to ignore the fact that women relatives do a great deal – sometimes most of the jobs on which the family's livelihood depends. They tend to describe a wife not as a farmer and manufacturer of cloth, clothing, shelter, but as a 'housewife'. A daughter doing similar work tends to be entered on forms as merely 'daughter'. In industrialized societies the easiest answer on a woman combining part-time paid work with the work of a housewife is that she is a housewife and no more. Also homeworkers may have an interest in not declaring taxable earnings, so that sometimes they conceal their work. In more modern times employers may want to avoid social security payments and so do not admit to employing part-time women workers or homeworkers.

Governments as well as individuals sometimes ignore unpaid family helpers, however great their contribution to the economy.

For example in its returns to the International Labour Organization in 1974 on women and men economically active, Algeria listed only 12,702 women family agricultural workers, but added in a footnote that there were besides 1,200,000 unpaid women family workers.*

The member states of the International Labour Office use their own categories of workers which may not be those of all other members. Standards of international classification are being ever more widely adopted, nonetheless countries still have difficulties in defining work done by their people. Because of this comparisons with numbers of workers in other countries may be impossible. Similarly, earnings statistics are based on averages which hide the range of pay and rates for different grades of work.

Such a survey means selection of material on the part of the author who is deeply aware of how much has had to be omitted because of limitations of space in a book of this length. It also depends on the work of many other people, on all those who, over the centuries, noted the facts of women's work and the economic and social settings in which it was carried on, in particular Otis Tufton Mason's pioneer study, *Woman's Share in Primitive Culture* and Robert Briffault's *The Mothers* in which he has so marvellously collated the sources of evidence of women's role in early cultures. My immense debts to them are duly acknowledged in the footnotes.

I should also like to express gratitude to library staffs without whose help it would have been impossible to amass the material, among them the Mitchell Library, Glasgow, the Birmingham Central City Library, especially the Social Sciences and Science and Technology Departments, the libraries of the London office

* International Labour Office 1974 Yearbook of Labour Statistics, Table 2B, 142–3; the official figure given for all female agricultural workers is 23,150; p. 236n.
For comments on this failure to include female family workers in statistics of workers see:
Jerzy Berent, *International Lab. Rev.*, vol. 101, No. 2, Feb. 1970, 182, n. 2.
Juan C. Elizaga, 'The Participation of Women in the Labour Force of Latin America', ILO *Women Workers and Society*, 129, 139.
K. A. Patel, ILO *Labour Education*, 'Women's Studies', No. 31, June 1976, 32.
Guy Standing, ILO Bull., *Women at Work*, No. 1, Autumn 1977, 4–5.

of the International Labour Organization, the University of London, the Museum of Mankind, the British Library, the Fawcett Library, the libraries of the United States Embassy and Indian High Commission in London, and the Hillingdon Central Library.

I should also like to record my thanks to Helen Fraser of Fontana Paperbacks, and to Heather Gordon Cremonesi, for their constructive and helpful criticisms; to Dr Genevieve Frank, Head of the International Educational Materials Exchange at the International Institute for Labour Studies in Geneva, the British Anti-Slavery Society, Mrs Krishna Swami of the Commonwealth Secretariat in London and Mr B. A. Pockney, Head of the Department of Linguistics and International Studies at the University of Surrey, for providing very useful information and to my friends Gerde Chambers, Jenny Daems and Janine Tiffon; and above all to H. K. Lewenhak, my husband, who put equality into practice, not only offering encouragement but rating the work much ahead of domestic comfort and accepting willingly the work of reading and criticizing many drafts when he himself was often under extreme pressure of work.

Thanks are also due to Sundial Office Services Ltd, and the Uxbridge Photo Printing Service Ltd, both all-female firms, and to Mrs J. Palmer of the Broadstairs family firm, the Swift Typing and Duplicating Service Ltd, for their work on Tables and on copying the MS.

My hope is that the book may prove to be a small contribution towards restoring omissions on the importance of women's work in much historical writing, since until these are repaired no true historical perspective can be reached of the achievements of both men and women.

Table 1 Time scale of technological change

Climate	Year approx.	Technological Change
	AD 1980	Socialism — National independence movements / Industrial capitalism
		— Merchant capitalism
	1000	Feudalism in Europe and West Africa
	0	Development of mass use of slaves
	BC 1000	Iron Age starts. Steel and Brass working. End of New Stone age
	2000	— Silver extracted from Galem
		— Bronze
	3000	
		— Melting & casting metal & New Stone age.
	4000	
		— Gold
	5000	— Slavery
		— Copper
	6000	
	7000	
	8000	Pottery making
	9000	Regular farming: Natufians at Hoth & Belt caves, Caucasus
Fourth Ice Age	10,000	Start of Middle Stone age
	11,000	Migration from North Asia
	12,000	via Bering Straits to North America
	13,000	
	20,000	— Needles
	25,000	— Semi-lunar knife
	50,000	
	100,000	
Third Ice Age		— Hoes
	200,000	— Digging sticks
	300,000	Migrations from Africa
Second Ice Age	400,000	
		Peking fire-users.
	500,000	— Makers of stone Scrapers Choppers
First Ice Age	600,000	— Australopithecus.
	1,000,000	Start of human cultures in Europe
	2,000,000	Stone tools, Africa. for cutting, Digging, Scraping.
	12,000,000	— Proconsul
	25,000,000	Dryopithecus

Right-margin brackets (top to bottom):
- Plough and Wheel
- Hoe culture / Shifting cultivation
- Nomadic herding
- Pottery, Weaving.
- Food gatherers, Fishers, Hunters, Stone tools, Domestication of animals

Chapter 1

HUNTERS AND GATHERERS

Xhooxham stretched as the sun touched her and eased her shoulders and neck. She had risen at dawn, starting the day's work by collecting firewood from round about the camp. She had raked the embers of last night's fire in the cooking hearth of three stones set on the ground. There was no fire left, so she made more by twirling a hard stick in a notch cut with a stone knife in a softwood stick until the sparks flew and caught a bunch of dry grass she had ready. She flicked it into the cooking place, covered it with dry leaves and blew on it until the wood caught fire. It was a widespread means of making fire among Stone Age peoples, an elaboration of the method of rubbing two sticks together or striking two flints against each other. Women made fire more than men; many peoples believed that they had received the gift of fire from a deity or that a goddess first provided fire.[1]

Xhooxham was a young woman of the San people, the race, it is thought, who were the common ancestors of many of us, of the same blood group as the Ainu of Japan and the Aborigines of Australia, people who survived through extreme climactic changes including Ice Ages. San people like Xhooxham were in Africa 12,000 to 10,000 years ago when the land north of the Mediterranean was covered with ice and Africa wet and rainy.[2] We have a picture of them living in several places in Africa, among them the area we know as the Kalahari Desert, from a number of explorers and anthropologists, for instance David Livingstone in the mid-nineteenth century, followed by G. W. Stow and others, as they were before other civilizations, both black and white, overwhelmed them.

For Xhooxham's people, the morning meal did not require much work as it was just last night's left-overs. As they finished, the men and some of the women started to prepare for hunting. They set to work sharpening their spears and arrow heads which they dipped in poison they made themselves.

Women like herself with a small child to breast-feed, and also
the older women, looked to their digging sticks. Whatever the
implement, each of them made it serviceable unaided, whether it
was tuning a bow, sharpening an arrow or spear-head, a digging
stick or an axe. Each time she handled her axe, Xhooxham remembered, for however brief a flash, how she had crouched at the base
of a cliff, searching for the right shape of stone, then, while the
sunlight was at its strongest, chipping at it for long, hot hours
with another stone, fining the edge. When it was tapered to a thin
edge, she used it to slice into a piece of hard wood in which she
set the head, wedging it tight. She had made her mallet and spear-
head in the same way. They all used appropriately shaped stones
to scrape and plane these cutting edges which were used to make
bows and arrows, to skin beasts and to scrape fat and tissue from
their hides. But women especially had extended this technology,
cutting out sinew for thread and cutting grasses and branches with
which to build their huts.[3]

Xhooxham wore a skin garment, part of which was a bag in
which to place the food she collected and hunted. She had
given her baby son the breast and he was contented. She placed
him in his leather bag which she slung over her right shoulder,
so that he rested on her left hip. Then she strolled off into the
plain, chatting desultorily with the rest as they did early in the
day.

For long now she had known every stick, stone, bush and tree
in her land, every cliff and rock, the way they changed in the brief
rainy season that had just ended and in the long, hot days that
stretched ahead. Like all San people she had been spending her
days working at the search for food since she could walk. Every
girl knew that the main responsibility for providing food was hers.
The men fished and hunted, but they did little gathering.

When you hunted big game, you had to move fast to cover a
wide territory. But searching after small game, insects, vegetables
and fruit, women and children walked slowly, their eyes ranging
over the ground, alert for the tracks of iguana or tortoises or the
trails of ants. They listened for bees to lead them to their honey.
They were on the look-out for every tiny leaf that indicated wild
melon or cucumber, yams or nuts buried in the sand. When
Xhooxham found a root, she put her baby down and set to work,
stabbing the ground with her pointed stick to break up the hard

surface, then crouching and scooping sand and earth with her hands, working furiously like a dog digging a hole, but always carefully so as not to damage the root, going four feet, sometimes six below the surface. The sweat poured off her as the sun rose. If she dug out an iguana from its burrow, or came upon a snake, she would stun it with a quick blow from her digging stick, then kill it. Everything she found went into her bag,[4] which weighed ever more heavily as the day wore on.

The women played a game about their work of foraging further and further afield as the ground round a camp site dried out, or was worked out, but never to the point of exhaustion. They sang a song:

> I went into the plain to look for melons,
> And on the way, what do you think I saw?
> I saw a blue wildebeest,
> But the blue wildebeest just flicked his heels at me
> And ran away.

They went on verse after verse, imitating the movements of the animals they met as they searched over the desert.[5]

Xhooxham rested for a little in the shade of a bush. She fed her baby when it woke and munched some nuts and melon, and then started on another quest. She had to collect water while it was still near the surface of the sand. That was why she took with her a net in which there were empty ostrich shells. They had bottle necks of black wax fitted to them and some had fine black patterns etched on them by the older folk who spent more time at the camp. She found a place in a circle of bushes whose shade slowed down the rate at which the ground dried out. There was grass and even a few reeds. Xhooxham cut a stick and took the pith out of it so that it became a tube. She did the same with a reed and picked a tuft of grass. She made a hole in the sand as deep as she could reach, inserted the hollow stick and began to suck. The muscles and veins on her neck began to swell and bulge, but drop by drop the water rose into her mouth, trickled along the reed, through the filter of grass and into a waiting ostrich shell. As soon as one shell was filled, she plugged it with grass.[6]

Her first job back at the camp, after depositing the food she had gathered out of reach of ants, and her baby on the ground, was to dig a hole deep enough in the sand to be in the moist layer and wide enough to hold all the shells which she then covered over again with damp sand. Each camp site centred on a water hole or a store of these eggs. As the earth dried out, the deeper you had to dig to reach the water. It was a job men did too. Here in the Kalahari Desert, life depended on water.

If Xhooxham had not had her egg-shells to carry, on her way back she would have collected wood for her hearth. Once she had deposited her three loads, child, water and food, she went to gather some and got her hearth fire going. Then she went to her hut for her pestle and mortar of iron wood and settled to pounding grasses, seeds, including melon seeds, and nuts to make meal. She scraped water into a shell from the water hole that was fast drying out to mix with it to make a dough. Next, using her stone knife, she skinned her iguana, making a slit at its throat, loosening the skin on the head and feet and ripping it off in one piece over its head. She checked the fire in her oven-place, shaped the dough into flat cakes and put them on the stones to bake. She hung the iguana on a stick to roast. She then pounded some dried meat and mixed it with water in a little clay pot which she herself had moulded and gave it to her great-aunt who had once been the mother of the family. Now old, the great-aunt spent her days lying at the camp, trying to keep cool by scooping damp sand over herself. The family showed their respect and affection for her by feeding her and caring for her. Next Xhooxham sifted her ants through a loosely woven reed mat, wrapped them in leaves and put them to roast on the stones.[7]

POTS AND CONTAINERS

Cooking rested upon another group of processes and manufactures carried on by women. Where seed-bearing grass grew, the seed had first to be extracted. One method was to bring the grass to camp or village and tap, or, as we should say, thresh it so that the seeds fell straight into the mortar bowl ready for crushing. Or, they were beaten out as the grass was gathered, a technique evolved for instance by the Pannamint women of Death Valley in California. Late nineteenth-century European Americans saw them hold the heads over small funnel-shaped baskets with one hand, and beat them with a sort of wicker-work tennis racket with the other. James Ramsey travelling in Scotland in the eighteenth century saw women had developed the process so that grain was 'dressed, winnowed, ground and baked' within an hour after reaping from the ground.[8]

Next seeds, ants, roots and all the other items used to make meal had to be pounded up. The obvious way was to follow the example of the apes or squirrels in dealing with nuts, and bang them with a stone. Women refined the process. Less was lost, and small stuff like seeds could in any case only be successfully dealt with in an enclosed space. They selected bits of hard wood from trees that had fallen or been chopped down and used a stone to chip out a hollow in the centre of one of these to make a bowl. Or they chose stones already hollowed by nature and so requiring less work, but light enough to carry around when they moved camp. North American women found holes in flat rocks that bordered streams and used those as mortars or pounding bowls. They also discovered that a smooth stone or piece of hard wood made pounding easier than a roughly shaped piece. So they chipped and honed pestles.

In cooking, their way of keeping foodstuffs like locusts together is to wrap them in leaves. But there are parts of the world where there are few leaves, and none at all at certain seasons. Stone Age woman discovered that soapstone, potstone or steatite could withstand heat without cracking. If they hollowed it and put water in it, and then dropped in stones heated in their hearths, the water became hot. A whole system of cooking developed from this. Alternatively these stone pots could be placed directly on hearths. Then again women lined baskets with pitch to make them waterproof or hardened leather in water to make pots. Where all these materials were available a single woman might make use of all these different processes.[9]

The men also prepared food. They skinned, jointed and roasted the game or fish they brought in, but women did most of the cooking since they collected most of the foodstuffs.

WEAVING

Gathering and hunting depended on having containers not only to cook in but also in which to carry home food and to sieve it as Xhooxham sieved her ants. These might be of leather, but they were also woven from whatever materials were available. As well as reeds and other plants like vines, people used grass, bark, bast, roots and strips of skin. Their teachers, as with the pestle and mortar, were birds, fish and animals. The twining of vines round tree trunks inspired crochet. New Guinea women made nets with uniform meshes, the fibres knotted at the interstices using our reef knot or square knot.

No early Stone Age person ever made anything half so complicated as a weaver bird's nest. But they learned the principle of making a base with ribs springing from it and the threading of filaments over and under them, as in darning. Women found they could carry on the process flat on the ground to make mats for sieves, beds, or roofs for their shelters. They went from simple utilitarian articles to patterned ones by letting each woof strip overlap two or more of the warp, or by using 2-ply weft.

Where natural materials were not ready-made for use, they made their own filaments. Polynesian women and all those living on the American Pacific coast from Washington State to the Arctic north of British Columbia learned to use the fact that tree trunks grow in layers. By beating a log at a particular season the *outer* layer or rings could be made to peel off, providing large shavings of a uniform thickness. These they cut into ribbons.

Some Amerindian women chose fresh shoots and broke off the tender tips. They bit one end so that the wand started to split into three nearly equal parts. They split pith and less flexible tissue from the inner surface, making flat strips to use as weft or to whip coils together. Samoan women also used straw and leaves. They began to weave a mat starting at one corner using small pieces and wove diagonally working with ever larger pieces until they reached the middle. They then continued across to the other corner, decreasing the size accordingly. By leaving the ends of strands loose Polynesians and Maoris made not only fringes, but produced cloth with a raised pile.[10]

CLOTH-MAKING

There was another use for bark where game, and consequently leather, was scarce. Either bark fibres or whole rounds of bark were used to make cloth. All over Oceania, in equatorial Africa, all over Central America and south at least as far as the Tropic of Capricorn, people obtained material by beating out the *inner* bark of trees. Polynesian women signalled to one another over long distances by their beating; it was one of the characteristic sounds of the Pacific Islands. They evolved a variety of tools for this job: clubs and other beaters, containers for water and fluids to splash on the bark to make it supple. In some of these places, men as well as women had this skill. But in others, Hawaii for instance, it was wholly women's work. It was there that they made the finest of bark cloths, a lace-like fabric. Polynesian women chiefs took great pride in producing paper-thin material. Some of the pieces they beat out were huge, up to 40 feet long by 10 feet wide.[11] Their fine fabrics were the ultimate development of beaten cloth production.

But weavers using strands went much further. They progressed from mats and baskets which included fishtraps to making their woven containers watertight. Shoshone and Apache women dipped their baskets in hot pitch to make unbreakable water bottles, much lighter and more durable than those of skin or pottery. Other North American Indians packed the spaces between the fibres with grass or thin splints to make a kind of caulking.

Here and there, men wove as well as women, particularly in Central and South America. Often each sex specialized in different fabrics and articles. Amerindian and Hawaiian men made their own ceremonial gear, war bonnets and, in Hawaii, magnificent woven feather cloaks. Or, while Carib Indian men twisted fibres into ropes and lines, women used them to make cloth. However, weaving, to a greater extent than beating out bark cloth, was a female speciality, a monopoly in some places. More commonly men wove baskets, mats and traps.[12]

Women everywhere using fibres noticed that these had different colours and with these they began to weave patterns. Some American Indian women for instance used year-old willow and aromatic sumac of light wood colours with black yucca root and the long black horns of the pods on the unicorn plant.

At the same time they developed the loom. Women in Bakah in Palestine foreshadowed it when they stretched warp threads on the ground tying them to pegs driven into the earth. As they passed the weft threads in and out, they pressed them down with rough wooden combs. The simple vertical square frame spread all over the world. Women carried their frames with them from one camp site to another, for these were precious, cherished possessions.

The overwhelming preponderance, a downright feminine monopoly in some places, of women in basketry, netting and weaving points to their having been early mathematicians. Making a basket demands much mental effort, for it is constructed by means of an intricate series of numbers. The patterns of Stone Age women show that they could count at least to ten, for on their counting depended the development of uniform designs. The end result was geometry, shown in regular zigzags using triangles and going on to squares, and, much more difficult, cycloidal curves. They progressed from abstract patterns to representations of their universe of birds, beasts, clouds and people. To do this they formalized them and then further simplified these conventionalized forms into sophisticated forms copied in carved totems, Oriental carpets, in modern fabrics and lace.[13] Women were as much creative artists as the men who traced figures in yellow ochre and other pigments on cliffs and on the walls of caves.

Weaving gave rise to another art, spinning, a job done in Stone Age times in southern lands by women and men alike. Australian aboriginals used their own hair. Polynesian women and men braided sennit (cords) from cocoa fibre, using it in place of nails and screws for boat building. Women in Africa, Sicily and Alaska twisted fibres in their fingers, two working together, one twirling, the other holding taut and coiling the finished twine. The most widely used method was to hold fibres in one hand and twist with the other. An alternative technique, a later development was to fasten a bunch of fibres to a stick, its lower end resting in a hole in a rock; or it was rotated down the thigh. From this developed the spindle hanging free with a hook on to which fibres could be fastened – as in many Egyptian, Greek and Roman paintings. In desert country there were few sticks: in ancient Palestine, for example, instead of attaching the fibres to a stick, women attached them to a stone drawing them away and twisting them simultaneously. Here was the spindle whorl.[14]

The same process was used in making fibres of varying thicknesses up to that of rope, vegetable fibres being plaited or twisted, the person twisting while walking backwards pulling out the strands until the desired length was reached. The trailers of vines, bast and hemp were used in rope-making, while in arctic conditions women made ropes of animal intestines or leather strips.

CHEMISTRY

Because of their role as gatherers of plants, women acquired a specialized knowledge of the uses of plant juices to make colouring matter and dyes. But spinning and weaving further encouraged this science. They found that thread made from fibres or indeed whole pieces of cloth could be dyed a uniform colour. This process and the fixing of dyes was entirely women's work and therefore presumably women's invention. Navajo Indian women produced black by boiling sumac leaves and stems giving, as we now know, tannic acid. They mixed the decoction with baked yellow ochre (iron) and pinon gum to produce a rich blue black. They also made red and blue dyes, and green from a mixture of blue and yellow. To fix their dyes, they used, for example, alum on yellow material and juniper ashes for red. Polynesian women had a similar wide range of pigments including grey from charcoal which they beat into cloth.

To make patterns they ground the dyestuffs in oil in stone mortars and either drew them with cords dipped in fluids or snapped the cords so that the liquid spattered off. Alternatively they drew with bamboo pens and brushes. They used natural objects like stones as die stamps or cut patterns on bamboo strips, sometimes making stamps several feet square to enable them to print over a large area.[15]

This hard exacting work was done with pleasure, the women sometimes carrying on a friendly rivalry. A good piece of finished cloth was a triumph.

POTTERY

Women not men almost everywhere were the sole practitioners, and so we must conclude the originators of a whole artistic and scientific process prompted by the simple need for containers in which to transport food and water – hand-made pottery. The word for 'woman' among some Amerindians is the same as the word for 'potter'.

Stone Age women like Xhooxham who had clay soils available saw lumps of it baked hard in the sun. Children played with it, digging holes in it with their fingers when it was damp. So women started moulding and baking clay into pots and containers. They learnt to use only certain clays. They found that their pots turned out better if clays were cleaned by washing so that stones and other impurities sank to the bottom, thereby discovering specific gravity. The fine clay soil cracked in cooking, but it stood the heat, they found, if it was mixed with sand. The simple process of hand modelling clay vessels gave rise to sculpture, or perhaps it was the other way round, sculpture of animals, birds and people came first. It has also been claimed that the idea of heating kinds of earth, i.e. ores, the basis of the later process of metallurgy, arose from the precedent of firing pottery.

Women found that they could use natural objects to give clay shape, lining gourds with it or building it up round a stone. Finally they found they could plait it, and coil these clay plaits round and round on top of one another, pinching each layer into the one below. Their pinching made marks and produced the idea of decoration. They decorated the clay objects they modelled with the impress of fingers, teeth, plants and woven materials.

Xhooxham had learnt to glaze her clay pots by dipping them in a solution of finest clay, another of women's contributions apparently to the development of chemistry.[16]

MEDICINE

Stone Age women's knowledge of plants and herbs led to their establishing another specialization – medicine. This pre-eminence was noted in the Andaman Islands, among the Kamchatkans, the Eskimo, the American and Mexican Indians. Medicine and pharmacy are wholly women's work among the Araucanians of Chile and in Indonesia, while women medical practitioners predominate in Patagonia, Fiji, New Guinea, the Marquesas group of islands, Tonga and Savage Island. Similarly in the West among ancient German and Scandinavian tribes medicine was a women's monopoly. It remained a recognized women's occupation in Arabia until medieval times and in East Africa until this day. Through observation and accident women found that plants and herbs could not only poison but could also induce oblivion or ecstasy, could deaden pain, cure and heal. Their knowledge was the basis of their monopoly of magic in parts of Africa.[17]

HUNTER GATHERER WOMEN'S STATUS

Xhooxham who handed her aunt food in a clay pot was artisan, scientist, doctor and artist; she was no mere drudge or scullion using utensils that others had made for her by processes Man had invented. She was a primary creative force. Weather and the seasons to some extent dictated how time was allocated to all these different jobs. Making things was a job for bad weather. But to take time off, a Stone Age woman had to be able to store food. The universal method with meat and fish was wind or sun-drying, hanging it up or sometimes just laying it on rocks or the roof of a hut and turning it in order not to let flies get too much of a hold. It was tough, but it was very sustaining.

By the time Xhooxham had prepared a meal it was mid-afternoon and she and the other women were scanning the horizon for their hunters. They started to sing them home:

> The grass in my hand before it was cut
> Cried in the wind for the rain to come:
> All day my heart cried in the sun
> For my hunter come.

The men hearing the song in the clear air, left off hunting and ran and leapt over the sand and scrub to the camp, apparently overcome by longing.[18] Romance and desire were intermingled with practicality. No man had a home by right. He had to earn one with his hunting. For Xhooxham, the centre of existence was her own family. The core of it was the women who gave her, and any child she might have, security. She would never leave the family, the motherhood, and they would never let her go. It was quite otherwise for her brothers. As soon as they were proficient in hunting, fishing and warfare they would be expected to go off to seek acceptance in another motherhood. The matriarch and older women would judge over a certain length of time whether a man's skills were adequate enough to justify his admission. Admission conferred the right to mate with one or two of the girls. But he was there on sufferance; if his behaviour proved displeasing or he did not provide enough food, he would be driven out and have to seek acceptance in another clan.[19]

Trouble was liable to arise when food was scarce. Had not Xhooxham's sister torn down her hut and beaten her hunter with her digging stick when he stayed out in the plain with his male hunting companion, the two of them cooking the game they had caught there and then instead of bringing it in? He was foolish to think the women would not see the smoke of his fire or notice his distended belly. The Pleiades, so the tale went, had cursed one of their hunters who had not brought in game, so that he could not return to camp, but had to shiver out the cold night, thirsty, hungry, alone. They had said to the other men:

> Ye men, do you think that you can compare yourselves to us and be our equals? There now, we defy our own hunter to come home because he has not killed game.[20]

So Xhooxham had a mate, Bauxha. No youth or man was forced on any girl. He had to win her favours. They fulfilled each other's regular sexual needs and some economic needs. Love between woman and man sometimes happened at first sight; more often it grew slowly born of loyalty and common struggle. The greatest love was that between mothers and children.

A mother taught her son, as she did her daughters during their early formative years, some of her multifarious skills. Segregation in the matter of teaching was not rigid, for the men in a camp played with and taught children too. But it was not until puberty that a boy passed out of his mother's hands into those of men.

It was a sociable life. People were always within call, although the ground round a hut was enough to give privacy. As meals became ready they all wandered to each other's hearths for a nibble here and there. They were always ready to lend a helping hand to each other.

Stone Age people did not always understand the link between sex and procreation. Girls and boys played at sex, provided the girls wanted to do so. If they became pregnant, they aborted. Among Australian aboriginals, if a girl was not successful in aborting, she went into the bush with her mother, or an older woman, who killed the child immediately it emerged, and buried it. The sex of the child made no difference. Unless it was wanted, its life would not be spared. Women alone created children helped by spirits. Girls were preferred to boys as they were the more productive, self-sufficient and valuable members of society who would carry on the matriarchal elite. People living in feudal, or even in some modern industrialized societies, may find it hard to believe that there was ever a time when a girl was considered superior to a boy child.

Even after girls mated officially, they resorted extensively to abortion and infanticide. Providing as she did the major part of the family food and breast-feeding a child over a number of years, usually three but sometimes up to six years, a girl felt she could not cope with another child while she was already feeding one. Also she liked to be free to travel. For example, with one child at the breast, an Australian aboriginal girl would be annoyed to feel, stirring within her, another spirit child. She would consider it was due to her own carelessness in going to a place where she knew there were spirit children. Perhaps she went near a deep water hole to take a snake, although she knew it was one of the places where Kaleru, the great serpent, kept spirit children as frogs and fish. As she knelt on the ground, one of them must have climbed up her leg and entered her body. To get rid of it she danced as energetically as she could at corroborrees, put hot stones on her stomach and drank special draughts. Abortion and infanticide were the converse of woman's primary responsibility as provider upon which was based her economic superiority. On the other hand, a child that was accepted was cherished. At the age of six a child would be able to help with gathering and could mind the new baby while she foraged around. What mattered to a woman was her ability to work. She could always go to where spirit children lived and get another one. Her mate had spiritual rights in children and might be angry, although her value to her mate was primarily as a provider of food, shelter and warmth. She might abort once or twice and only agree to bear a child if her mate insisted.[21]

Rituals to placate or intercede with deities in order to ensure supplies of necessities promoted social life. As guardians of these ceremonies, women danced themselves or with the men to celebrate the new moon which dispelled the dark nights, and the full moon, and the first thunderstorm of the season which betokened rain. They dressed up, the men in the skins and head-dresses representing animals they hunted, the women wearing animal ears, or they decorated themselves to represent frogs, baboons or bees, creatures which provided them with food. To halt famine, war or disease, men of the San had to perform the dance of blood, dancing until the blood gushed from their noses. They were revived by the women so that they might continue. It was the women, as guardians of ritual dances, who insisted on them. But in order to dance you had to have rhythm and music. Women made stringed instruments, based on the twang of a bow string. They held the bottom of the bow firm with a foot and blew on the string of antelope sinew at a place marked with a quill feather striking it with a small switch. They made bells of stiffened skin with pebbles for clappers which they tied to ankles, wrists and waists. They had flutes. We do not know of San women making a flute, but only women played flutes. They would leave camp when the spirit moved them to challenge another group in a fluting competition. They took with them, and their hostesses and hosts made ready, huge quantities of food. Then for three or four days they gave themselves over to fluting, dancing, sex with their male hosts and feasting until all the food was consumed. Then they walked fluting back to their own camp. It was an assertion of their freedom. No man dared follow them, although they too went off on visits.[22] We can see something of these masquerades and dances on the walls of caves in south-western France and north-western Spain.

For neither the gods nor necessity, but for pure joy, they made decorations. They carved beads from a red root, or a golden wood, they cut rings from ostrich shells, chipping away with great delicacy and patience, producing sometimes only three rings from one whole shell. They used these to decorate bags and the hems of garments, to make necklaces and fillets for their foreheads, sewing and stringing them with leather thongs, a knot between each bead.[23]

All over the world, women carried on a similar daily round of a huge variety of jobs. In addition, however, to their productive work, they were traders where barter exchange developed. For instance, an Australian aboriginal woman in the north of the continent, like a man, might be a partner on the 'road', the trading chain that ran from the north-west coast eastwards to link with another road running still further east. If she was in territory where two 'roads' intersected, she might be a partner in both. A partner knew only her immediate partners in the chain, four or five of them on either side of her, who were members of her own family. A woman in the north-west territory would hand on eastwards bamboo or pearl-shell necklaces and ornaments from the coast and send back spears, dilly bags for food-gathering which she made herself, and red ochre for people to decorate their bodies and for rock paintings. The woman or man who wanted to buy had to pay in honey or flour. Women always did but men did not and then there were quarrels. Women who received objects always gave a public party, inviting whoever they liked. No one kept pearl-shell ornaments for long, except youths who needed them to show that they had attained manhood. It was not right to be selfish, so exchanges went on the whole time.[24] It was part of social life.

SKINS AND LEATHER

People converted animal skins into leather all over the world. In temperate and warm climates, it seems to have been work done by both sexes. The leather for the garment of Xhooxham, the San woman, for instance, had been made by her maternal aunt and uncle. They had processed and softened hide by squeezing on to it the juice of a bulb and working it in their hands. Xhooxham herself had stitched her dress with sinew from the back of an antelope, threaded through her needle of fine bone in which she had pierced an eye. You could also make needles from large thorns.[25]

But it was the north that was the land of hunters. The nearer to the Arctic you lived, the less vegetable food, so that people spent a greater proportion of their time hunting and fishing than gathering vegetables and fruit. The killing of a beast was only the start of a sequence of laborious and exacting work which only women did. They took charge of the carcasses. An Eskimo woman made for herself the famous half-moon shaped, or semi-lunar, stone knife used by women from Asia to Greenland, shaped like a mincing chopper with the blade set in the straight edge. With this they slit the hides off walrus and seal. After making a small cut, they could draw off a seal's skin whole, as they did with the pelts of smaller animals and the feathered skins of birds. The hides might be up to 30 feet square and the first job of processing was to scrape off the inner layer of fat. For this they used the scraper, said to be the oldest craft implement in the world, and the most widespread. Made of whetstone or oilstone, or reindeer or musk ox bone, it has been found right round the northern hemisphere. The women gave it a serrated edge to roughen up the inner side of the skin and to give it flexibility.

Kala, an Eskimo woman, knelt in front of the huge expanse of hide and pushed her scraper forward, carefully keeping the precious blubber which had many uses and rolling up the finished part of the skin in front of her as she worked. After this primary process, the curing and drying of the skin had many variations. Some women rolled it in the snow to clean it thoroughly. Skins of large animals were best pegged out on the ground to dry. They

were rolled up – Kala and her friends used then to sit on a hide
to help squash it – and then the skins were left to 'sweat' until
the hair rotted off them. The hair was then scraped off in large
flakes, one of the filthiest jobs in creation. After this a hide was
treated by rubbing it with the brains of the animal from which
it had been taken, or by soaking in urine (ammonia), just as urine
was used in medieval Florence or in England to clean wool. The
skin was then soaked in water and pulled and hauled about while
it was drying, the heaviest of all the kinds of Stone Age work
about which we know. Kala used feet, hands and teeth for pulling,
pounding and breaking the grain of the leather.

Kala learnt all the highly specialized uses of different skins and
parts of skins: that the skin of a reindeer's forehead, for example,
was the thickest and the best for boots; that wolverine fur alone
did not freeze with the droplets of sweat on one's face and so
had to be used for fringing the hood of a parka; that the smooth
black pelts of seals were best for dress on land. She knew how
to stretch and oil her raw hides in order to make her own and
the hunters' kayaks. She and her relations found they could make
wonderful soft inner parkas from birds which they skinned all in
one piece, using the skins of a number of birds to make one garment. The women worked on such garments in a group, sitting
together chewing the skins to make them supple. They stitched
them together, whipping the edges. When the seams were stretched
and the garment straightened no one could say where one skin
merged into another and they wore them with the soft feather side
against their skins.

The load of work in autumn was enormous, for supplies of food
had to be caught and processed and stored for the winter. The
making of clothes for all the family was in itself a huge and non-stop
task. In winter they wore double suits, two long fur tunics, two
pairs of fur trousers, the inner with the fur against the skin. On
their feet they all wore fur slippers inside their boots which were
made of leather so processed that it appeared yellow. The stitches
made on boots were invisible because the sewing had to be very
fine and close to ensure that they were watertight. Kala's tunic
housed her small son who sat there, warmed by her body, with
pads of sphagnum moss under his bottom as nappies. Collecting
a huge mound of moss was one of her autumn jobs, for she had
to have enough for winter. She also used it as a sponge. She would

carry him around until he was three years old. They took measurements for suits by knotting a length of sinew or leather thong for length of arms, legs, width of waist and so on. They left plenty of room for working muscles and each suit was made with love expressed in decorations, bands and patterns of white fur, leather fringing or wooden beads.

Generally the older women made most of the clothing, and it was they who kept the hearth, for woman had been given the gift of fire. But that entailed fetching the fuel. Old Howmik went out every day, walking perhaps up to 10 miles through the snow to a stand of willow that would yield enough fuel for the next twenty-four hours. When she did not have her head down against a blizzard, it was fine to look up at the sky, at the clouds, to hear the long-tailed geese talking to each other down on the frozen lake, to see the icicles glitter on the stream in a glint of sun. Then the children went with her, to learn and to play. She made up the wood and twigs into a great bundle which she carried on her back the ten miles back to the camp. She was also a great teller of tales as they sat in the dark round the sorry fire of green willow which produced a thick smoke. The skins of the tent were torn and rent, yet no one repaired them because they formed vents through which the smoke found its way out. When the temperature reached 60° or 70° below freezing, the dreaded moment came when they had to make a snow house. Then there would be no fire, only the dark, for the smoke was intolerable. How much more comfortable was the light and warmth from the great stone bowl in which the seal oil burned in the snow houses of the coastal people. For they had the bountiful fat of seals and walruses as well as deer, hare, fox, stoat, birds and – when the streams thawed – fish. Those who lived inland had only the animals and they disappeared in the black night of winter. Then the lesson of interdependence was burnt into their brains with the frosts. They survived. They are still with us. But the law of survival was harsh. It evolved into an order of dying when food became scarce in the late winter. First their dogs, whom they loved as themselves, were killed and eaten. Then the old were asked to go out into the icy dark. Then women past child-bearing age, then the children, for two adults could always make more children. Here in the enclosed snow houses people learnt more quickly the reality of how a child was conceived. Then the younger women, the oldest first, because there were always more women than men of whom hunting took a heavy toll. Families ignored the law sometimes, preferring to stay together, and died for it. Sometimes, however, the tender children were eaten, even by those who begat them. Since many men died, a woman took a new mate quickly and was generous with her body to male visitors who had travelled many hazardous miles. In order to survive, all had to have their feelings under control. Once when Howmik's hunter had become ill and their neighbour had refused to help, she had not let anger cloud her wits. She had simply taken her first child out and buried it in the snow and walked five days through a blizzard for help.

The law of survival gave priority to men. But they did not there-fore, in everyday life, act in a crudely superior way towards women. On the contrary a man showed the high value he put on his wife by giving her what pleasure he could. For example, a white man who came to some of these people who lived by Stone Age tech-niques offered the husband he came to know best some tobacco. The man thanked him and at once handed it to his wife, although he himself loved a smoke. The woman smoked nearly all of it, leaving him very little.[26]

The conditions of existence of inland Eskimos give some idea of life and a woman's work which brought humanity through the arctic conditions of the Ice Ages.

The creative urge that drove women beyond supplying their own and their children's wants to accepting responsibility for men as well, was spurred by a search for security of food sources, for comfort, for labour-saving devices. Such was their surplus energy that they went beyond mere usefulness to the creation of adorn-ment for its own sake. To them must go much of the credit not only for human survival through the terrors of darkness and ice, or through the gloom of endless rain. They took the first steps to many, perhaps most of the artefacts and processes that have turned human life for some from short bursts of ease and joy, alternating with passages of black disaster towards a continuing well-being so that in modern industralized societies disaster is becoming less familiar.

Women's creative contributions in the field of work did not end mid-way through the Stone Age level of civilization. There were yet more marvels to come from their observation and adaptation of natural objects and processes.

NOTES

1 The name, 'Xhooxham', is taken from Laurens van der Post's *The Lost World of the Kalahari*, 211; Schapera, *The Khoisan Peoples of South Africa*, 92, 94; O. T. Mason, *Woman's Share in Primitive Culture*, 29, 30, 32, 259, 265–6; G. W. Stow, *The Native Races of South Africa*, 44; Kaberry, *Aboriginal Woman, Sacred and Profane*, 5, 17–18, 162, 165; J. J. Batchelor, *Ainu of Japan*, 258–9.

2 Pilbeam, *The Ascent of Man*, geographical distribution; Mourant, Kopec, Domanewska-Sobczak, *The Distribution of Human Blood Groups*, 84; Freedman and Lofgren, *Nature*, vol. 282, p. 298 *Man*, 1936, 255, Sri Lankan Veddahs and Australian Aboriginals: B. Davidson, *Old Africa Rediscovered*, 26ff.

3 Kaberry, op. cit., 5, 163; B. Spencer and F. J. Gillen, *The Native Tribes of Central Australia*, 22, 26–7, 33–4; McGee, *Seventeenth Ann. Rep. of the Bur. of Ethnology*, 152ff, 274; Mason, 21, 270–1, 277; E. S. Hartland, *Man*, vii, 50.

4 Daryll Forde, *Hist. of Technology*, ed., Singer and others, i, 163, 172–3; Mason, 21; Stow, 44; Schapera, 92–3; Kaberry, 5–6, 20; Spencer and Gillen, 22, 24, 26–7; van der Post, 214, 217–18.

5 ibid., 222. I have made a slight alteration to his translation.

6 David Livingstone, *Missionary Travels and Researches in South Africa*, 59; van der Post, 211, 213; Mason, 25–6.

7 van der Post, 209–10; Schapera, 42; Stow, 148; D. Forde, 174; Mason, 19–20, 27; Spencer and Gillen, 222; B. Spencer, *The Native Tribes of Northern Australia*, 323, 392–93; Kaberry, 32–3, 182, 207–8.

8 D. Forde, 174; J. Ramsey, *Description of the Western Isles of Scotland*, 1, 4; Mason, 16, 20.

9 ibid., 9, 15, 29–38, 144; Spencer, 393; Spencer and Gillen, op. cit., 27, 323, 392, 445; van der Post, 209.

10 Mason, 42–9, 62–4, 278, Spencer and Gillen op. cit., 30; S. Leith Ross, *African Women*, 94: A. S. Bickmore, *Trans. of the Ethnol. Soc.*, N.S. vii, 17; Marco Polo, *Travels*, R. Latham trans. (Penguin), 58–9; J. Hemming, *Red Gold*, 392–3; D. Forde, 173–4: G. Turner, *Samoa & etc.* 120; W. Ellis, *Polynesian Researches*, i, 185–6; vol. iv, 109, 179, 184.

11 ibid., iv, loc. cit.: Mason, 54–5 (quoting Brigham, *Bishop Mus. Catalogue*, Honolulu, 1892, 23), 225, 227–8.

12 Crowfoot, *Hist. of Technology*, eds. Singer etc., i, 415–16; Spencer, 379–82, 388; A. F. Bandelier, *Papers of the Arch. Inst. of Africa*, Ser iii, A. de Herrera, *Genl. Hist. of the West Indies*; F. C. Nicholas, *The Amer. Anthropologist*, N.S. iii, 613; Leith Ross, 95; Kaberry, 163; Mason, 49ff.

13 ibid., 52–3, 55, 60, 169–71: F. V. Colville, *American Anthropologist*, vol. v, 558; H. H. Bancroft, *The Native Race of the Pacific States of North America*, vol. i, 766; W. M. Thomson, *The Land and the Book*, 1, 195: I. L. Bird, *Unbeaten Tracks in Japan*, ii, 92: H. Ling Roth, *J. Roy. Anthrop. Inst.*, xlvi, 292; C. Hill Tout, *J. Roy. Anthrop. Inst.*, xxxv, 135f.

14 Bancroft, i, 698; Kalm, *Travels*, ii, 131; H. H. Johnston, *George Grenfell and the Congo*, ii, 589; H. Ling Roth, *Jour. of the Roy. Anthrop. Inst.*, xlvii, 113f; M. Dobrizhoffer, *An Account of the Abipones*, ii, 128, 130; Spencer and Gillen, 40, 558–9, 613–14; Spencer, 10; Kaberry, 79, 162–3; Garrett, *Proc. of the Roy. Geog. Soc.*, Lond. 1892, xiv, 436; Mason, 55–9.
15 ibid., 65–7.
16 Ibid., 94–113; Tothill, *Agriculture in the Sudan*, 9: Hemming, 625–6, n. 395; G. E. Church, *Aborigines of South America*, 121, 235; Werner, *The Natives of British Central Africa*, 197, 204ff: Livingstone, *Last Journals*, vol. i, 59, 79; Bleek and Lloyd, *Specimens of Bushmen Folklore*, 343ff; G. M. McCall Theal, *The Yellow and Dark-Skinned People of South Africa*, 245; H. H. Johnston, ii, 812; also *British Central Africa*, 197, 204ff, 459; Tylor, *Primitive Culture*, i, 45; P. M. Kaberry, *Women of the Grassfields*, 86; G. Elliott-Smith, *The Evolution of the Dragon*, 182, 199; A. Macmichael, *Sudan Notes and Records*, v, 35ff: F. L. Griffiths, *A Collection of Hieroglyphs*, 3; Strabo, iv, 4, 3, (Gaul); *Ann. Reps. Bur. of Ethnol.*, Fourth, Cushing, 511; Eleventh, Stevenson, 11; Twentieth, Holmes, 163; Twenty-third, Stevenson, 273; Twenty-sixth, Russell, 128; *J. Anthrop. Inst.*, 1870–1, Ross King, 40; xxiii, Wray, 25; Man, 21ff; xxxv, Randall-MacIver, 22; Torday and Joyce, 406; xxxvi, Parkinson, 321; xxxix, Latcham, 339 etc.; C. Lumholtz, *Unknown Mexico*, vol. i, 250; A. E. Jenks, *The Bontoc Igorot*, 117f; (Both suggest reason for loss of pottery skill was due to determination to keep the secrets as a female monopoly); For breaks in the female monopoly i.e., e.g. of men making pots see J. P. Mills, *Man*, Sept. 1935, 134; A. R. Brown, *The Andaman Islands*, 473; Basden, *Among the Ibo of Nigeria*, 177.
17 Mason, 149–50; R. Briffault, i, 485–88, 485–8.
18 Van der Post, 223.
19 Briffault, i, 148–51, 268ff, 543–4, iii, 183; W. Crooke, *Tribes and Castes of the North-West Provinces and Oudh*, ii, 43: Howitt, *Native Tribes of South-Eastern Australia*, 185: Kaberry, *Aboriginal Woman*, 55, 58. A. Werner, 254; *Bur. Ethnol. Reps.*, Powell, First, 65. Dorsey, Third, 259; Fifth, 252. MacCauley, Sixth, 496: Stevenson, Eleventh, 19; McGee, Seventeenth, 9–11, 15211, 269–79 etc. Also *J. Anthrop Inst* and *J. Roy. Anthrop Inst* Reps. etc.
20 Schapera, 94.
21 Kaberry, *Aboriginal Woman* . . . 42–3, 49, 54, 58–9, 74, 90, 186, 233, 271; L. C. Lloyd, *Further Bushmen Material*, 21; J. Barrow, *Travels in China*, 473, 376; W. Crooke, *Intro. to the Popular Religion and Folklore of Northern India*, i, 11; Macfarlane, *Geographical Coll. Relating to Scotland*, ii, 520; *The Kalevala*, J. Crawford, ed., ii, 719ff; Briffault, ii, 451–2; Pliny, *Nat. Hist.*, viii, 67 etc.
22 Stow, 109ff; Spencer and Gillen, 53, 420, 547; Mason, 174ff, Leith Ross, 26, 54; Kaberry, *Aboriginal Woman*, 60, 186, 204–17, 219ff; *Women of the Grassfields*, 9, 48, 96–101, 105–6.
23 Stow, 46; van der Post, 219.
24 Spencer and Gillen, 24; Kaberry, *Aboriginal Woman*, 167–74.

25 van der Post, 211, 218; Australian aboriginals did not convert skins into leather, Spencer and Gillen, 30; Mason, 43; Crowfoot, 413.

26 Mason, 27, 72–7, 80–2, 85–92, 206–7; Crantz, *Hist. of Greenland*, 154; H. Egede, *A Description of Greenland*, 126; Rink, op. cit., 27ff; F. Mowat, *People of the Deer*, 93–5, 105, 120, 128, 147–8; Murdoch, *Ninth Ann. Rep. Bur. of Ethnol.*, 109–38, 294–302, figs. 209–302, 412ff; E. W. Nelson, *Eighteenth Ann. Rep. Bur. of Ethnol.*, 291; F. Boas, *The Bull. of the Amer. Mus. of Natural History*, 115; Father E. Pettitot, *Les Grands Esquimaux*, 198; Bancroft, vi, 787; Dall, *The American Naturalist*, iv, 187–8, xii, 5n; Warburton Pike, *The Barren Grounds*, 75, 160; J. Georgi, *Description de toutes les nations de l'Empire de Russie*, iii, 13, 55: de Charlevoix, *Hist. de la Nouvelle France*, v, 264ff; Carruthers, *Unknown Mongolia*, 221; Rasmussen, *People of the Polar North*, 62, 65: Sam Hearne, *Journey from the Prince of Wales Fort to the Northern Ocean*, p. xxx: For cannibalism, Daisy Bates, *Rev. d'ethnographie . . .*, no. 21, p. 31: Hemming, op. cit., 31–2; Evans-Pritchard, 133f; E. McNeill, ed., *The Lays of Fionn*, (Irish Text Soc.), 122; J. Chalmers, *Pioneering in New Guinea & etc.*, 62ff.

Table 2 Technological and Cultural Development

```
2000  ─
      ├─Nuclear power, Electronics, Automation Europe, North America, Japan
1900
1800  ├─New developments in medicine & nursing   ⎱ Gas & Electricity
      │ West European power revolution            ⎰ Water & Steam
      │                                           Decline of
      │                                           feudalism starts
1700  ├─World population rise. Feudalism starts in Russia & Japan
1600  ─
        Colonization of South by North African tribes

1500  ├─ Start of European voyages & colonization
1400  ├─ Start of women's emancipation, West Europe
1300
      ├─Renaissance – Women at medical school
1200  ─           at Bologna
1100  ─
1000  ─
      ├─Norman Conquest      West African feudalism

 800  ─
      ├─Charlemagne
 600  ├─Hypatia teaching at Alexandria ──── Arab Conquest
      ├─Mohammed
 400  ─

 200  ─
AD                             Roman Empire
 O    ├─Christ
        Confucius/Lao Tse
BC      Buddha
1000  ─
      ├──────────────── Agricultural communities
      │                 in Mexico & Andes
      ├─Iron tools & Wheel
      ├─Silk production
2000  ─
        Indus valley        Settlers        Irrigation
      ├─brick buildings      in      God    Egypt    Sumeria
3000  ├─Start of Old        Greece  kings   Pyramids Ur tombs
      │ Testament                   Nile valley, Tigris and
      ├─Copper tools                         Euphrates
      ├─Silver              Settled farming  civilizations
      ├─Start of using iron Yellow River
4000  ├─Gold                valley China
      ├─Jarmo village
5000  ├─Copper
6000  ├─Pottery

7000  ─
                                              Slavery starts
8000  ├─Patriarchy starts, Near East

9000  ─
      ├─Settled farming, Caucasus
10,000├─Women as hoe users
        Shifting cultivation
        Digging sticks
        Stone scrapers, Knives in use
```

Feudalism starts in Egypt, Near East, India, China

Hinduism

Chapter 2

EARLY FARMERS AND HERDERS

From stone, bone and wooden tools the grater, the quern and the mill developed, implements made and used in Stone Age societies apparently only by women and so possibly owing their origins to women. Brewing and food preparation including some quite elaborate recipes were also, so far as we have evidence, wholly 'women's work'. Women almost certainly initiated some of the techniques we still use today in building. But greater than all these technical changes, they brought into being and organized the supreme revolutions in Stone Age technology, the domestication of birds, fish and animals, and the cultivation of crops. Growing populations put pressure on food supplies and were one spur to the development of more intensive food production methods. Original techniques were also modified in response to changes in climate and to the impoverishment of the topsoil. But there was also technological development without such compulsion, an urge towards finding labour-saving devices and, in a contrary direction, towards the elaboration of existing technology, towards greater fineness of material or more ornamentation. No one can say positively when these new technologies and forms of work first appeared. But there was considerable alteration in methods after the last retreat of the ice about 10,000 BC, followed by the slow improvement in the climate, permitting vegetation to grow in hitherto ice-bound regions and diminishing the rain in the tropics and equatorial regions.

DOMESTICATION OF FISH, FOWL AND ANIMALS

The diet of gathering and hunting peoples included a lot of fish. Long before the last Ice Age they were gathering shell-fish around shores of lakes and seas. There are still large mounds of shells they piled up. Collecting shell-fish and fishing in inshore waters was work done primarily by women.

Australian aboriginal women fished in the creeks when they were full of water. A woman might take as part of her spoils of the day perhaps fifteen fat perch which she had speared. They went into streams not only to collect fish, but also to gather lily roots and buds. When the creeks ran fairly full, you could see the little, black faces of the women and girls just above the water among the leaves as they groped for the roots.[1] In summer sometimes they spent nearly all day in the water.

Labour-saving methods of fishing included the use of poisons to quieten or kill fish, traps and dams built both around seashores and in fresh running water in imitation of dam-building creatures like beavers, and of natural formations of rocks and pools which enclosed water. Freshwater fishing was often a co-operative effort, with men helping to make the dams or driving the fish to where women waited to catch them. Agatharchides, a Greek historian and tutor to the Egyptian Pharaoh, about 116 BC noted a people of south-east Persia and Baluchistan who lived almost entirely on fish and seals, an illustration, incidentally, of the then much colder climate of the Arabian Sea. They used stones to block up channels of the sea that wound inland, and caught the fish that were carried in twice daily by the tides. The division of labour was that women and children took the smaller fish and the able-bodied men those 'hard to overcome' because of their size. In stormy weather when fishing was more difficult, they gathered mussels – some of them huge, weighing about five pounds. After some days spent gorging themselves on their catches, they journeyed inland to freshwater springs. The men took charge of the older children who could walk, and the women carried the infants. There they drank until their bellies were distended and then walked back to the coast to fish again.

A similar division of labour in fishing persists to this day among Polynesians. The women have entirely taken charge of the construction of dams and of inshore fishing. The shores of many coral islands are indented with small bays, almost enclosed to seaward by rocks and coral reefs. To such islands around Hawaii, Polynesian women would set out in their canoes through the heavy surf, before the sun was really up. They shot the narrow entrances, beached their canoes, deposited their babies under the shade of palms on the soft sand and, in the calm waters of these small lagoons, protected from the rollers, with knife and hatchet they set to work. They cut lumps of coral rock and lifted them into the narrow entrances, trying not to scratch themselves, for some coral is poisonous. To cool themselves off they dived and swam, regaling themselves with fish and coconuts, working until the mouth of the bay was closed. A canoe or catamaran can shoot a wall of coral that is only slightly submerged so the Hawaiians could thenceforth go in and out, bringing older children with them to help spear and capture the captive fish trapped in the lagoon. It was almost a game. When supplies ran low, the men went out into deep water and brought in fresh stocks of fish. The sea sluiced through the encircling corals of the women's dams and kept the water fresh. Occasionally sand and weed silted up the bottom and they had to spend a day or two cleaning it out, depositing it in their canoes for dumping on the beach. The artificial lagoon helped to remove much of the uncertainty of obtaining a food supply. It gave the women leisure to make and decorate their bark cloth, to make and play musical instruments like the nose-flute, to sing and to dance.

Women also did deep-sea fishing. Among the greatest Stone Age women experts were the women of Terra del Fuego who built their own canoes. They went out naked in all weathers in the terrible waters off Cape Horn, and at certain seasons provided the whole of their people's diet. Only women could swim. It was a skill not transmitted to boys. For fishing lines they used roots of certain plants weighted with a stone to which the bait was tied. They used no hook. The fish followed the bait as the line was pulled through the water. Late nineteenth century Europeans saw them 'take large quantities of fish when our own sailors at the same time and place barely succeed in securing a few using European lines and fish-hooks.'[2]

Everyone took birds' eggs as part of their normal gathering work, from nests in the ground, in bushes or trees and, more perilously, from cliffs. Anyone could snare or bring down a bird with bow and arrow. They may have been first sought for their feathers, not as food. Men wanted feathers for decoration to attract women, since roles in mating were the reverse of those in most modern cultures, and for ceremonial and warlike dress. It was the birds themselves that suggested their own imprisonment. The unsuspecting wildfowl flew down near huts to peck at spilt seeds and food scraps. They could be enticed to stay by the same means and so save people the trouble of stalking them and searching far afield for their eggs. They made enclosures for them knotting vines round tree trunks, or driving stakes into the ground close together, roofing them with nets or matting. Wherever birds were domesticated, it was women who as food providers fed and cared for them.

The domestication of animals was equally easy when people brought in baby creatures orphaned or abandoned in the wild. Human mothers and children petted them and cared for young wolves, kids or lambs, mothers sometimes even feeding them at their own breasts. When they grew up, the animals provided not only food, but skin, sinews and bone. Eventually women thought of putting animals to work. Eskimo women provided shelter and food for wild dogs in return for the dogs' pulling sleds.[3]

The greatest help came from the horse, the ass and the camel. Perhaps mounting and riding them began as a game, but it ended with the realization that, riding on a four-footed animal, people were more evenly matched in fleetness with the herds from which the animals came. They could trek with them over great distances following them from their winter to their summer pastures. It became a way of life.[4]

Animals were found to have another use. They could carry burdens. The carrying of their own kind and of objects is natural animal practice. Birds, bees, ants, all kinds of wild cats, beavers and lamprey eels all carry things, mainly nest building materials. Spiders and various mammals carry their young. Human creatures followed this instinct, mothers carrying their babies until they were able to walk or became strong enough (in the case of the Eskimo) to withstand ferociously cold temperatures of 40° below zero without additional heat from their mothers' bodies.

When Stone Age people moved camp, the division of labour was for women to carry small children and life-sustaining tools and totems while the men walked free, carrying only their weapons to guard them from animal and human enemies. Men were also on the look-out for game. Europeans, coming with pre-determined notions of male supremacy upon such a party, tended to assume that women with their heavy loads were the inferiors and the free-ranging men their superiors. But, as Dr W. H. Keating remarked of the Chippewas Indians, 'A woman would object to travelling with men who were not ready to defend her at an instant's notice, and the supposed "beast of burden" is often the ruler of the household.'[5]

However, women were only too glad to lift the burdens of tent skins, tools and children from their backs and heads on to the backs of animals. Moreover, riding on animals, the whole group from infants to the oldest adults could keep up with the life-giving herd. Meat was always fresh and besides they had milk. If women gave suck to small animals, sheep, goats and wolves could give suck to their infants and save some of the hardship of prolonged breast-feeding. Even more than men, women had an interest in domesticating animals.

There was no need for a child to take the risk of a kick or a nip by sucking direct from an animal. Women and men squeezed the animal milk out of the udders into buckets and containers. From this there arose the whole sophisticated process of dairying, of culling calves in order to have female beasts in milk, of fermenting mare's milk to make koumiss, of making butter and yoghourt.[6] Men joined women in milking larger animals, a highly dangerous job, for one blow from the hoof of a camel was enough to kill. Women did all the rest – they milked the smaller animals, and did all the work of processing milk into dairy products.

First catch your horse or camel. In the clear air of the steppe in what today is north-east China, Rigtso and her daughter thundered over ground hard with frost towards the herd of horses, weaving and manoeuvring to separate out one mare. They did not have to waste energy in calling to one another for this was an everyday job. Yet it was always different and they loved its excitement. In a cloud of misted breath, Rigtso reached the mare first and leapt from her own horse on to its back as she galloped neck and neck with it. She pulled hard on its mane and dug her bony knees in their high boots hard into its sides as her daughter came up and threw a leather lasso round its neck. Rigtso knew well how to quiet a captured horse and at the same time call back her own mount. She was 70 years old and had literally lived all her life on horseback. This was the life of women nomadic herders for the last five thousand and more years. In central Asia, in the twentieth century, it was going on unchanged. Three English women missionaries who made an epic journey from China to Russia in the early 1920s, saw Rigtso and her like still exercising their consummate riding skills. And their way of life has been well attested since then, even in the 1970s in post-Revolutionary China.

Children were reared on horseback. As soon as she was born, Rigtso was put in a wooden cradle with a built-in channel to carry off her excrement. She was not taken out for feeding. Her mother being busy and the air cold, she simply stooped her breast to the infant where it lay. When they moved with the herds, her cradle was tied to a horse's back.[7] Once Rigtso could crawl, she had been placed on the back of a horse with a supporting hand behind her. By the time she was four, she could ride well enough by herself to keep up with the rest.

Their herds of horses, cows and sheep roamed over 1000 square kilometres and two hundred families lived off them supplementing their wardrobes and their diet with game like deer, marten and marmot from the woods and valleys. The year was punctuated and enlivened by horse race meetings, wrestling matches between women or men and archery contests in which Rigtso, in her younger day, excelled.[8]

Among such central and northern Asiatic tribes, as among most Stone Age peoples, sexual licence was considerable until official mating which was governed not by love, but by the laws of kinship. A man who mated with one daughter was accepted by her sisters and the laws of hospitality extended to strangers as with the Eskimo. Despite the kinship rules, it was a free sort of life, their horseriding enabling them to move over great distances.[9]

The revelation of the advantages of domesticating a quadruped did not strike all those peoples for whom herds provided a major part of their food. The San people never domesticated the zebra, for example. Sparse though their food became in the dry seasons, they did not apparently trek south with the herds. They could find sustenance in the south central African desert when animals could not.

For herding slow animals such as cattle, or small creatures like sheep or goats, people did not need to be mounted on horse or camel, but mostly followed the flocks on foot. Women not only milked sheep and goats, they also collected tufts of their hair caught on thorns and cacti, using them to spin yarn. From this they progressed to the idea of shearing the hair off animals at the hottest time of year. Shearing among Stone Age nomads and right up to modern times among many peoples was women's work, the men lending a hand sometimes to hold an unwilling animal still.[10] Using the spindle-whorl women perpetually spun the wool as they walked or rode, providing thread for the never-ending need for clothes, carpets, cushions and saddle-bags.[11]

WOMEN AS CONSTRUCTORS OF SHELTERS AND BUILDINGS

Partly from women's business of skinning animals and processing their hides developed their monopoly in the construction of temporary dwellings. People all over the northern hemisphere used tents. Some established permanent winter houses, digging holes in the ground and roofing them over, or digging into hillsides, a communal job. They could then leave at some permanent camp or settlement the children, the sick and the old who could not keep up with their summer migration. They did not need to abandon them to starve or die of exposure if they reached some natural barrier impossible for them to cross, such as a river swollen with melting snow. But whether all year round or only in the summer, they nearly all used tents made and erected by women. Thus Amerindian women stitched the huge buffalo skins together to make tepees, sewing them from top to bottom except for one seam which they left open five feet from the bottom. To this split a woman sewed leather laces as fastenings and a loose piece of buffalo robe or cloth as a door. It was left to hang except in bad weather when it was tied with the thongs. Women gave each other a helping hand in the raising of their tepees, or their young female relatives helped. They spread the heavy cover on the ground, then thrust under it three poles tied tightly together at their tapering ends, raised them upright and splayed out the ends as far as possible. One woman flicked a thong or rope attached to the top of the tepee over the three crossed poles, pulling on the end while another adjusted this tripod until the tepee was thoroughly taut. They carried in other supporting poles, pushed the thin ends through the opening at the top against the tripod and carried the thick ends as far out as possible to the sides of the tepee, arranging them equidistantly in a circle. They knocked a few wooden pegs into the ground through slits in the bottom of the covering. To prevent the wind blowing directly down through the hole at the top, they made a sort of cap, manipulated from below with thongs of deer skin according to the direction of the wind. They also set two poles to windward of the opening, shifting them as the direction of the wind changed. This whole complicated operation, when timed by early European explorers, took three experienced women only five minutes.

To take the tepee down took only three minutes. They removed the pegs and all the loose poles, loosened the rope holding the cover in place, brought the lower ends of the tripod together and the covering came down of its own weight. They folded, rolled and bundled it up ready to be transported.

In the building of tents and tepees, women used the principle that a triangle can bear enormous stress and remain rigid whereas a quadrilateral will move. This principle is used today in the metal framework of bridges and in buildings precisely for the same reason: its strength. They also hit on the idea of the pulley operated by a counter-weight and on the use of wind power, draughts, to expel smoke and foul air.

Not only putting up tents, but also the erection of solid buildings was 'woman's work'. It was only natural in the sense that many female animals make nests and burrows. So in human as in some other species, making a home was sometimes a wholly female job. Among Central Asian Turkoman and Kirghiz, men made the framework for the yurts (circular tents); however, in the extreme north-east of Siberia, Chukchi women made not only the skin covering, but also the wooden framework. Similarly in Africa Bantu women, for example in Botswana, did all the work of putting up huts. They used either clay or cow dung for walls and floors. Livingstone noted that the dung was the better, since dung huts were never verminous, while mud huts were. Following weaving techniques, they thatched roofs. The only job men did was the felling of timber from which the women made the framework. Australian and Andamanese women made family dwellings. In Samoa and Madagascar, where homes are made mainly of thatch, women still do the thatching work. In Melanesia and Indonesia, men make the frameworks of the pile dwellings and women thatch the sides and roofs. In the Americas Patagonian, Botocudos and Seri Indian women all built their homes; Plains Indian women largely made their long houses; Omaha Indian women excavated earth lodges. In New Mexico and Arizona traditionally they build their mud houses in terraces, the flat roof of one house serving as the step to the next. Using Pueblo women's mastery of building, Spanish invaders had them make bricks and build convents and churches, helped by girls and boys. The women's own mud homes were the models for the stone buildings of the Mexican Mayas. Similarly in Egypt, where women still do a great deal of the building of their reed and mud huts, architecture derived directly from

African women's huts.[12] Women were also builders in stone. Herodotus tells us that one of the greatest of all the buildings of Egypt and Babylonia, the monument to the hero, Alyattes, at Lydia, had an inscription attesting that most of it was built by women.[13]

This mastery of building was the final touch in women's self-sufficiency. Samuel Hearne, journeying in Canada from the Prince of Wales Fort to the North Ocean in the late eighteenth century, instances an Indian woman, taken prisoner by a hostile tribe, who escaped and lived cosily for seven months, having built herself a hut, made traps, snares and knives with which to hunt, and also needles so that she had not only a good store of food, but new clothes which were not merely utilitarian but also highly decorative.[14]

SETTLED FARMING

To their development of the key technological processes for making tools, containers, fabrics, homes and domesticating wild creatures, women added one more innovation. They observed a miracle on which was based an economic revolution.

A group of people of the race we now call Natufians temporarily made a home for themselves in the Belt Cave in the Caucasus about 9000 BC. A millennium earlier their ancestors had been at this same spot fishing for seals through the ice. Patiently carrying on their new economy of herding flocks of sheep and goats, later cave-users remarked of a regular succession of hot and cold, dry and rainy seasons, which regularly brought forth plants and saw them wither. Watching and passing on their observations from one generation to the next, by about 5500 BC they had discovered the miracle: trees, flowers, fruit, and edible grasses like emmer wheat which they picked to pound in their mortars sprang anew from the soil each year at a particular season, because some months before, seeds, fruit pips or stones had fallen to the earth and rooted. So the women helped the process, poking holes in the earth and dropping in grass seed instead of putting it all in the supper pot. Some idea of how the transition from gathering to cultivation of food plants may have been made was given by the American ethnologist, Stephen Powers. He found Yokaia women in central California working the soil with their bare hands and in this way making little gardens in which they planted maize, obtaining a better yield than European Americans with newer methods.[15]

Stone Age people found ways to speed up the process, one person walking ahead with a stick making holes for seed, and another coming behind, performing the key task of dropping in the seed. Since the spirit of earth was a goddess, a mother,[16] and the plants that would sprout had female spirits, women had to plant them to ensure success. Today in the Sudan, the man walks in front making holes in the earth with a digging stick and the woman comes behind, dropping in the seed. Europeans saw this division of labour in terms of the status of the sexes in their own society, as showing man's superiority and women's inferiority. Those who studied ancient religion and society realized it was a survival from days when women were supreme as food providers.

In Asia Minor, the planting of grain went on at the Belt Cave, perhaps also round the nearby Hotu Cave; at the Tell of Jericho, near a spring, in Jordan; and at Qalat Jarmo on a spur of the Kurdish hills above the River Tigris. In the three and a half thousand years, 8500–5000 BC, a longer stretch of time than lies between ourselves and the birth of Christ, agriculture and farming became an established way of life. There were two distinct ways of farming dictated by geography and climate. In the cold north people worked all year round to produce a single harvest. In the lush tropics the aim of farming was to ensure a continual supply of fresh food all year round. There was no single great harvest. Planting and gathering went on simultaneously the whole time. The collecting of one crop went on over weeks and others were growing to replace it. Some plants fruited the whole year.[17]

But for both systems women produced another tool, the hoe. Hoe culture spread right round the globe from the tropics north almost to the sub-arctic wherever farming was possible. It was associated with shifting cultivation, as opposed to settled farming in one spot. When farming began the ratio of land to people was very high. The earth was virgin and rich even in the north, so when one site was worked out, the community moved to another which they cleared by chopping down trees and burning off scrub leaving the ash as fertilizer. Meanwhile jungle and scrub soon reclaimed the old site, hence the system is sometimes called 'long fallow'. The frequency of these removals depended on the fertility of the land: they might have to shift after two years, or even one;

they might stay four or five years at the same place.[18]

Kengeran and her two daughters, members of the Bantu-speaking peoples who came from the north in successive waves into the forest lands and hills of central Africa, were such hoe farmers, shifting cultivators using the slash-and-burn method to clear new sites. Like the rest of the women, Kengeran owned her own crops and farmed her own land allocated to her personally. When they moved to a new site, they expected the able-bodied men to help burn the undergrowth and clear it, and to chop down trees with their big axes. Sometimes women worked alternately with them, chipping away layers of bark and trunk which the men loosened until the tree creaked and crashed to the ground. The men, however, were sometimes lazy about this as about their hunting. When Kengeran was first married and her husband had been disinclined to help, she took his axe and chopped the trees down herself, rather than be late planting and so lose her bean harvest. Once land was cleared, women established their claim to farm it simply by starting to hoe it in preparation for sowing.

One of the lessons of the profusion of natural growth was that plants thrive in association with one another. The trick was to know how to associate those which humans could eat. So Kengeran grew sweet potatoes on one field as ground cover to keep out weeds together with maize which came up through them. In her fields round the village in the wooded valley she grew gourds to give ground cover and not only maize but oil seed too was grown up through them. Finger millet was grown through ground nuts. On one of her patches, five different plants, sorghum, hyptis, sesame, maize and finger millet were grown. Trees were left standing to provide support for vines or to act as posts for enclosures.

On the uplands women went later to their fields than in the valleys because, they said, it was colder up there. Dr Phyllis Kaberry observed them in the Cameroons in the late 1940s and early 1950s still working at this traditional farming. She saw them setting off carrying their hoes, small knives, a calabash pipe, a little tobacco, a flint or glowing charcoal in a pot, a bag of woven raffia palm or a basket if they were harvesting and, in the rainy season, wide, woven head-covers as portable umbrellas. At sowing time they tied round their waists baskets from which to dispense the seed. They generally brought back enough root vegetables, greens or plantains and kindling to cook meals for three or four days so that they did not have to go to their hill fields every day. However, women of some tribes lived in small huts at their plantations, only coming to the village on market days, in the slack season or for religious festivals.

Kengeran's two teen-age daughters worked with her as they had done since they could walk, gradually progressing from what was almost a game of balancing a basket on their small heads, to a full adult's share of the work, by the time they were teenagers. Young women liked working together, singing, chatting and encouraging each other. Men worked in teams too, when clearing new ground; women did so less often. But they would co-operate, for instance in opening ground for a plot for a bride and sometimes also in cleaning and preparing beds for planting. The hostess of the day, on whose land they all worked, gave a meal to her co-workers at the end of the afternoon to which her husband was expected to contribute a little fish. Older women, however, preferred to work individually at their own slower pace, chatting to a neighbour on a plot alongside, as Kengeran did with old Biy. Resting at noon, each of them watching the blue smoke from her pipe curl upwards into the bluer sky, they discussed the crops and weather – two experienced, independent women who could well fend for themselves.

Women and men were always teasing each other about what was 'women's work' and what was 'men's work'. Normally there was no hope of Kumbu, her husband, doing her work of growing plants other than his own special yams and medicinal tobacco. Tobacco was a male plant which no woman must touch for fear of destroying the crop, and, incidentally, breaching the men's monopoly. But once when she was ill of a fever he had good-naturedly done all the work in her fields, including the interminable weeding and cleaning of crops, reduced but not eliminated by the growing of ground cover plants. He had endured the chaff about doing 'women's work' because the work had to be done if they were to eat and not be a burden to the community. Some of the women had lent a hand as they always did if anyone was sick.

On her side Kengeran liked to fish and hunt; she had a head-dress decorated with the teeth of leopards she had killed. It had been difficult to go out when the girls were little and had to be breast-fed. When, however, she could move about freely again, she found that the division of labour had sharpened. Hunting and fishing had become Kumbu's specialized job and farming hers. That had not stopped her taking her bow and arrow and knife and going out if she felt like it. But it was sport, not essential for their livelihood. In a whole day's hunting, she might or might not bring back enough meat for the evening meal, whereas her fields, unless they were devastated by natural disasters, could be relied on to provide the staple foods, just as the uncultivated earth provided for her gathering forebears.[19]

Half a world away, Mexicans worshipped their staple, maize, as the goddess Chicometcoat[1]; the Cherokee Indians knew her as the Old Woman, indeed all Indians except the Jibarros regarded maize as female. Peruvians invoked her as the Maize-Mother along with the Quininoa-Mother, the Coco-Mother and the Potato-Mother, each of whom had the power to give birth to and nourish many plants. Amazonian Indians credited a greater number of plants with male souls, but almost all food plants were female. Because 'like is best known and served by like' the responsibility for their cultivation rested on women. Religion provided a reason and a justification for the allocation of work between the sexes. In the twentieth century, Brazilian Indians working in sugar factories still sang incantations to the Earth Mother, Nungui, and to her husband Shakaema, who did the same work as men, clearing the plantations.[20]

COOKING AND FOOD PROCESSING

Kengeran did not mind farming. Weeding was tedious and you sweated in the sun, but it was nevertheless skilled work. It was creative, and it was interesting to watch the crops ripen, to pit yourself against pests and weather. What Kengeran did not like was the women's speciality of preparing food and drink which took a lot of time and effort and was so quickly consumed. The maize had to be ground and pounded in a mortar. To lighten the work, in some places two women would sit one either side of a large mortar and pound with a log, raising it and letting it fall, slipping through their guiding hands to smash the grains. Some found large, rounded stones with holes worn right through the middle so that they could be suspended with straw rope from the branch of a bush, touching the flat grinding stone on the ground. A woman could then make the upper stone turn and crush the maize or seed merely by turning the straw rope. Some thought of setting handles into the tops of round flat stones which two women worked together, sitting facing each other, both holding the handle, one catching up fresh seed and throwing it in through a hole in the upper stone. There were innumerable local variants of these grinding processes.

Women developed their ways of reducing hard roots like cassava to an edible consistency. Instead of simply pounding, Kengeran rolled a smooth round stone forwards and backwards, forwards and backwards, rocking on her heels as she knelt to the work. Carib Indian women in the Amazon and Orinoco deltas and West Indies invented graters, setting sharp pieces of stone in wooden boards, glueing them with resin to deal with the same root which they called manioc. Ground or grated, the mush was hung up in nets and left so that the poisonous juice would drain out of it, to be kept for tipping arrows and spears or to be used for medicine, while the pulp would be rendered fit for human consumption. The quern, the grater and their variants may well have been women's inventions.[21]

When Kengeran's daughters were small and she had all the work to do, like other women she was sometimes too tired of an evening to cook. Sitting at the doors of their huts in dejection and utter lassitude, the women sometimes reached a state of semi-starvation from which men might rescue them by bringing in supplies of meat.

Women also developed the processing of sugar and of salt. In the south-western parts of north America, in early summer when the sugar plants were nearly half-grown, women cut and dried them in the sun. They ground the dried leaves and stalks, sieved out a 'moist, sticky flour' which they moulded into a gluey mass and roasted over their fires until it swelled and browned slowly, producing a kind of toffee.[22] As gatherers they procured salt which Stone Age people used for seasoning, a more sophisticated approach than that of animals who merely lick it raw. Nature provided it in places where salt lakes evaporated and left it piled like sand dunes, to be scooped up. It was not merely hard work. It burnt bare feet and hands. But women also obtained salt from water by process of evaporation, from the sea, from lakes in East Africa and in Mexico where it was a great staple of trade, or from salt springs in Ohio. They danced at the feast of the salt goddess.[23]

Women were also Stone Age brewers of alcoholic drinks, spruce beer in the north, fermented spirits and beer from all sorts of grains in Asia, Europe and Africa. They found out the process of fermentation and artificially induced it. The preparation of beer for a big party or religious festival took days. But for some it was easier. In Angola, Quissama women climbed palm trees, cut the bark to let the sap run and hung a gourd to catch the dripping liquid. Twenty-four hours later, they climbed up again, sealed the slit with wax or resin and collected the gourd, now full of palm beer.[24]

There were two significant factors about the progression in women's work among Stone Age communities in so far as we have knowledge of it. One was the variety of work done by either men or women, their interchangeability and co-operation as a matter of course. The other, even more impressive to people living in the most modern technologies where women's work has become severely limited, was the range of women's work and the large number of processes they monopolized and dominated.

NOTES

1 Spencer and Gillen, *The Native Tribes of Central Australia*, 27, 394; Spencer, *The Native Tribes of North Western Australia*, 27; Kaberry, *Aboriginal Woman*, 5–8, 11, 15, 17–22.
2 J. G. Wood, *The Natural History of Man*, ii, 431; S. Löven, *Origins of the Tainan Culture*, 16, 672; Torday and Joyce, *J. of the Anthrop. Inst.*, xxxv, 405; *Narrative of the Honourable John Byron*, 96; Bonwick, *Daily Life and Origins of the Tasmanians*, 55; Hyades and Deniker, *Mission Scientifique du Cap Horn*, vol. ii, 368ff; G. Bove, *Patagonia. Terra del Fuoco. Mari Australi*, 131; Garrett, *Proc. of the Roy. Geog. Soc., 1892*, vol. xlv, 436; P. Kaberry, *Aboriginal Woman ...*, 18, 22; *Diodorus Siculus*, vol. 11, Bk. 111, 15.1–15.3.
3 O. T. Mason, *Woman's Share in Primitive Culture*, 152; Las Casas, *Apol. Hist.*, 114, 532; Briffault, *The Mothers*, iii, 274; W. Crooke, *Hastings's Encyl. of Religion and Ethics*, iii, 442; F. W. Fitzsimons, *The Natural Hist. of S. America: Mammals*, vol. i, 58; Zeuner, *Hist. of Technology*, Singer & etc. eds., vol. i, 330–1; L. H. Morgan, *Ancient Society*, 26; Hemming, *Red Gold*, 25, 324; Mason, 151; Pike, *Barren Grounds ...*, 160; P. Beveridge, *Aboriginals of Victoria and Riverina*, 117; E. Thorne, *Queen of the Colonies*, 337; Gason, *The Diererie Tribe of Australian Aboriginals*, 12ff.
4 Peake and Fleure, *Peasants and Potters*, 37–8; Hemming, 387, 394; Tothill, *Agriculture in the Sudan*, 12.
5 Keating, *Narrative of Expedition to the Source of St. Peter's River*, vol. ii, 242; Heckewelder, *History, Manners and Customs of the Indian Nations*, 155; Pelleschi, *Eight Months on the Gran Chaco of the Argentine Republic*, 64.

6 Evans-Pritchard, *The Position of Women in Primitive Societies* etc. 189ff;
Marco Polo, op. cit. 67–8. Among some herding people, animals were kept
solely for meat and hides, and they never carried on any kind of dairying,
see Leith Ross, *African Women*, 63–4.
7 Cable and French, *Through Jade Gate*, 53; A. Migot, *Tibetan Marches*,
188, 214; *China Pictorial*, Feb. 1976; 40–1; Mar. 1976, 33; July 1976, 26–9;
C. Aymard, *Les Touaregs du Sud-Est*, 94ff. 202; Skeat and Blagden, *Pagan
Races of the Malay Peninsula*, vol. ii, 67ff; E. Huntington, *The Geog. Jour.*,
xxv, 154ff; F. Halle, *Women in the Soviet East*, 52, 59, 61; Marco Polo,
Travels, (Penguin), 168–9; U. Johansen, *Altaic Aspects of Civilisation*,
Sinor Ed., 210 and etc.
8 Halle, 59–60 for the famous Jangul Mursa; J. Palafox y Mendoza, *Hist.
of the Tartars*, 582; J. Deguignes, *Hist. des Huns*, iii, 5; Matthew Paris,
Chronica Magna, iv, 77; J. Creagh, *Armenians, Koords and Turks*, ii, 168.
9 Marco Polo, op. cit. 146, 149; Rockhill, *Land of the Lamas*, 213, 230;
Bogoras, *The Chukgee*, 578–83, 602–7; A. Henry, *Travels and Adventures in
the Years 1760–1776*, 241; Petitot, *Les Grands Esquimaux*, 141; Jochelson,
The Koryak, 754; *The Yukaghir*, 62–4; G. A. Farini, *Huit Mois au Kalahari*,
190ff; Lewis and Clarke, *Travels to the Source of the Missouri River*, ii,
291; L. H. Morgan, 47ff, 180–1, 372–6, 39ff, 467n.; Levi-Strauss, *Elementary Structures of Kinship*, 39–41, 69ff; Briffault, i, 132 and Chs. xi
and xii, 613ff for detailed analysis; Halle, 62–4, quoting A. Nukhrat, *Legend
of the Steppes*, 94, 99; Thurnwald, *Memoirs of the Amer. Anthrop. Soc.*,
iii, No. 4, 383–4.
10 Halle, 107.
11 *Woman's Work for Women*, Nov. 1888, 296.
12 O. T. Mason, *Woman's Share in Primitive Culture*, 152–4; *Man*,
'Andaman Islanders', 38, 40; Dodge, *Our Wild Indians*, 233; E. Boserup,
Woman's Role in Economic Development, 79; V. Gordon Childe, *What
Happened in History* (Pelican), 37–9: Skeat and Blagden, *Pagan
Races of the Malay Peninsula*, vol. i, 374ff; Kaufman Kohler, *Jewish
Encyclopaedia*, vol. vi, 504ff; Briffault, i, 373–4, 'tent' as synonym for
'woman' also 480; Bogoras, 547; André Migot, *Tibetan Marches*, 148;
Vambéry, *Travels in Central Asia*, 316; E. and P. Sykes, *The Deserts and
Oases in Central Asia*, 121; J. O. Dorsey, *Thirteenth Ann. Rep. Bur. of
Ethnol.*, 269; W. McGee, *Seventeenth Ann. Rep. Bur. of Ethnol.*, Pt. 1,
152ff; A. C. Haddon, *Jour. of the Anthrop. Inst.*, xix, 342; A. Harvey, 'Some
Types of Egyptian Women', *The Cosmopolitan*, xxviii, 276; H. H. Johnston,
George Grenfell and the Congo, ii, 731; G. Lindblom, *The Akamba...*,
137; T. H. Hood, *Notes of a Cruise of HMS 'Fawn' in the Western Pacific*,
32; A. F. Bandelier, *The Delight Makers*, 14: and etc.
13 *Herodotus*, vol. 1, 93.
14 S. Hearne, *Journey from the Prince of Wales's Fort...*, 262.
15 J. Hawkes and L. Woolley, 'Prehistory and the Beginnings of Civilisation, UNESCO Ser., *Hist. of Mankind: Cultural and Scientific Development*, vol. i, 222–4; Stephen Powers, *Contribs to North American Ethnology*,

iii, 167; J. B. Davis, 'Some Cherokee Stories', *Annals of Archaeology and Anthropology*, (Liverpool Univ.), iii, 47; G. A. Dorsey, *Field Columbian Mus. Pubns., Anthrop. Ser.*, ix, No. 1, 40; J. V. Couto de Magelhaes, *O Selvagem*, 134ff; De Sahagun, *Historia general de las cosas de Nueva Espana*, i, 5ff; vol. ii, 250; Lumholtz, *Unknown Mexico*, i, 295; Bourke, *J. of Amer. Folk-Lore*, vii, 136; J. Sanchez, *Annales del Museo Nacional*, iii, 29; P. Ponce, *Annales del Museo Nacional*, vi, 5, 8.

16 For the Earth Mother in various guises – E. Seler, *Hastings's Encycl. of Religion and Ethics*, vol. vii, 614; L. Paton, *Hastings's Encycl. of Religion and Ethics*, vol. vii, 430; M. A. Czaplicka, *Hastings's Encycl. of Religion and Ethics*, vol. xi, 175; Graves, *The Greek Myths*, (Pelican) i, 27–8, 30; Briffault, 63–6, 90f, 119 etc.; Jacob Grimm, *Teutonic Mythology*, 250; David Cusick, in *W. M. Beauchamp, The Iroquois Trail*, 2ff; Al-Kindy, *The Apology*, 17; C. K. Meek in *Essays Presented to C. G. Seligman, Evans-Pritchard and others eds.*, 210–11 etc.

17 Löven, 353, 357; Las Casas, *Historia*, vol. 64, 22; French-Sheldon, *J. Anthrop. Inst.*, xxi, 362; Mason, 148–9; Kaberry, *Women of the Grassfields*, 59.

18 Ling Roth, *J. of the Anthrop. Inst.*, xxii, 26; C. O. Sauer, op. cit., 56; Boserup, op. cit., 16–19; also *Conditions of Agricultural Growth*, 28ff.

19 F. Braudel, *Capitalism and Material Life, 1400–1800*, 115, map; Briffault, 660–1; Löven, op. cit., 374, 533; Hemming, 25, 27; H. Baumann, *Africa*, i; de Schlippe, *Shifting Cultivation in Africa*, 14–15, 140ff; Kaberry, *Women of the Grassfields*, 47–8, 53–60, 67, 70n., 71, 91 (the name 'Kengeran' taken from this work); Leith Ross, 84, 90–2, 197, 254; Lévi-Strauss, 38–9; Karsten, 322–3; Hearne, 262; Lumholtz, *Unknown Borneo*, 182ff; Bonwick, 55; Bogoras, 601 and etc.

20 Cushing, *Thirteenth Ann. Rep. Bur. of Ethnol.*, 13; Magelhaes, op. cit., 134ff; Rink, op. cit., 39ff; Heckewelder, *History, Manners and Customs of the Indian Nations ...*, 429; T. Falkner, *A History of Patagonia*, 114ff; Karsten, op. cit., 300–1, 316–17, 319, 322–3; G. B. Grinnell, *J. of Amer. Folk-Lore*, vi, 112.

21 Mason, op. cit., 21–4, 37–9, 156; Im Thurn, op. cit., 65, 259; Löven, op. cit., 358–66, 374; Kaberry, *Women of the Grassfields*, 71, 82–3, 85; A. Richards, *Land, Labour and Diet in Northern Rhodesia*, 104–5; Evans-Pritchard, op. cit., 99–100; Coville, *Amer. Anthropologist*, v, 354.

22 Ibid.

23 Mason, op. cit., 145–6; Bancroft, *Native Races ...*, vol. ii, 363; Sellers, *Popular Science Monthly*, xi, 573–85.

24 Kaberry. *Women of the Grassfields*, 82–3; de Schlippe, op. cit., 147; Price, *J. of the Anthrop. Inst.*, vol. i, 259; Boserup, 164.

Chapter 3

DECLINE OF THE MOTHERHOOD AND WOMEN'S STATUS

The wealth of women's inventiveness, their energy and dexterity did not preserve their status and authority. On the contrary, the waning of the power of the Motherhood as a world-wide social change was due partly to women's very ingenuity, resource and capacity for hard work, that is to say their economic value. Women lost their economic status, too, because of their own actions and attitudes as well as those of men. Also of crucial importance was the accumulation of property, property of very different sorts.

The deterioration in the standing of women's work has been an enormous and complex process, developing in step with changes in climate and technology. Hardship and disaster strip away hierarchic power and force people to recognize their inter-dependence. The best chance of survival for each individual is through the group. Easing of conditions allows for greater individualism, facilitates survival and diminishes the status of Mothers. Birth and life become much less mysterious.

Women assisted their own decline by initiating hierarchies in Stone Age societies in place of earlier unstratified communalism like that of the fish hunters and gatherers of the Arabian Sea. As a social elite and as producers of wealth, women to a great extent were responsible for ending early egalitarianism and for the development of a society graded according to material possessions, age and sex.

PHYSICAL SIMILARITIES BETWEEN WOMEN AND MEN
The consequence of women's primary economic responsibilities was that the differences in physique of the sexes was not as marked as in modern industrialized societies. Xhooxham was 4 centimetres taller than her hunter, Bauxha. Like many San men, Bauxha had highly developed mammalian glands so that, as Frater Joao dos Santos noted, sometimes men were able to suckle. The similarity of females to males was a world-wide feature among Stone Age

peoples. It was noted in Polynesia by Captain James Cook, among the Bantu, and among West Europeans and north and central Asian peoples. The muscular development of women in hunting, gathering, and strenuous work like processing hides, was further encouraged by their role as warriors and defenders of their camps and villages. It is no part of this book to consider their military exploits. But they not only accompanied their men to battle on sea or land, they often fought themselves. When fighting became formalized, they formed their own war-bands and battalions under their own leaders. Much later the Chinese Emperor, Fu-Hi, decreed that women 'should distinguish themselves by their habits,' so difficult was it to tell the sexes apart. While the Kuki and Marring tribes of Assam introduced different hair-styles to make clear the distinction between females and males.

ILL-TREATMENT OF MEN BY WOMEN
When women dominated society they were often overbearing and sometimes savagely cruel to outside attackers, mutilating both corpses and wounded, delighting in slow tortures, instigating their men to eat their enemies. There was, however, a difference in kind between this ferocious hostility to outsiders and their much less bloodthirsty brow-beating of their own men. Fuegian women towered over their men and were apt to knock them down or beat them if they displeased them. Seri Indian men were similarly cowed. The right of a woman hunter gatherer to beat her husband has been noted among the San people and Australians. With some it extended beyond mere correction for the men's failure to fulfil their share of food providing. Women of the Ladrones Islands of Micronesia had the right to punish husbands who did not show them due deference, or who conducted themselves irregularly. They could use them as butts to relieve their own bad temper. They could collect their children and leave altogether, or call in female relatives who came, armed with spears and clubs, took the unhappy husband's possessions and sometimes pulled down his house. Among the Dayaks of Borneo, a woman beat her mate with a stick, but a man who beat his woman mate was severely punished. The dominance of hunter-gatherer women carried over into the hoe-farming Stone Age societies and often their domineering behaviour with it. The Ba-Gesu women of Uganda, like the northwestern Australians, attacked their husbands with hands, sticks

or knives. The more sophisticated a society became, the more sophisticated were the women's methods. Among the Tibbus, a Berber people of the Sahara, 'men were nothing, idling and lounging their time away, kicked by their wives as so many drones of society'. The women maintained them as stallions, to preserve the Tibbu race from extinction. They permitted men to enter their houses only if they sent word in advance of their coming. The gynaecocracy of Tuareg women were the custodians of culture and literacy; the men were kept illiterate. The women of Dongola in the Sudan, and of Beni-Amer in Egypt set out deliberately to ruin their husbands economically. The Dongola men had some redress; they could report major crimes committed by women to the women's guardians who had the right to beat them. The Beni-Amer men had no such right. If a man uttered a cross word, he was turned out of his home, his wife's commotion bringing all her brothers to her support. He was allowed back only in return for quite a heavy payment, for example of a horse or a camel. He had to give his wife a present for every child she bore him. Gradually a wife acquired all her husband's property and when he was beggared turned him out and looked for another victim. Both Dongola and Beni-Amer women considered it weakness to show husbands the least sign of affection. All over the Americas, among the Bantu-speaking peoples, among the Nigerians of West Africa, Tibetans, Aleuts, the people of Kamchatka, the Giliak of Sakhalin, the Ainu (the aboriginals of Japan), in some of the Melanesian Islands, particularly New Britain, and New Guinea, the general rule, enquiring Europeans found, was that women had the upper hand.[2]

It is against this background of female supremacy that the decline in women's status must be judged. It has been to a large extent due to the revolt of the inferior class, men, against the superior governing class, women.[3] This rebellion succeeded among hunter-gatherers thus in a number of cases it pre-dated herding. Their vestigial sense of property pertained to food supplies and so extended to the territory where these occurred, but both were *communal*. So the accumulation of *private*, personal property whether of lands, herds or any other form of personal wealth was not necessarily a primary or a main cause of women's subjection.

THE MALE TAKE-OVER OF RITUAL AMONG HUNTER GATHERERS

When climate warmed up, populations grew. To ensure food supplies, groups fixed territorial boundaries which they defended against infringement. At the same time, rituals became more elaborate so that a failure to observe the necessary respect at the death of even a distant relative might spark off a blood feud. Warfare therefore became more likely. It also became more of a male specialization and less of a communal activity shared by both sexes.

Men's desire for self-assertion, even revenge against women's hegemony was expressed inevitably whenever they found women wandering some distance from the matriarchal hearth. They were fair game. They were raped automatically and often killed, unless cunning or superior strength saved them.[4] While women had some chance when numbers were more or less even, if they encountered a group of men when alone or with only a few companions, their own guile and men's awe of their ritual powers were their only hope.

Tribal groups became known by faculties or other characteristics which suggested similarities with wild creatures; good weavers, for instance, were spider people. Or they chose group identities which would make them appear ferocious to would-be attackers. Women as well as men had these totems. For example, a girl in north-western Australia might inherit a totem from her mother. But men as the specialists in warfare established a superiority in totems. It was part of their take-over of the initiative ritual. Sir Baldwin Spencer and F. J. Gillen in their account of the walk-abouts of the Arunta (Wild Cat) people in central Australia in the Time Long Past, remarked the conjunction of the custom of raping women and of taking ritual secrets from them. There was no set pattern of behaviour. Sometimes women from other totemic groups successfully hid their sacred objects. Sometimes the Arunta men took ritual secrets from old men, or showed women their own ceremonies.[5] The wresting of ritual secrets and sacred objects from women was more important in diminishing their status than the momentary enforcement of physical domination through rape. For by learning their secret rites, men took from women their role as intermediaries with the deities which was part of the basis of their social pre-eminence. They broke women's claim that they alone could intercede for the fertility of the earth and that therefore they alone were able to ensure a plentiful food supply. By depriving women of their religious role, men not only undermined their power, they also took from them a means of intellectual fulfilment.

THE GROWTH OF SPECIALIZATION

Women's function as mothers, with children in the womb or at the breast made it more difficult for them to take part in military expeditions, to fight and lead their people into battle. Also when women took to long-fallow hoe farming, they were tied to their settlements more than hunter gatherers. They had to stay where their fields and gardens currently were. Women farmers expected protection from their male kin while they hoed, planted and weeded crops. Men accepted that they should stand guard with spears and shields while woman carried on their magical specializations of providing the essentials of life.[6] People who feared attacks selected the ablest male fighter to organize their protection. It was only common sense.

Women's function as mothers also made it more difficult for them to take part in long-range hunting. However, they undermined their own status by avoiding hunting not only when they had infants dependent on them, but also because comfort induced them to specialize in work nearer their homes. Long-range hunting is a more arduous job than gathering as the anthropologist, Dr Phyllis Kaberry found when she tried to keep up with Australian men on their expeditions:

It is true the woman provides the larger part of the meal, but one must not automatically assume that her work is more onerous. Actually it is less so than the men's, as I speak from experience. Merely to follow them in their hunting over rugged hills and the blazing sun left me so exhausted that after two attempts, I was content henceforth to amble with the women over the plains and along the dry river-beds. The element of sport distracts attention temporarily from fatigue, but too often it ends in the disappointment of seeing one's dinner leaping into the distance over the hills.[7]

Men's specialization in hunting was encouraged in another way. Women's concentration on endless daily gathering and local hunting of small game was not mindless as B. Malinowski has suggested[8] but on the whole they produced less interesting and less nutritious food. However, they loved meat and with reason, since it is the most concentrated source of protein. They gave their favours to the men who provided the most succulent meats, the ablest hunters. Among North American Indians, a good hunter could take his pick of women – provided the weather was kind to him and animals plentiful. If he failed to satisfy their craving for meat, women were apt to switch their attention to a man more fortunate.[9] A large part of happiness after all was having enough to eat, and if the food was enjoyable that was a bonus. But this practice had within it the germ of prostitution and the mercenary view of marriage summed up in the Victorian adage: 'Don't marry a man for his money: but don't marry a man without any.'

Women's concentration on the cultivation of crops, the domestication of birds and animals, more elaborate food preparation and skilled craft work all tended to build up men's specialization as fighters and hunters; so did female appetites and inclinations. It was not only the result of women's maternal function.

THE BREAKDOWN OF MATRILOCALITY
There was another process tending both to take girls from the maternal hearth and to elevate the status of men. Men learned how to use bribery to escape the onerous services imposed on them as the price of acceptance at a matriarchal hearth. In return for presents of game, the older women rulers might excuse a man from the labour, say, of chopping down trees. A man could use the same means eventually to buy his wife's way out of her Motherhood.

The successful male hunter who bribed his way out of jobs for the matriarchs, who could provide spears, bows and arrows, shields, traps, ornaments to the family of the woman whom he wanted as his mate, would also be sought after by his own women relatives, his own Motherhood. Until he left to live with his bride's family, they would want him to hunt for them and protect them. Thus his influence among his kin increased.

Moreover the affection so often lacking in mating was present among blood relations. To break the very strong tie between mothers and sons elaborate ceremonies were evolved as part of initiation ceremonies at puberty. Mothers suffered from this practice. New Caledonian women, for instance, so desperately wanted to keep their sons with them, they purchased infant girls as brides for them, and these children came to live in their households until they reached puberty.[10] The mothers themselves thus undermined the crucial rule of matrilocality.

The value of bride gifts or price rose as people accumulated property. The exaction of high payments ensured the wealth and social standing of the husband, hence, in this phase, girls sometimes favoured bride price. By making payments, a man shortened the length of time which he had to spend living as a stranger at his bride's settlement or village, far from his own people.[11] He paid a price for his food provider, provider of his children, creator and keeper of his own particular private hearth, a continuing price at fixed intervals before his marriage and at fixed intervals during their life together. In return for his gifts sooner or later he took her away from her Motherhood to live with his people as a stranger. The women folk of his family would help her, teaching her the features of new camp sites where she must hunt and gather, or hoe and plant as the case might be. She was still protected by her own kin, by her status as a worker and enricher of the family. She still had the right to walk off to visit her mother and blood relations when she felt like it. Like other women she was still consulted about community and family matters. But the family was her husband's family. She relinquished her own totem or family name and became a member of his group. She could still beat her husband if he displeased her, but then he had the right to beat her, which the Motherhood would not have allowed.[12] Furthermore a particularly able or lucky man could, in time, buy a second wife so that he would no longer be dependent on a single woman's work.

Another aspect of men's growing influence was that male relations obtained an increasing say in the disposal of a girl of their family to another man. Mothers and their brothers wanted the best price for a girl, and her well-being was less and less important, her consent less and less asked. The temptation to turn mating into a commercial transaction was too great. Families in the eastern and central Australian tribes, like the Diery, handed over girls of seven or eight years old to men old enough to be their grandfathers. A. W. Howitt, who described such practices in the 1880s, and European anthropologists who followed him, recorded the cruelty with which many Australian aboriginal girls and women were treated by their husbands. Here, in Melanesia and in an increasing number of places throughout the world, they lived at their husband's whim, liable to be killed for the least misdemeanour. Australian women were often speared through the fleshy parts of arms and thighs, or their skulls were cracked. But apparently this did not impair their ability to work, for anthropologists described them continuing their gathering and food preparation immediately after such attacks. In the north-west, as Phyllis Kaberry described, where they seem to have lost matrilocality later, punishments were less harsh and wives as apt to beat their husbands as vice versa.[13]

The effects of maltreatment of women by men were exactly the same as those of the ill-treatment of men by women. Women who were beaten and bullied had a physique and intellect inferior to that of their men and were fearful. Or they became like punch-drunk boxers, good-natured or seemingly impervious to injuries.

The cruelty shown by men to women may have been provoked by the extension of desert areas and generally worsening living conditions. But it occurred in dissimilar areas, for example among both the Australian desert tribes and the Melanesians, whose technological level was, however, similar. It certainly seems to have had in it the elements of revenge against earlier oppression by women since men in all primitive societies continued to dread their mothers-in-law. There were taboos even against meeting them.[14]

INCIDENCE OF THE ECLIPSE OF MATRIARCHAL POWER

Yet none of this adequately explains the subjection of women among some hunter-gatherer people, but not among others; in New Caledonia and Fiji, for instance, but not in New Britain and Java, in southern and central Australia, but much less in the north west. An examination of the circumstances of peoples among whom men turned the tables on women may suggest causes but cannot altogether resolve the question.

The North American Indians operated the same licence with lone women as Australians and Melanesians, yet the Iroquois, the most ferocious of all the tribes holding land from the Mississippi to the Atlantic, from the St Lawrence to the Cumberland River, not merely accepted the rule of women, but upheld it in face of the male-dominated policies of white settlers. Their chief negotiator of an alliance with the European incomers, led by Governor Clinton and the Commissioners of Indian Affairs, declared at Albany in 1814:

> Brothers! Our ancestors considered it a great offence to reject the counsels of their women, particularly of the Female Governesses [i.e. matriarchs]. They esteemed the mistresses of the soil. Who, said our forefathers, brings us into being? who cultivates our lands, kindles our fires and boils our pots, but the women? Our women, Brother, say that they are apprehensive their uncles have lost the power of hunting.... They entreat that the veneration of our ancestors in favour of the women be not disregarded, and that they may not be despised ... The Female Governesses beg leave to speak with the freedom allowed to women and agreeable to the spirit of our ancestors. They entreat the Great Chief to put forth his strength and to preserve them in peace. For they are the life of the nation.

Similarly among the Plains Indians, the Cheyenne, the Navajo, those from Virginia, the Indians of the Mexican Pueblos and throughout the continent among many tribes until the early twentieth century, women remained 'the guardians of the nation', preserving the family structure, the social hierarchy which they dominated, and determining war and peace.[15]

There was, however, one great difference between these peoples and the Melanesian and Australian tribes in which women were brutally treated. American Indian, Tibetan, Ainu, Bantu, Celtic and Polynesian women who had a high status became hoe farmers. The Melanesians and Australians were among those who did not. With them women's technology stagnated, as, indeed, did that of men. They never made this great cultural leap. So they provoked no new wonder at their abilities. On the contrary, over thousands of years, their skills were taken for granted, although much in demand. Whereas hoe farming elsewhere gave women a new lease of power. Yet many hunter gatherers did not experience this corrosion of male-female relationships. All that can be said is that technology is one of the facts that must be taken into consideration in considering the shifts in the balance of power between the sexes.

There does not seem to have been any special male proclivity for cruelty as some ethnographers have claimed. They themselves make clear that cruelty was common to both sexes, and kindness too.

Women fought back against men's attack on their power. Women gatherers and hunters went off to live alone, or banded with others in groups. The Arunta men on their ancient walk-about were careful to avoid a 'devil-woman' held to have strong magical powers and hid from a group of 'Dancing Women' who practised violent behaviour to escape being molested by men. One result of the threat from men was the establishment of women's realms, enclaves in which a matriarchal group of women dispensed with men except for the purposes of mating and for certain heavy work. Once they had fulfilled these functions, they might, if they were lucky, simply have to leave. They might be killed. An Island of Women in the West Indies, women's territories along the Orinoco and Amazon rivers, the women's countries in Mongolia and the Caucasus (see pages 98–9) and many more show the Amazons were not the phenomenon some European writers and historians from patriarchal societies have claimed. These gynaecocracies seem to have been a common defence of women of various levels of civilization against men's efforts to limit their ancient power.[16]

The custom of paying for a bride persisted after men took power, as did the custom of buying a bride by labour service to her family as witness the Old Testament story of Rachel and her cousin, Jacob. After seven years' labour, her father, Laban, tricked Jacob into marrying first his less prepossessing daughter, Leah. In order to have Rachel a few days later, Jacob had to agree to work a further seven years. In central Asia there were instances of men denied wives altogether after years of service.

POLYGAMY

The workload of women determined their attitude to polygamy. More often than not they welcomed it particularly in societies where mating was commercialized as in parts of Africa. After a woman had borne and reared a couple of children, she did not want to be burdened with more. She was glad to have a companion to share the daily work and the pains and risks of child-bearing, maybe too, the blows and wounds from a brutal husband. These advantages had to be weighed against any threat to her status from a second wife and a lessening of her husband's sexual attentions. Among many African hoe farmers the first wife generally had precedence. Second and subsequent wives she treated virtually as servants. Still a second wife had land of her own to cultivate and was economically independent. She insisted on having her own hut, and grainstore too, if possible. She could grow a small surplus to trade and gradually raise her status. Children added to her prestige and she had her kin behind her.[17]

But where social class became sharply defined and women lost their economic importance; where, as in northern Fiji, for example, men became unequivocally dominant, they took not one or two, but large numbers of wives. Women's status increasingly depended not on their economic role, but on their attractiveness to men. In such a situation, wives feared each other as rivals who might divert a husband's attentions to the extent that they were left sexually unsatisfied.

The main objectors to polygamy were the younger men. For it was the older men who accumulated wealth and therefore wives. So much did they feel deprived that there were instances of their making raids and carrying off wives, not simply out of passion, but because they then acquired skilled workers of their own. The women who were taken were placed in a position of utter dependency upon their new mates, although the exchange of a young for an old man might not have displeased them. This practice disrupted the entire bride-price structure. The women's relatives would have no further payments coming to them and would, like the old husbands, be very angry.

The decline in the status of women workers was certainly due in part to the development of personal private property. But the property was not initially herds, land or permanent buildings, as a number of anthropologists and sociologists have claimed since the 1880s, following Lewis Henry Morgan. In the first instance it was woman herself the invaluable worker, who constituted valuable private property.[18] The groups of young bucks who ran off with the wives of older men showed a way of escape from the Motherhood and from the continual drain of the bride price. While the older men who took little girls away from their maternal relatives demonstrated very clearly that the power of the matriarchy resided less in matrilineal descent of property than in matrilocality and the protection extended to a woman so long as she remained with her own family. Once away, once a man was no longer having to work in order to possess her, she became the servant and he the master. Women found wandering were no longer raped, killed or abandoned. They were captured and used as workers – as bed-mates, too, of course – but their value was as workers.

NOTES

1 Briffault, *The Mothers*, i, 443–7; U. Beier, *African Poetry*, 73, War Chant of the Fon of Dahomey's women's battalion.

2 Spegazzini, *Annales de la Sociedad Científica Argentina*, xiv, 171; le Gobien, *Histoire des isles Marianes*, 59ff; de Freyanet, *Voyage autour du Monde*, vol. ii, Pt. 1, 376, 475; Schwaner, *Borneo*, vol. 8, 161; C. Brooke, *Ten Years in Sarawak*, i, 70, 97, 130ff; Roscoe, *The Ba-Gesu*, 35; J. Richardson, *Travels in the Great Sahara*, ii, 343ff; Duveyrier, *Les Touaregs du Nord*, 334, 339ff, 420; de Zeltner, *J. Roy. Anthrop. Inst.*, xliv, 359; Crowfoot, *Sudan Notes and Record*, i, 121ff; Munziger, *Ostafrikanische Sudan*, 325; Grinnell, *The Cheyenne Indians*, i, 128ff; L. H. Gray, *Hastings's Encyl. of Religion and Ethics*, vol. vii, 421; Bandelier, *Rep. of an Archaeological Tour in Mexico*, 138; de Herrera, *General Hist. of the West Indies*, iii, 297, 299; de Andragoya, *Proceedings of Pedrarias Davilas*, 133; del Techo in *A Coll. of Voyages and Travels*, Churchill, Awnsham and John, vol. iv, 722; Livingstone, *Missionary Travels … in South Africa*, 622ff; Poix, *Rev. de l'Anthropologie*, xvi, 272; P. A. Talbot, *In the Shadow of the Bush*, 97ff; Felkin, *Proc. Roy. Soc. of Edinburgh*, xii, 329; Junker, *Travels in Africa*, 132; Dall, *Alaska and its Resources*, 396; Georgi, *Description de toutes les nations de l'Empire de Russie*, iii, 89; F. Halle, *Women in the Soviet East*, 152; Rockhill, *The Land of the Lamas*, 213, 230; Father Desideri in C. Puini, *Il Tibet*, 132; Bastian, *Die Völker der oestlichen Asien*, v, 866; Mama Rinso, *Nippon Archief voor de beschrivijving van Japan*, vii, 169; Powell, *Wanderings in a Wild Country*, 17; *Ann. Reps. of the Bur. of Ethnol.: ninth*, Murdoch, 413; *sixteenth*, L. Carr, 211; *seventeenth*, McGee, Pt. i, 9–11, 152ff, 269–79; J. Batchelor, *Ainu of Japan*, 191–4.

3 *Man*, May 1935, 67–8; R. Graves, *The Greek Myths* (Pelican), vol. i, 59–60, paras c–d; 71–2, paras 1–7; *Strabo*, ix, 402; Augustine, *De Civitate Dei*, xviii, 9; L. H. Gray, op. cit., 421; *Mission Scientifique du Cap Horn*, Hyades and Deniker, vol. vii, 257; L. F. Martial, vol. i, 214.

4 Spencer and Gillen, *Native Tribes of Central Australia*, 405, 407–8, 410–411, 416, 419; Dodge, *Our Wild Indians*, 198, 203ff, 210, 212ff; D. Macdonald, *Africana*, i, 131ff, 173; Livingstone, *Missionary Travels and Researches*, 146ff; C. O. Müller, *Hist. and Antiquities of the Doric Race*, ii, 318ff; Burton, *First Footsteps in Africa*, iii, 80ff; W. T. Pritchard, *Polynesian Reminiscences*, 149ff; O. Temple, *Notes on the Tribes … of the Northern Provinces of Nigeria*, 36, 60, 220, 340, 345; Cushing, *Thirteenth Ann. Rep. Bur. Ethnol.*, 13. Bogoras, *The Chukgee*, 455; Jochelson, *The*

Yukaghir, 62; Briffault, i, 730–1 and etc. ...

5 Radcliffe Brown, *Proc. of the 4th Pacific Science Congress*, 1929, 304; Spencer and Gillen, 336, 392, 404, 407–8; Coudreau, *La France equinoxiale*, ii, 186ff; C. M. Doughty, *Travels in Arabia Deserta*, ii, 515ff; J. Rhys, *Lectures on ... Celtic Heathendom*, 124, 572ff; Kaberry, *Aboriginal Woman*, 42, 44–5, 194–6, 201–2, 235 etc.

6 A. Werner, *The Natives of British Central Africa*, 135ff and see below, Ch. 7, Women as Burden-bearers.

7 Malinowski, *The Family among the Australian Aborigines*, 287; Kaberry, 6–7, 15, 22–4; also introduction to her book by A. P. Elkin (see Chs. 4 and 7 below).

8 Kaberry, 15, 25, 165; Heckewelder, *History, Manners and Customs of the Indian Nations*, 155, 157, 234; Schoolcraft, *Indian Tribes*, ii, 63; Dorsey, *Third Ann. Rep. Bur of Ethnol.*, 237; Spencer and Gillen, 32, 58; Hemmings, *Red Gold*, 387; Guiacuru men could outrun deer.

9 Briffault, ii, 272; A. I. Richards, *Land, Labour and Diet in Northern Rhodesia*, 55–9; *Hunger and Work in a Savage Tribe*, 81; Roscoe, *The Baganda*, 439; Heckewelder, 162, 234; Rasmussen, *People of the Polar North*; Georgi, *Description de toutes les Nations de l'empire de Russie*, iii, 129; Murdoch, *ninth Ann. Rep. Bur. o. Ethnol.*, 410 and etc.

10 L. Danks, J. Anthrop. Inst., xviii, 288.

11 Lévi-Strauss, *The Elementary Structures of Kinship*, 63ff, 275, 468–70; Evans-Pritchard, *The Position of Women in Primitive Societies ...*, 21, 181ff; Powers, op. cit., 22, 26, 259; Schoolcraft, iv, 24; v, 654; Briffault, i, 266, 304, 307; Roscoe, *The Northern Bantu*, 39, 209 etc.

12 Kaberry, 127–9, 136, 140ff; Spencer, *Native Tribes of North Western Australia*, 328.

13 Howitt, *Native Tribes of South Eastern Australia*, 193; T. H. Hood, *Notes on a Cruise of H. M. S. Fawn in the Western Pacific*, 141, 218; J. Barrow, *Travels in China*, 138; H. H. Johnston, *George Grenfell and the Congo*, i, 403; Burton, 120; W. J. Reid, *The Cosmopolitan*, xxviii, 452; Halle, *Women in the Soviet East*, 78, 'spouse' synonymous with 'slave', 82, 84–5 etc.

14 Frazer, *The Golden Bough*, iii, 83; A. Werner, 132; J. H. Weeks, *Among Congo Cannibals*, 130ff; Torday and Joyce, *J. Anthrop. Inst.*, xxxvi, 285ff; Grinnell, *The Cheyenne Indians*, i, 128ff; Junod, *Life of a South African Tribe*, i, 230ff and etc.

15 *Colls. of the N. York Hist. Soc. for the year 1814*, vol. ii, 128ff; Gray, loc. cit.; Ratzel, *Hist. of Mankind*, vol. ii, 130; Grinnell, loc. cit.; Bandelier, 138; de Herrera, iii, 297, 299 etc.; de Andragoya, 133 etc.

16 Spencer and Gillen, 220, 415, 417, 442; S. Löven, *Origins of the Tainan Culture*, 697; Sauer and Brand, *Aztatlan, Ibero-Americana*, 42 (my thanks to the Roy. Geog. Soc. Map. Lib. for confirming an Isla de Mujeres in Yucatan); Coudreau, 208f; Halle, 39ff.

17 Boserup, *Women's Role in Economic Development*, 43–4; Spencer, 41, 48; Livingstone, *Narrative of an Expedition to the Zambesi*, 284ff; M. H.

Kingsley, *Travels in West Africa*, 212; Leith Ross, 154–6; Kaberry, *Women of the Grassfields*, 37, 93–4, 98, 114–16; Bogoras, 600; Dorsey, 261; E. and P. Sykes, *Through Deserts and Oases in Central Asia* . . ., 121; Graham, *J. Asiatic Soc. of Bengal*, xii, Pt. 11, 636 etc.

18 J. R. Swanton, *Handbook of the American Indians*, i, 205; Kaberry, *Aboriginal Woman*, 25; A. C. Haddon, *Reps. of the Cambridge Anthrop. Expedition to Torres Straits*, v, 28; F. A. Monfat, *Dix années en Melanesia*, 265; A. Hadfield, *Among the Natives of the Royalty Group*, 183; J. Bailey, *Trans. of the Ethnol. Soc.*, S., ii, 294; H. H. Risley, Tribes and Castes of Bengal, i, 226; Rasmussen, 65; J. Roscoe, *J. Anthrop. Inst.*, xxxix, 182f etc.

Chapter 4

SLAVERY AND SETTLED FARMING

The date at which slavery appeared on earth is, of course, unknown. It was present at least by New Stone Age times, that is by the fourth millennium BC (see Table 1). Capturing in place of killing enemies and forcing them to work could only occur where food supplies and the techniques of exploiting them could support extra people outside the tribal group, where the captives would help to produce more food and raise the living standards of their captors to compensate for their own food consumption. By the fourth millennium BC in the Near East, tribal warfare was providing an increasing number of captives who would be potential slaves. At the same time, new farming techniques had provided the basis for social change.

THE GROWTH OF SLAVERY AMONG WOMEN
A captured woman was even more defenceless than a child wife who, however ill-used, had still to be negotiated and paid for within the bride-price system. A full-grown woman was also more useful and stronger than a mere child. Among hunter gatherers and hoe-farmers she would not have to be taught anything beyond the features of the new camp-sites. Because women in these economies were prized as workers more than men and theirs were peaceful arts leaving their captors less fearful of a violent uprising, the status of women tended to decline more rapidly. There were no niceties for captured men about doing oniy 'men's work'. Too much 'men's work' was warlike and of little use. They were therefore often put on 'women's work' which when performed by slaves was classed as 'servile'. Slavery thus altered the whole allocation of work between women and men, the specializations that had grown up amongst hunter-gatherers and hoe-farmers.

All slaves, male and female, were wrested from their kin. Their only safeguard against ill-treatment was their potentiality as workers. They would not be starved, beaten or misused to a point that would make them incapable of work, unless supplies of captives became extremely plentiful. The frequent fate of male slaves came to be castration, so that they would not then seduce or disturb free women.[1] Women slaves have always tended to be concubines. In communities in which the practice of paying bride price was on the increase, or where there was group marriage, enforced sexual relations were less of a departure from custom than in strong matriarchies such as those of the San people or Amerindians where a woman could refuse a hunter she did not like.

The advent of female slaves and slave wives ended the mystique and holiness of birth. It assisted the observation that man was the fertilizing agent in the process of procreation and so destroyed the idea that it was an entirely female process. At the same time improved food supplies which permitted populations to rise and to keep slaves made motherhood more common and devalued it further.

UNPAID FAMILY LABOUR
The key factor in creating the male-dominated hierarchy of work and of society in modern times was men's transformation of women's 'right to work' into 'forced labour' for them personally within the family. The great leap in the status of men came when they established the right to use captive women as wives; when their women relatives who were their rulers accepted not only that men had sexual rights over captive women, but rights of possession over them; when men could regard their women captives as their private workers and providers, as their personal property in per-petuity and keep the children they bred off them. Once this right was established they went on to establish that their heirs were the children bred from their slaves thus by-passing matrilineal in-heritance. This right was ultimately extended to the inheritance of land. The disadvantages to a bride of the commercialization of marriage which eventually made a slave of a girl sold into matrimony, were reinforced by this more direct and intensive slavery.

The advantages of capturing a woman and not having to pay for her were so great that the persistence of the bride price appears extraordinary until one remembers its profitability to the relatives of the girls. It was primarily through the institution of the captive wife that women's work for their husbands and children lost status and they came to constitute the bulk of that vast army now classi-

fied in censuses as 'unpaid family labour'. The change was the
result of deliberate male effort.

In countenancing the enslavement of others, of course, free
people not only increased the risks of slavery for themselves, since
the practice of taking slaves became generally popular, they also
undermined their own free status. For free rich women, in some
hoe cultures as well as in later civilizations, *not* working and a
consequent lack of economic importance became a status symbol.
Over time they delegated the manufacture of textiles and clothing
to household slaves, in very wealthy households to whole workrooms of them, small factories. Work within the home was more
and more associated with slavery, whether slave workers were
taken on, or wives and female relatives who continued to do work
undertaken by slaves for the better-off, were treated as slaves. Its
value was down-graded.[2] So wealth itself led to the decline of
women's status. All that was left to a woman from a rich family,
was the portion of land, or other property given her by her father
or husband, and her power to produce children. Women gradually
lost the right to be heard on the conduct of communal policies
and business. The use of women's intellectual powers was discouraged, their achievements belittled or ignored. However, clever
they were at their work, they were classed as inferior beings and
derided in order to destroy their supremacy. The same destructive
process was used against poor and servile males. But it was used
because of their poverty and servility and to perpetuate it, not
because of their sex.

WOMEN'S CONTINUED DESIRE FOR SKILLED WORK

However, slavery began when Motherhoods were still powerful
and when 'chief' as a male prestige position meant merely 'war-
chief', often an elective and not an inherited office. Women's wish
to exercise their skills survived the accumulation of wealth. Among
hoe farmers there were still in the twentieth century examples of
women working at their own insistence at jobs that in later societies
came to be regarded as menial. In Uganda, for instance, no woman
of high or low degree would stay with a man unless he gave her
land and a hoe with which to dig it. She would return to her family
and demand a divorce. On the Pelew Islands in the South Pacific,
the richest woman not only went out to superintend poorer women
who worked on her taro patch, she worked with them in deep

mud which coated them up to their hips, wearing mats on their backs to protect them from the burning sun.[3] They regarded work as their right in the same way as men came to consider warfare their prerogative.

Where, however, slavery undermined women's status, the change took place slowly and the majority of women continued to do skilled work inside their households. Even the comparatively wealthy still span and carried on the intellectual pursuits of weaving, dyeing and decorating of cloth, of embroidery and the making and decorating of pottery. For thousands of years it was only temples and royal households that were rich enough to employ slaves.[4]

SETTLED FARMING

Another motive for enslaving people arose through a new and fundamental change in food production. Shifting cultivation within tribal boundaries required continuous occupation of the same tribal territory all the time. But within the tribal area hoe-farmers moved around. There were no pieces of lands that belonged to families forever. When the land of a settlement was worked out, they looked for a new site on land long fallowed under natural growth. They established a claim to it by clearing the wild growth and opening it up. Where, however, cultivable land was in short supply, nomadic herders like the Natufians returned again and again to the same spot. With the growth of population and so of competition for food-bearing land, their descendants had to settle permanently at their water-source to ensure their continued access to its fertilizing and life-giving properties. The first known continuous farming settlements arose around three places in the Middle East: in the Caucasus, in Iran and in Jordan. Settled farming, the sort of farming most people think of today, was going on by 5500–5000 BC and spread along the valleys of the great rivers, the Tigris, the Euphrates, the Nile and the Indus. It extended across Asia to the Yangtse and the other great Chinese river basins.[5]

Since the amount of fertile land was limited in Asia Minor and North Africa, it was continually cropped. People were hemmed in by mountain and desert and could not move off to another site. At first, when population was sparse in ratio to the cultivable ground, and the climate wetter and colder, the living was good.

In order to speed up and ease the work of preparing the ground for planting, people improved digging sticks and hoes. Livingstone in the mid-nineteenth century found women and men in South Africa using double-handled hoes, pushing them through the ground to make a continuous furrow.[6]

Because the food supply was relatively certain, population began growing. Later generations of people who had not established territories of their own and were consequently landless, were given a new reason for armed raiding. To obtain land cultivable under known techniques, they had to conquer others. At one and the same time they secured a food supply and people to work it for them. Nomadic herding increased the incentive for armed robbery. The movements of animals as well as the growth of population sustained by regular annual harvests, tied people to territories even more tightly than tribal organization. People who wanted herds knew where to go to steal those belonging to others. Armed robbery of this kind and the taking of captives were great new labour-saving devices. They were the specialties of the out-group, the younger and poorer men. As the ancient Cretan warriors' song stated:

> My wealth is my long lance
> With which I cultivate and harvest
> The sweet wine of the vine.[7]

There was no sudden shift from hoe to plough cultivation, no dramatic decline in numbers of women in agriculture. The slowness of the change from gathering to shifting, and from shifting to settled cultivation is illustrated in India. By 2500 BC the Indus valley civilization in the west of the sub-continent, based on settled cultivation, was established. But it was not until a thousand years later, in 1500 BC, that the earlier form of shifting cultivation was creeping along the Ganges valley to the east, among people still at the hunter-gatherer stage.[8] In Russia shifting cultivation was spreading northwards to the Baltic only from the late fifteenth century AD. It was still used in parts of Russia and Finland in the nineteenth century, women and men burning off the under-growth together. For a settled village did not necessarily turn to settled cultivation if shifting cultivation of different sections of the surrounding land sufficed for its needs. No more did the use of the plough instead of the hoe to open up land, signify a change from shifting to settled cultivation. For example, in the Danube basin, in Central Asia and in southern Siberia between 3000 and 2000 BC, the plough was used in conjunction with shifting cultivation. People lived in large permanent villages, for instance on the land between the Rivers Dnepr and Pruth, a tributary of the Danube, with up to two hundred dwellings of clay and timber, some with separate rooms and compartments, heated by stoves. They still used 'slash and burn' methods in opening plots in rotation around the villages, leaving spent plots to fallow. It was an early kind of field system, possible because land was plentiful in relation to those who had to live off it. Such a system could only be operated communally by a village council – in the case of Russia, the mir, in which women played a part.[9]

Food surpluses were created not only through short-fallow plough cultivation, but also through irrigation. As a further means of ensuring the fertility of the soil that was constantly farmed, Mesopotamians and, almost simultaneously, Egyptians and the Indo-Aryans of Mohenjo-Daro and Harappa in the Indus valley hit on the idea of building canals. There is a connection between the building of dams referred to in Chapter 2 and the diversion of water into artificial channels. The connection between the plough and the digging stick is plain with women in South Africa using very early types of ploughs at the beginning of this century, just as men used digging sticks. The respective contributions of women and men to the development of the plough and irrigation cannot be determined.

Cantabrian, Thracian, Scythian and Celtic women all tilled the soil with ploughs in historic times. Slave and poor women agricultural workers in plough cultures illustrate the tearing away of mystery from childbirth since for them there was no privacy or aid from some wise woman. They gave birth to children in fields, pausing only to bathe them in nearby brooks. But they did so out of harsh economic necessity, not hardihood. The idea put about that because they hardly stopped working, they felt no pain at childbirth was a myth. Poseidonius, visiting the estate of a friend at the port of Massilia (Marseilles) learnt that he employed women and men on ditch-digging. One day he noticed a woman 'seized with the pangs of child-birth go aside from her work and, after having given birth to her child, go back to work at once in order that she might not lose her pay.' Seeing the pain she was in as she worked, he drew his friend's attention to her. And this man, Charmoleon, more generous than some twentieth-century employers in textile factories, paid her and sent her away. So she took her baby to a brook and washed it before leaving.[10]

In much of China, India and the Middle East – all rice and plough cultivation areas – the allocation of work was the same, but women became much more, sometimes entirely, subject to men. The aggressive assertion of male authority, women's loss of economic independence, harsh climate and infertile country, population pressure, and the marriage market contrived to reduce women to the status of slaves. In the south of China and in the rice-growing area of the Lower Yangtse, there was more than one harvest a year and the members of a family with land worked at cultivation without regard to sex or age. In the northern subdistricts of this region, fields were kept in cultivation during the year by means of crop rotation, wheat, beans, rape-seed and barley being sown in winter when the paddy-fields were dry. All over China women pulled light ploughs. Only much later, due to big population growth, many women in northern areas were needed much less on the land. Then peasants copied the foot-binding practice of the middle and upper class women. These became the foot-binding areas. Yet even in the twentieth century in the north and north-west there were places where women's feet were not bound and where respectable women maintained a freedom and independence at odds with conventional Chinese ideals of female behaviour. It was not only the labour requirements of agriculture that determined women's economic status, but tradition and women's determination. There were, for example, groups of girls pledged to refuse marriage and even to commit suicide rather than accept marriage that was not matrilocal.[11]

Society was increasingly divided by wealth and the divisions became more and more complex. Free women saw captives as men did as a means of labour-saving. Slave women therefore particularly took over the eternal, infernal grinding and milling of grain and the carrying of water and other burdens. The rise of the non-working woman and the growth of women's subjection were telescoped in the history of Rome and are therefore more clearly visible than when these processes were spread over thousands of years. Dionysius Halicarnassensis related that in the days of Romulus women customarily gave long speeches in the Senate.

Horace [in *Carmen*] referred to the old Roman custom whereby youths hewed wood and drew water 'under the orders of a severe matron'. Most of the important events in the early days of Rome were ascribed to women. Yet years later Cato the Elder, defending the State Law, declared:

> Our fathers have willed that women should be in the power of their fathers, of their brothers, of their husbands. Remember all the laws by which our fathers have bound down the liberty of women, by which they have bent them to the power of men. As soon as they are our equals, they become our superiors.

Just because the change was relatively quick, within the compass of a few centuries, Roman free women retained more privileges than their peers in Asian countries, most notably religious observances, relics from the heyday of the maternal clan. Robert Briffault claimed that this accounted for 'a strange combination of patriarchal principles and matriarchal sentiment which persists in modern Italy'.[12]

A girl became property from her birth. First her parents owned her. The bride price became institutionalized. Prices paid for wives came to be fixed by tribal law in Africa, for example among aristocratic families on the Gold Coast. The Shambaa of Usamba had a fixed price of so many goats. In Uganda in the 1920s, there was a universal rate of 13*s* 4*d* whether the girl was a peasant or a princess. Sometimes chiefs tried to check this mercenary traffic. The Nanzela for a time limited the price to two or three shoes, presumably pairs, but they could not hold it down. Among the Mkamba in East Africa, wives were customarily bought and sold as goods.

But the trade did not stop there. In Warega in the Congo, a man could buy an already wedded woman from her parents, by offering more than her current husband was paying in bride price. Among the Samoyeds of the far north of Asia and the central Asian Sifan, parents sold daughters over and over again to the highest bidder.

As men established their ownership of wives, they also established the right to sell them, the transactions always being based on the working capabilities and child-bearing prospects of the women. This was common practice among the Tartars. The Russian historian, J. D. Georgi, recorded that one man had sold eight successive wives and was courting a ninth.

The necessity of owning a woman as a means of obtaining a worker was well understood. Hesiod, a Greek poet of about 700 BC, advised his young brother on how to succeed as a farmer. At the age of about 30 he should get an allotment, a ploughing ox and 'a woman, purchased', preferably a virgin 'so that you may teach her chaste morals'. He must be careful to have only one son, that is only one heir, unless he grew so old that he was in danger of outliving his middle-aged offspring. It was then advisable for him to produce a second, younger son to ensure the succession.

Or the Chinese had a saying: 'A wife married is like a pony bought; I'll ride her and whip her as I like.' And the Japanese still say today: 'Get a horse, or get a bride.'[13] A woman's status became like that of a draught animal, an aid in work with the additional advantage of being able to produce children if required. And like an animal she cost no more than her keep whatever a man considered that to be.

As men gained in economic importance, male children were preferred to females. Men's primary responsibility for warfare increased the risks of their being killed when young and so expanded the demand for sons. Rachel mourned because she could not give Jacob a son to the extent that she had her handmaid deputize for her. The maternal function was narrowed still further: it consisted not of producing children, but of producing sons.

Women consented to their own sale partly because they had little choice, when wife-beating was customary. But even when it was not, the development of patriarchy, women's loss of initiative in work, the fact that they were intended always to be in the possession of some man, meant that if left on their own, the best they could do for themselves was to find a new male protector as in the Old Testament story of Naomi and her widowed daughter-in-law, Ruth, whom she helped to a new marriage. It was no worse than a woman giving herself to a good hunter in return for meat. But the woman hunter gatherer was free and self-sufficient; she was under no pressure but her own appetite, whereas for Ruth and Naomi the alternative was destitution.

PATRIARCHAL MARRIAGE

The solidarity of the group was less necessary because herding

and armed raiding alike facilitated the provision of food and necessities. The old idea of property as something communal for the
sustenance and pleasure of all, of land belonging to the group, of
moveables being handed on for others to enjoy was submerged
increasingly in the idea of individual personal property. Under
motherhood and matrilineal succession, men looked to their sisters'
sons as heirs, or to their in-laws' families. In group marriages,
no man could positively identify a child as his own. In both these
social arrangements, sexual licence made this difficult. But when
a man began to acquire property, including a wife-cum-worker,
he could identify his children. Fathers tended to favour their own
rather than their sisters' sons, keeping them near them, constantly
supporting them, giving them villages in their own territory. They
established the right to attach themselves to their fathers' clans
if these ranked above those of their mothers'. The total possession
of a woman and a desire definitely to establish paternity resulted
inevitably in the limitation of a woman's sexual freedom. Proof
of paternity required that women's right to free sexual relations
be ended. But women were accustomed to freedom, even after
marriage, even in patriarchal societies that imposed purdah. The
Hausa poet, Imrul Kaisi, loved women and attested in his verses
that they could meet men freely on ordinary occasions. He bears
witness to their sexual activities telling how he came secretly to
them in their palanquins on the backs of camels and braved 'many
guards and hosts of dangers', for to be caught visiting a woman
meant death to a man, and a woman leaving her tent at night to
go with her lover for some hours under the stars, trailed the fringes
of her cloak to wipe out their footprints in the sand.[14]

Women were discouraged and hobbled not by chains, but by
a variety of methods, including guards. The protection they had
created for themselves against sun, wind and sand or against mosquitoes in the way of veils or face masks was turned from its original
purpose in order to hide their faces from men so that none might
desire them. Some Jewish sects required wives to shave their heads
and render themselves as unpleasing as possible to the opposite
sex. A method not used by the Hebrews, but in much more general
use was an extension of female circumcision. The circumcision of
males was regarded as an hygienic if painful measure among people
who lived naked and who often coated themselves with grease and
ochre, risking dirt and insects damaging their genitals. The removal

of folds of skin was a preventive and protection against disease. Among some peoples it was elaborated for men so that it became a rather painful ritual to demonstrate their courage. And it was also extended to girls for whom it came to consist of the partial or total excision of the clitoris which left the vaginal orifice inelastic and reduced its diameter to half an inch. For a man to have entry to a woman's body, never mind the egress of a child, the services of a midwife and surgery were required. Sexual intercourse was thus made so painful that it became absolutely repugnant to a married woman. Her chastity was ensured. These extreme methods of female circumcision were built up into such a powerful social convention that no man would marry an uncircumcized girl. The practice became rife in North Africa and the Near East. It created the most frigid wives in the world so that it was customary for the men to find their sexual pleasures with poor women, family slaves, or prostitutes. In patriarchal families wives were strictly for breeding purposes and, in all but the wealthiest, for work.

The iron chastity belt of Europe and the binding of the feet of little Chinese girls so that they were badly crippled were other aspects of maintaining a girl's chastity. It was impressed on her that this was her supreme gift. Most common of all, the threat of severe physical punishment or death were discouragement enough and no permanent physical disfigurement was required in advance to ensure that her children were those only of her owner, her husband. The result of these harsh methods was considerable success in imposing monogamy on women, reserving sexual licence only for men. It also helps to explain the preference of women for prostitution. It is arguable that the independent prostitute suffered less than a servile, slave wife purchased for breeding purposes.[15]

It is curious, however, and an instance of the durability of human conventions that the desire to ensure paternity by a husband did not destroy the custom that a male guest or a stranger should have the comforts provided by a female relative of his host in his bed, be it his host's wife or daughter. The shreds of group marriage remained.[16]

Men accumulated wives according to their wealth as they did other forms of property. Wives became status symbols. With the growth in population and a surplus of women who were not killed off to the extent men were in wars, wives of chiefs and kings were sometimes in a worse situation than ordinary working women. One reason for their vulnerability would appear to have been their own property, the dowry.

THE DOWRY

The establishment of patriarchy altered the direction of payments in marriage. Instead of men paying bride price to a girl's relatives, parents virtually bought sons-in-law by giving their daughters dower. Dower was property which a girl brought with her to her new family. It could be in the form of herds, land, jewels, household goods, even armaments. Married women retained some rights in their dower. In some cases husbands were allowed use of herds and land and controlled their wives' dowries; later they could invest the cash and obtain interest although they had no right to the principle. In this way, if a man predeceased his wife, his widow had some of this dower left, off which she might live.

The change from bride price to dowry is co-terminous with strict patriarchy in China, India, the Near East and, later, much of Europe. But it was limited by class and wealth, that is, the dowry became characteristic of those societies in which women lost work or left off working, employing poorer people to do the work for them. Sometimes it was a matter of handing back to the bride the bride price, sometimes quite other property was given her. But whatever form the dowry took, and although her husband might have the use of it during her lifetime, it was hers.[17]

However, the dowry provided an incentive to her husband's family to encourage her to commit suicide on his death, or even to kill her when the only way to obtain her property was through her death. In Northern Fiji, for example, a chief's wives were killed at his death by the populace whose co-operation was ensured by paying them with presents, including women. In certain Indian states, wives were induced to immolate themselves on their husbands' funeral pyres. In Benin, Natchez and New Zealand, as in ancient Scythia, aristocratic women committed suicide on the deaths of their husbands.[18]

It has been argued that the women wanted to do away with themselves. Their life as widows could be made so unpleasant that they might prefer this alternative. Or they could be 'brain-washed' into suicide, even by the very painful method of self-immolation. A few might kill themselves out of grief. But the custom of arranged marriages made such deep love less likely. It became part of the price a woman paid for *not* working.

The working woman, on the contrary, was much in demand once she was widowed. As a part of a husband's property, on his death she was inherited by one or other of his male kinsmen, a practice called the Levirate. The original intention had been benevolent, the protection of a woman so that she avoided the destitution which threatened Naomi and Ruth. But with the subjugation of women, the system was increasingly used to over-exploit women as workers. The Levirate was prevalent in the whole vast area from the Balkans to China. A Kalmuck proverb ran: 'If an elder brother dies he leaves for heritage – his wife. But if a horse dies, it leaves for heritage – its hide.'[19]

PATRIARCHAL RELIGIONS

Men sought religious sanction for their social supremacy. The first phase of any patriarchal religion enjoined complete submission on the part of women to men. For men had but lately thrown off the matriarchal yoke and matriarchs in their struggle to maintain their ascendancy had not been too nice. Their human sacrifices tended to be male. So men made new pantheons in which the supreme Earth Mother was subject to a male deity as his wife or daughter. Many goddesses retained immense power. For example in the twentieth century in the Nigerian provinces of Onitsha, Owerri, Agoja and Benin, the goddess Ale was the deity to whom all prayed. But over her ruled Chuku, father of the sun, of lightning, the supreme Earth God, sender of rain who makes crops grow, thus symbolizing men's seminal role in childbirth.

Similarly the Sumerian goddess Inanna, in the third millennium BC, retained pristine powers:

My father has given me heaven, has given me earth: ... Rule over men, rule over women he has granted me. The hurricane he has given me, Heaven has he set as a crown upon my head. Earth has he put as sandals for my feet....

But she derived her powers not even from the chief god of the pantheon, but from his son, Enlil, her father, and shared them with other gods. At the fertility ceremony to mark the start of spring, a priestess who represented her was ritually married. She went below ground to her realms of death and darkness where male priests awaited her and a new Inanna arose. So was the golden bough turned against women. The king for a day, who became a king for a year before sentence of death was carried out on him, became a permanent priest king and a woman became the sacrifice.

Kings now claimed divinity, but they had still to acquire it through marriage to a queen who represented the Earth goddess, Aditi in Hindu mythology and Sri among the Fijians, the equivalents of the Roman goddess Ceres.

The Indo-Aryans imposed upon the animism and Mother Goddess cults of the Aborigines whom they conquered in the Indian sub-continent, a male-dominated cult which gradually crushed all women. A woman was forbidden to study the holy tenets of the Vedas, to know the Shastras, to perform sacrifices. One dictum ran:

> In childhood a woman must be subjected to her father, in youth to her husband, and when her lord is dead, to her sons. A woman must never be independent.

The pharaoh became a god-king greater than the female Isis with whom he shared power. Among the Hebrews, goddesses were eliminated and there was only one supreme God. The tale of Eve's revolt suggests a rising of vanquished people led by a woman against their conquerors, or a male revulsion against a bloodthirsty Mother-goddess cult.[20]

But while patriarchal religions institutionalized the downgrading of women, it was through them that humanity moved away from human sacrifice, for example in the Hebrew law, 'Thou shalt not kill'. Confucianism required no ritual letting of blood although a Chinese wife's utter lack of rights permitted her husband to kill her.[21] The Hindu Ramayana enjoined a husband to be concerned about his legal spouse however much she was his inferior. No woman could hope to attain the rank of Buddha simply because she was female, but she could attain a secondary grade in the Buddhist hierarchy. The greatest step towards equality was the Hebrew Christ's equal concern for women and men of all classes and his assertion of their equal value to God.

Nonetheless where slavery persisted so did the slave wife, hence the word of St Paul: 'Wives submit yourselves unto your own husbands, as unto the Lord.' But he also preached the absolute physical equality of man and wife in marriage and equality of behaviour in divorce. He gave to women of his church an equal right to speak. For women Christians, like men, in the Roman Empire put their lives at risk.[22]

Six centuries later Mohammed accepted women's inferiority but opposed Arab harshness to them. He laid down that a man must make financial provision for his wife. A Moslem marriage contract is only valid when a man has signed an agreement that he will pay over a dowry, which must be itemized, to his wife. It can be in any negotiable form and it is hers, not her father's, although her male relatives settle the sum in hard bargaining. It is quite distinct from the dowry provided to a bride. And it is very necessary because of the ease with which Moslem men may divorce their wives, although instant divorce is condemned by the Koran as 'an injustice and a manifest sin'. Usually only half the dowry is paid on marriage and the rest on divorce, or the death of the husband. A wife's rights to her sons, during their early boyhood, and to her daughters are also safeguarded. Moslem law lays down a specific right of inheritance for a daughter of one half that of a son.[23] Thus if Hindu, Christian and Moslem girls and women have been ill-treated it has less been owing to religious precepts, but rather in spite of them through a clinging to traditional customs, the 'shanat' and 'adat'.

Husbands took over from priests and kings the role of personification of male deities, epitomized in the Turkman saying: 'A woman has two gods, a senior god in heaven and a younger one on earth.' If a man acknowledged the full value of jobs done by wives and daughters, he must allow them a status equivalent to this value and this no man would do.

Yet, perhaps the most remarkable feature of the reversal in the balance of power between the sexes was the survival of the Earth Mother the world over. The new creeds of the wealthy were slow to change the ancient creeds of those who grew their food.

Neither the plough nor irrigation necessarily caused women to lose work and economic independence. Proof of the maintenance of balance and harmony in a plough economy comes from the small independent farmers of warm and fertile Burma. There animal-drawn ploughs and irrigation are still used. Out of long habit, a Burmese woman, Mi Mi Gyi, would wake at dawn. Lying on her sleeping mat she could see through the woven bamboo blind that covered the window that the sky was turning pale gold, the light through the mesh making a faint pattern on the wooden floor. After changing into her day-time sarong and winding up her hair, she customarily lit a cheroot and went down the verandah steps to fetch firewood from under the house to start the cooking fire.

Today was different. It was the first of June, the beginning of those three months when they left the house and, with stores of food and tools and their water buffalo, set off for their paddy fields. This year it was easier for her because her son was old enough to be left with her niece who would also do some weeding in her vegetable and fruit garden. For four years now, they had returned from the paddy fields to find weeds knee-high, so that she had no respite from the hard work with the rice, but had to clear them at once, before they grew worse.

Up at the paddies, she opened the hut, put away provisions and hung her new baby, Ni Ni, in her sleeping basket out of the way of deadly snakes and insects like scorpions and tarantula spiders. Maung, her husband, had the buffalo harnessed to the plough, so she tucked her sarong up and went to join him. It would go on like this, day after day, first following his furrows, planting; then weeding, although the plough cut down that job; then harvesting, passing the grown rice to Maung who followed her, and who carried away the loaded baskets, always bent double, feet in mud and water until they turned greyish, watching for leeches that slyly crawled up your legs to suck your blood. From the time she was nine years old she had been going up each year to work in the paddies, first with her parents, then with her brother, now with her husband. Only age and infirmity stopped women and men working in the paddy fields. But older women, like Maung's grandmother, still went on working in their gardens round the house with help from sons and grandsons. Yet while she and Maung sweated, she knew they lived among splendour, wading in sapphire during the day, and flaming amber and gold in the evenings as the water reflected the changing skies, watching the piercing green of the young rice shoots pushing up. At the end she would be sitting stripping off the heads of rice so that there would not be the weight of leaves and stalks to go home in the cart. She would know they had enough for the next year.[24]

Theirs was a land of plenty. There was always enough to eat

so long as Mi Mi and Maung pulled together. Only when wife or husband did not or could not co-operate was there trouble. It was accepted that a wife, like a husband, should work and earn. There were two main differences between them: while Maung had time of an afternoon to sit and read or visit friends, she rarely did. She could not read in any case, for that came from temple education given by Buddhist monks only to boys. It was of no great consequence when literacy played little part in life and work. Her visiting usually arose out of business and when people visited her her hands were always busy, rolling cheroots, spinning, sewing. She still strolled up to the temple of an evening, but much more seldom than when she was a girl, and she had to carry her babies with her. If Maung disapproved of any of her activities, she would have to drop it, whereas he would not necessarily respond to her complaints, although he might listen to his grandmother. Women's leisure and status increased with age.

The degree of a woman's subservience varied from place to place. If a family was poor and had no paddy fields, it was common for women, like men, to work as paid labourers for those more fortunate. Even in relatively well-off families in Burma, teen-age girls like Mi Mi hired themselves out when family work was slack, shifting earth in baskets for building and road and canal-making. In Thailand there was a saying: 'Your husband is a shading umbrella to protect your head. He makes you look pleasant and respectable in all eyes. Therefore obey him.' There the difference in the work contribution of either sex was clear in any natural disaster, flood or famine. The man was concerned to save the plough and other equipment, while the woman's role remained that of family nourisher. If their own crops failed, she found paid employment to provide as much food as possible for her family.[25] But her importamce was recognized in her status. Women not only worked in the family fields, they still had their own plots, carried on by-industries and marketed their products.

NOTES

1 A. Richards, *Land, Labour and Diet in Northern Rhodesia*, 401; J. Hunter, *Memoirs of a Captivity Among the Indians*, 384; H. W. Bates, *The Naturalist on the River Amazon*, 199; T. W. Atkinson, *Travels on the Regions of the Upper and Lower Amoor*, 250ff; *Exodus*, ch. 1: Dionysius Halicarnassensis, *Antiq. Rom.*, ii, 30·5; Marco Polo, 161; Greenidge, *Slavery*, 27.

2 R. J. Forbes, *Hist. of Technology*, C. Singer and other eds., i, 591; Gordon Childe, *What Happened in History*, 235, 270–72; Sir J. Marshall, *Mohenjo-daro and the Indus Civilisation*, pp. vi, 33, 194; E. Mackay, *The Indus Civilisation*, 103, 137–8.

3 Kubary, *Ethnologische Beiträge zur Kentniss der Karolinesen Archipels.* 159; J. Roscoe, *The Baganda*, 426.

4 R. J. Forbes, loc. cit.

5 Gordon Childe, *What Happened in History*, 48; *Hist. of Technology*, C. Singer and others eds., vol. i, 47–8, 513; Hawkes and Woolley, *Prehistory and the Beginnings of Mankind*, UNESCO Ser., *Hist. of Mankind*, i, 220–223; Mortimer Wheeler, *Early India and Pakistan*, 34, 72–3, 76, 86–7.

6 Livingstone, *Missionary Travels in South Africa*, 442; Gordon Childe, *Hist. of Technology*, i, 539, 541.

7 E. Mireaux, *La vie quotidienne au temps d'Homère*, 111.

8 Mortimer Wheeler, 94, 113, 121–3.

9 Symons, *Russian Agriculture*, 18; Stepniak, *The Russian Peasantry*, vol. i, 129–30; Mackenzie Wallace, *Russia* (1912 ed.), 128, 133, 138–9; *Man's Role in Changing the Face of the Earth*, W. L. Thomas ed.: Narr, 140; Omer C. Stewart, p. xxx: Darby, 208 and fig. 64, 209.

10 Strabo, iii, 111–17, 113; v, 233–39, B xi, Cv3–5; Neuburger, *Technical Arts of the Ancients*, 84, photo; Livingstone, *Missionary Travels in South Africa*, 442; Boserup, *Woman's Role in Economic Development*, 33.

11 Lossing Buck, *Land Utilization in China*, 293; Dyer Ball, *Things Chinese*, 428f; *Li Ki*, xxvii, 38; J. Barrow, *Travels in China*, 73–5, 140–2.

12 Dionysius Halicarnassensis, *Antiq. Rom.* ii, Oldfather trans., ii, 45: Horace, *Carmen Seculare*, Way trans., iii, vi, 33–41; Livy, xxxiv, 2, 3, 5; Briffault, *The Mothers*, i, 428–30.

13 Hesiod, *Erga*, 405, 406; Halle, *Women in the Soviet East*, 78ff; Lévi-Strauss, *Elementary Structures of Kinship*, 36, n. 5; Boserup, *Woman's Role in Economic Development*, 47–8: Georgi, *Description de toutes les nations de l'empire de Russie*, ii, 23; Bove, *Terra del Fuoco Mari Australi . . .* 132; Majumdar in Appadorai ed., *The Status of Women in South Asia*, 61–2; Greenidge, quoting Sister M. André, 99; The mass of evidence contradicts Briffault's claim that marriage by purchase was exceptional; see ii, 223–4; Delhaise, *Les Warega*, 171; W. J. Reid, *The Cosmopolitan*, xxviii, 452; F. G. Jackson, *J. Anthrop. Inst.*, xxiv, 405.

14 *The Book of Songs of Imrul Kaisi*, Rattray trans. in *Essays Presented to C. G. Seligman*, p. xxx, Evans-Pritchard and others eds.

15 Anne Balfour Fraser, Supp. to *The Baptist Times*, 9 January 1975, 5; P. Montgomery, *The Contemporary Rev.*, vol. 223, No. 1291, August 1973; Daisy Bates, *Rev. d'ethnographie*, No. 21, 31; Greenidge 30; Davin, *Woman-work*, map facing p. 1, 10–11; W. G. Walshe, *Hastings's Encyl. of Religion and Ethics*, iii, 491.

16 Fled Bricrend, *The Feast of Bricriu*, G. Henderson ed. and trans. 69, 81; de Jubainville, *L'épopée celtique en Irlande*, 8, 23; and trans. *Tàin bò Cuàlnge*, 36; Paris, *Romans de la table ronde*, vol. iii, 166. P. Meyer,

Romania, iv, 394ff. E. Armstrong, ed., *Le chevalier de l'épée*, 16f. *La livre du chevalier de la Tour Landry*, 266. L. Meray, *La vie au temps des trouvères*, 76ff. G. Schoepperle, *Tristan and Isolt*, vol. i, 254ff. Fr. Michael ed., *Gérard de Rossillon*, 124; Halle, 94.

17 Briffault, *The Mothers*, ii, 225–6, 337–8.

18 *ibid.*, i, 133, 329–30; Hocart, *The Northern States of Fiji*, Roy. Anthrop. Inst. Occ. Pubn., No. 11, 156.

19 Halle, 95–9; Briffault, i, 672ff; 766ff.

20 Halle, 46; Taplin, *Folk-lore, Manners, Customs and Languages of the South Australian Aborigines*, 50; Savage Landor, *In the Forbidden Land*, ii, 6, 64; Dall, *Alaska and its Resources*, 416; C. H. Rao, *Anthropos*, v, 735; Jochelson, *The Koryak*, 751; Spencer and Gillen, *The Northern Tribes of Central Australia*, 510; Howitt, *The Native Tribes of South Eastern Australia*, 235; Charlevoix, *Histoire de la nouvelle France*, v, 419; Meek in *Essays Presented to C. G. Seligman*, 210–11; Leith Ross, *African Women*, 108, 117; O. Weber, *Arabien vor dem Islam*, 19; Moscati, *Face of the Ancient Orient*, 39–40; S. Langdon, *Tammuz and Ishtar*, 8, 10, 13ff; Seligsohn, *The Jewish Encyl*, viii, 678; I. Hershon, *Talmudic Miscellany*, 342; Eutychius, *Annales*, i, 72 in Migne, *Patrologiae Cursus*, Ser. Graec. iii, cols. 923ff; Briffault, i, 108, 225, 766; iii, 116, cf. Sauer in *Man's Role in Changing the Face of the Earth*, Thomas ed., 58, agricultural peoples preceded pastoral; *Kwang-Zze*, vi, 1·6.; *The Sacred Books of the East*, xxxix, 224, Legge ed.; Wake, *Marriage and Kinship*, 232; E. A. W. Budge, *The Gods of the Egyptians*, i, 388; Maspero, *The Dawn of Civilisation*, 164; Flinders Petrie, *History of Egypt*, ii, 183; Hocart, *Kingship*, 35, 76, 100–5, 162; *Rep. of the Committee on the Status of Women in India*, 40, para 3·15, Laws of Manu; Siriwardena in B. E. Ward ed., *Women in the New Asia*, 151, cf. Ni Ni Gyi, 141; Crooke, Intro. to Popular Religion and Folk-lore of Northern India, 13ff, 43.

21 Legge, *Life and Teachings of Confucius*, 106; Koyama, *The Changing Social Position of Women in Japan*, 10; Cable and French, *Through Jade Gate*, 42–3, 107–8, 131–2.

22 *St John*, Ch. 4, 7–28; Ch. 8, i–ii; *St Luke*, Ch. 7, 28–30; Ch. 10, 38–42; *1 Corinthians*, Ch. 7, i–ii; Ch. 11, 3, 7–9; *Ephesians*, Ch. 3, 22–5, 28, 51; *1 Timothy*, Ch. 2, 9–15.

23 Mogannam, *The Arab Woman*, 26ff; Muir, *Life of Mahomet*, 22ff; *Women in the New Asia*, B. E. Ward ed., for Subandrio, 230, 237; Swift, 267, 273, 275; Nazmul Karim, 311–14; Koran, Chapter of Women.

24 *Women in the New Asia*, Ward ed., Mi Mi Khaing, 125ff; Ni Ni Gyi, 39ff; Le Kuang Kim, 466–67; Majumdar, 51ff.

25 *Women in the New Asia*, Siriwardena, 151, 153, 162; Dickinson, 453–4, 458–9; Swift, 277, 283; Fox, 352; Grigson, *The Maria Gonds of Bastar*, 295; Caton-Thompson, *The Desert Fayum*, 46.

Chapter 5

TOWNS AND SPECIALIZATION

In terms of technology, work and social organization, the five thousand years from 3500 BC to AD 1500 constitute one sweep. It is the first age when machines and metals predominate and has a homogeneity akin to that of the millennia of the hunter gatherers of the early Stone Age and their descendants, the hoe farmers and nomads of the later Stone Age. By 3000 BC from the Mediterranean to China, cities and towns sustained by permanent agricultural settlements had become an established feature. Thinly populated expanses of territory where people lived by Stone Age technologies surrounded these centres like a vast ocean. But the urban centres prevailed, extending both in numbers and power, sucking in produce and people.

A citizen from a medieval Italian city state would not have felt too lost in Egyptian Thebes two thousand years earlier, certainly a great deal less lost than in a modern, motorized conurbation, much nearer him in time. A Parisian or a Londoner of the thirteenth or fourteenth centuries, accustomed to a dominant military land-owning and leasing aristocracy, and to streets and quarters dominated by one kind of trade, those of mercers, gold- or silversmiths, leather-workers and shoe-makers, would not have found Mohenjo-Daro of 2000 BC too unfamiliar. Village life in India or Mexico resembles more closely village life in Western Europe in medieval times than life in big cities in India and Mexico today.[1]

There was another overall similarity throughout these five thousand years, a gradual closing of occupations to women, their relegation to preparatory processes, a devaluing of their work simply because they were women, and a disregard of their skills. Men increasingly asserted as a principle that if paid work was scarce, they had a prior right to it.

SOCIAL HIERARCHY
The bondwoman or man of the Near East was not a slave, but

a kind of contract coolie working to pay off a debt which in the case of a woman was almost always one that a male kinsman or her husband and not she herself had contracted because men could pledge their families' labour in this manner. They were paid and so not truly slaves.

Below these again socially were craft workers who were slaves, but carried on their trades in workshops alongside free people, all of them in competition with individual families working from their own homes. This system was spreading between 200 and 250 BC. Below these again in rank were household and domestic slaves. Whereas only the wealthy owned slaves in early settled civilizations, now more and more ordinary households had them. Slavery really only developed on a mass scale after the start of Christianity. It was an aspect of conquests and also of a rising population.

Slavery became organized big business. There was a great west European slave market at Marseilles and others at Naples and Narbonne. Moors were sold in Gaul, Thuringians and English in the Mediterranean. Everybody irrespective of race or creed cashed in on the traffic. By the time Rome fell, slaves were so numerous even the poor owned them, being given ex-prostitutes as domestic servants. Nor did it stop then. Varangian dealers were bringing slaves from Russia to Italy in the ninth century, and there was still an export trade from the west of England in the early twelfth century.[2] Specialization was increasingly a response to a rising standard of living for a wealthy élite. It was built on declining standards for the mass of the people who had to feed and maintain them out of their own still largely subsistence family economies, or, as landless craft workers, they had to provide them with manufactured goods and so become wholly dependent on payment in goods or in kind. Free men, women and children had to stop working for themselves and labour on public works such as buildings at the orders of town governors, kings or queens. Like slaves, however, they had then to be fed by the authorities and sometimes men and women together stopped work in protest at bad conditions.[3]

PROSTITUTION AS WORK

Prostitution, far from being 'the oldest profession', arose only in urban city states and especially in ports. Instead of girls' families deriving an income from their alliances, girls derived an income themselves. For the slave inmates of brothels, forced into it, it was hell. For free townswomen it was sometimes better than love-less and commercial matrimony. For a few it was much better. It gave them intellectual status which no wife could claim, as companions of philosophers and writers. They were philosophers, artists, politicians themselves. Thais, Diotima, Thargelia although officially prostitutes, were renowned as philosophers in the classic age of Greece. Leontion was the companion of Epicurus. Aspasia opened a school for young women in which she herself taught and is said to have composed the famous funeral oration of Pericles in honour of those fighters who had died in the first year of the war with Sparta. It has been acclaimed as the finest of all statements of a political ideal. In some cases the liaisons were determined by affection, not commerce. Such women appear in plays, for instance, Plautus's *Mostelleria*, as spurning wealth and insisting on their self-respect and faithfulness to one man.[4] They were therefore not real prostitutes, but women who rejected the crushing conditions of contemporary matrimony. A Greek citizen's legal wife was little more than a prisoner. According to Xenophon she was 'not allowed to see, hear, or ask anything more than was absolutely necessary'.[5] There was a strong resemblance between her condition and that of wives in middle- and upper-class Confucian China or Western Europe in the eighteenth and nineteenth centuries.

However, women intellectuals survived in east Mediterranean and Roman cultures. The greatest was Hypatia, the pagan, rationalist mathematician, neo-Platonist, philosopher and metaphysician, who around AD 600 used to lecture in the museum at Alexandria. Her intellectual challenge to obscurantist male priests provoked them into having her assassinated.

WOMEN'S LOSS OF WORK
Into the ancient relationships of kindred group and family, there was now interpolated that of slave-owner and slaves, or employer and employees set to perform one or two specialized tasks. Homer in the *Odyssey* described the slave girls of Odysseus who spent their lives and strength in grinding grain:

> Twelve maidens, day by day, toiled at the mills
> Meal-grinding, some barley, some wheat,
> Marrow of man. The rest their portion
> Ground all slept ...[6]

It was soul-destroying, little but work and sleep. But there was a reason for keeping them alive. What became of such women, captives, or free but poor and obliged to hire out their labour when, about a hundred years later in the first century BC, a machine took over the work, as Antipater of Thessalonica described?

> Cease from grinding, ye women who toil at the mill; sleep later, even if the crowing cocks announce the dawn. For Demeter (the earth goddess) has ordered the (water) nymphs to perform the work of your hands, and they leaping down on top of the wheel, turn its axle which, with its revolving spokes, turns the heavy, concave Nisyian mill-stones.[7]

Family women could rejoice if they had money to pay a 'miller', always a man, instead of having to grind their own grain, but mill-girls were no longer wanted.

Thus early on in history the problem of unemployment caused by technological change was affecting women who depended for their livelihoods not on their own subsistence production, but on their work for others.

Labour-saving, so much a feminine development to allow women to carry their huge unspecialized work-load in Stone Age times, in order to free them for creative work, was grasped by men, partly to ease the 'women's work' which they took over, partly, as they gained the upper hand socially, out of sheer innate, human inventiveness, which they were more able to exercise.

When baking and brewing was paid work in the households of the rich and in private enterprises, men took over.[8] Women gathered the grain and, until water mills were installed, ground it, illustrating that the allocation of work among employed labourers had nothing to do with wanting to spare women the hardest jobs. Men were determined to keep the more interesting skilled and better-paid jobs once they had been forced into 'women's work', usually the finishing processes. Among non-slave workers, whoever handed over the finished order, woman or man, usually received payment for it. There was a 'family wage' and skilled and assistant workers within a family did not generally receive a share. Thus within slave societies attitudes on the division of labour were set which were to persist through the era of independent crafts into the late eighteenth-century industrial revolution and beyond, into the twentieth century. This is one of the ways in which job opportunities for women of the present day are linked to civilizations one hundred and eleven generations ago.

The take-over of women's work by men was speeded up by inheritance and property laws aimed at protecting and perpetuating patriarchal succession. Even low-born men rather than women were recipients of leases and official commands from the authorities to deliver produce, for example, honey, then a very precious commodity. In some places women's predominance in the gathering of wild honey was embodied in religion, in the Cretan goddess, Britomartis Diktynna, the honey maiden, and in Artemis, the huntress of Minoan Crete. The bee was sacred in the temple of the Egyptian goddess, Isis, and to the Hittite goddess, Hannahannas (grandmother).[9] But men, as purveyors of honey to their social superiors, developed bee-farming and, although wives and female relatives attended to hives, it was the men who were paid.

Tanning and leather work were increasingly taken over by men, a simple enough transition since in Africa it had been done traditionally by both sexes and was not rigidly 'women's work' as it was among American Indians and Eskimos. First the making of leather goods was split off, then sub-divided according to the kind of goods made. Men took over women's half-moon shaped knives with which they cut leather for sandals to be sold in the mass market that developed in the Mediterranean and south-east Asia. Women excluded from the primary process of cutting the leather still sewed soles to uppers and stitched on thongs. Tanning and leather work remained a family occupation in settled farming urban cultures in North Africa, Asia and Europe. The nomadic herding and Stone Age women of North and Central Asia and America, however, retained their absolute monopoly of tanning and leather work until the nineteenth and in some cases until the twentieth century. In the 1860s, Henry Dussauce noted that one North American Indian woman could completely process eight to ten elk hides in a single day, after an earlier initial washing in a stream. At that rate two women using their traditional methods could process about six hundred hides in 30 days, the same rate of production as that of two men using the most up-to-date mid-nineteenth-century methods in the most advanced cities.[10]

The wheel used for grinding, a development of the women's

quern, was adapted not only for milling, but also for transport and making pottery. To this day wherever pottery continues to be hand-made without the wheel, from Cyprus to South Africa, Morocco to the Amazon, it remains almost wholly a female occupation carried on with Stone Age women's techniques. Both the potter's wheel on which the clay is turned into shape and the foot wheel used for motive power, were developed in Sumeria from 3500 to 3250 BC, and were used in the Mediterranean, south-east Europe, India and China. Most potters using the wheel have been men. But not all; given the chance, women have proved as adept at the wheel as men and have continued to work at pottery decoration. O. T. Mason states that Pueblo Indian women evolved the principle of the wheel using an old bowl as a pivot on which to construct a new one. New Caledonian women also did this.

Women and men slaves mass produced lamps and bricks which became one of the great Roman export trade commodities. In Europe, brick-making remained a women's occupation as it has done in Africa and the East. To this day in the English West Midlands, women, some of them over 70 years of age, make odd-shaped bricks for corners which modern brick-making machines cannot turn out. In the West Midlands until after the Second World War they customarily lifted and carried weights of 28 tons of bricks a day and were reputedly able to do so because they wore very strong steel corsets.[11]

If women lost work, they also gained through the development of new processes. In aboriginal societies, cosmetics were used by men and women alike. Australian aborigine men monopolized them. In the urban states the arts of cosmeticians, barbers and masseurs were practised by men and women. It was a new craft specialization for both sexes. In general women attended to women's toilette and men to that of men. One of the earliest known female hairdressers, Innu, is shown on a relief dating from about 2000 BC, dressing the hair of Queen Kawit of Egypt. Those who did this sort of work were slaves, domestic servants, artisans, some of those attending on women being men. Juvenal in his sixth satire depicting wealthy Roman women, refers to the sexual thrill they derived from visits to male masseurs. Included on the staff of a rich woman's boudoir was a man or men charged with whipping the girls actually doing the work if they were slow or unskilful. Working women, as a mark of their low status, went bare-shouldered, bare-breasted, and with undressed hair, their shoulders ready, as Juvenal puts it, to receive the lash.[12]

METAL WORKING

Settled farming using the plough and irrigation had been a key change. Simultaneously with it there was another transformation in the basic material of tools from stone, bone or wood, hide or fibres to metals. In hunter-gatherer societies, men added to their status with the discovery of metal working. Just as all myths about growing food are associated with women, all myths about the start of metal working are connected with men. Like any craft it was regarded as magic, a mystery imparted by the deities for whom human beings were mere instruments. Not surprisingly, gold, flashing in the sunlight in the beds of streams, was the first metal to be collected and worked from about 4600 BC. Streams carried it down into valley settlements. There it was trapped either in troughs, pierced with holes to let the water pass through, or on fleeces, for example in the Caucasus, literally the land of the Golden Fleece, sought by Jason and the Argonauts. Later the Romans following this natural method artificially washed gold out of the mountains of Spain, collecting it on fleeces in the same way. No mining was involved at first. Women could as easily trap the metal in sheepskins as men.

The mining of gold developed in Nubia (Ethiopia) and a vast gold-bearing region between the Nile Valley and the Red Sea. The Egyptians, having subjugated Nubia and turned it into a province, exacted gold as tribute. Agatharchides, the Greek grammarian who in the late-second century BC was guardian to the Pharaoh Ptolemy VIII, described the gold mines at Baramia as being worked by war captives, political prisoners and criminals. The underground mining was done by able-bodied men with candles bound to their foreheads like the free Greek miners, the Cyclopes. Boys collected the hewn blocks and took them out of the mine to be ground in iron pestles, first by men. Then women and older men put the broken stone into hand-mills set out in rows in an enclosure and, working two or three to each handle, 'filthy and almost naked, women lay to at the mills until the measure handed to them is completely reduced' to the consistency of flour. Some seven centuries after the earliest known gold working, silver was being extracted from galena which is lead ore. But the real mass production of metals began with copper, being worked in Sumeria in South Mesopotamia, Cyprus and Egypt by 3500 BC. Five hundred years later the first copper tools were being produced. It was no accident that the use of this metal started in sub-tropical areas under intensive cultivation. The hoe and the wooden plough shod with copper delved deeper. Women in central and south Africa still use metal-shod hoes. Later its use for armaments was developed. Meanwhile about 3250 BC bronze was being made from copper ores and cassiterite. This marked the decisive change from the Stone Age to the Age of metals.

No one knows when iron working began among Stone Age peoples. In some tribes women were entirely excluded. In the Bangwa tribe in the Cameroons, for example, sacred iron working is taboo for women, children and outsiders, just as among the African Nandi no man may go near a hut where a woman is making a pot or watch her at work, for if he did, he would be sure to die. But among early Stone Age peoples, it was sometimes shared work. In Papua New Guinea women were collectors of ore. They sifted it in basket sieves; they were fire builders and feeders of furnaces, blowers of bellows. Among metal workers the distinction was often less between women and men than between slave and free. The smiths of conquered peoples were valuable to their conquerors, but they were treated as outcasts. Slave and free women were members of hereditary smithying families, some of whom were itinerant. The unit of work with these as with other specialists was the family.[13]

Proof of women's skill as smiths comes, as ever, from the Amazon kingdoms. A 'woman's kingdom in Albania noted by Strabo, was matched by others further east. There are accounts of several women's states around the Black Sea and Caspian from the fourth century BC. In Georgia women smiths made armour for women warriors who fought in historic times, one of the greatest figures in Georgian history being Queen Tamara who reigned between 1185 and 1214 AD over a realm that stretched from the Northern Caucasus to Persian Azerbaijan. An anonymous epitaph to her runs: 'My steeds penetrated to Osfahan (Isfahan). I buried my sword in the maidan at Stambul'. An Italian priest, Father Lamberti, spent eighteen years from 1635 to 1653 as a missionary in Mingrelia which had once been known as Colchis, the land of the Golden Fleece, and is now called Georgia. He told of the repulse of an army which included Amazons, by the Svanetians and Karachais in the Caucasus while he was there. In confirmation of this reported battle, the Prince of Mingrelia

> received several pieces of armour worn by these women ... The weapons that were brought to the prince were remarkably beautiful, the work of female hands, forged with exquisite taste. The helmet was just like that worn by horsemen.... a little woollen coat hung from the cuirass to the knees, so bright red that it looked like porphyry. The shoes were marvellous in workmanship and appearance, and the uppers covered with shining brass, no bigger than a pinhead. The arrows, ... were very long, made of the best steel, but well polished, not pointed like ordinary arrows.
> That is all that I saw and heard of these warrior women ... it was said that they were generally at war with the Tatars, known as the Kalmucks ...

A woman of the north-west Chinese frontier startled three English women missionaries bound, in 1923–4, on an epic journey to Russia, by pigeon-holing them to her own satisfaction: 'You,' she said, 'must be from the Women's Kingdom.' She may have been thinking of the Kingdom of Women in the Tsung-ling mountains, a division of Ch'iang, ruled and run by women, men merely acting as their deputies.[14]

SILK MANUFACTURE

Women's inventiveness had not dried up. They were not only keepers of hearths, but also of lamps. The only oils used in lamps with which men were in any way concerned were those of fish and coconut. Even so, while collecting coconuts was a job done by men and women, the pounding of the nuts to extract oil was sometimes done only by women. Women also fished and extracted oil from suitable specimens of their own catch as well as from what the men brought in. As processers of aquatic mammals and of animals, it was women who extracted blubber and fat to burn to give light. But inland, where no suitable animals lived, where there were no fish and no coconut palms, they thought up a process which was entirely original. It was so immensely delicate that no men could carry it out. They obtained the necessary grease from certain creatures known as tallow insects, which they collected and cultivated for this sole purpose.[15]

Similar to this process in its use of insects and delicacy was their one great technical innovation of the third millennium BC, the manufacture of silk. The Chinese ascribed it to the Empress Si Ling Chi in 2640 BC. It was almost certainly a Chinese innovation and was carried on wholly by women for thousands of years. A number of varieties of moths produce caterpillars which live on a range of trees, such as oak, ash and sycamore, and which spin themselves into silk cocoons. They are common to the countries of South-east Asia, including India, the Near East, Mongolia, Russia and the Mediterranean. It is not clear when the process spread westwards from China. Both Aristotle and, later, Pliny attested the female monopoly of silk manufacture in the east Mediterranean. Aristotle, about 342 BC described how

> ... some of the women unravel the cocoons of this animal by combing them out and spin them; and they say that Pamphile the daughter of Plateus in Cos was the first to weave ...

The lengthy involved process calling for extreme delicacy of touch must have begun with the observation of the cocoon filaments of wild moths, hence the term still given to the material obtained from these creatures is 'wild silk', more grainy, knotted and coarse than later diaphanous materials. The key technique was the unreeling of the gossamer filaments. Women found that dead cocoons yielded their silk more easily when agitated in hot water. They heated them in little pots of water over simple fires, the trick being to find the ends of the fibres with which to start reeling, then to loosen them and keep them reeling in a steady stream. Only a few cocoons went into the pot at the same time, women winding the filaments on to a little cylinder, twisting several into a single strand, the forerunner of the spinning wheel. What was not wanted for making family clothes, women like Mi Mi Gyi, the Burmese, sold like their other garden produce. The difficulty lay not only in the fineness of the cocoon threads, but in the fact that the lengths of the filaments caterpillars span all differed, hence the need for the most delicate operation of all, knotting together the short or broken strands and re-reeling the filament. Women used the gelatinous material with which the filaments were covered, to press and solder them together and later washed it off. One of the trees in low-lying country which silk-producing moths liked was the mulberry, and women cultivated mulberry trees in the vegetable and orchard plots round their homes. In spring they carefully collected cocoons as part of the daily round of work. They found that sudden heat killed off the worms inside the cocoons so special huts were constructed abutting their houses with fires to produce the requisite steamy temperatures. Eventually their forethought extended to artificial cultivation of eggs collected the preceding autumn and carefully incubated until the caterpillars hatched and produced their cocoons. Some were allowed to develop into moths to produce the following year's crop.

Over centuries they elaborated methods of twisting and spinning. They found it easier to use a spindle for longer lengths (see p. 26). The problem of using shorter lengths was solved by the spinning wheel used in China by the early thirteenth century, while the first known in Europe dates from AD 1280. By 1313 the Chinese were using multi-spindle machines.

The pain suffered by a workwoman in plunging her hands in the boiling water to retrieve ends of fibres was part of the job. Eventually she provided herself with a basin of cold water in which from time to time to cool her fingers. A Chinese poet, Lou Chou, in AD 1237 described the process:

> Steeping the weft, again is part of the mystery,
> And with hands as cool as the bamboo shoots in spring,
> The country maidens marry two fibres of silk
> And twist them together in one inseparable thread
> Fitted to play its part in a myriad patterns.
> And now, at last, in the slanting radiance
> The big wheel's shadow looks like the toad in the moon
> Yet still, here below, sweet Ah Hsiang speeds her turning
> And under a night blue sky the rumbling goes on.

During the Han dynasty in China (202 BC–AD 220), the export trade in fine silk textiles from mulberry cultivation developed westwards across the Asiatic 'roof of the world' along the 'Old Silk Road', carried by Parthians and Siberian nomads. The Chinese refused to yield their secrets of the very fine textiles produced from the mulberry culture, so Westerners sedulously unwove them to obtain yarn. The secret of the moth, Bombyx Mori, as opposed to wild silk manufacture, is said to have been smuggled out of China to the West by a princess who brought caterpillars and mulberry seeds in her head-dress when she went to Khotan in Tibet. But the cultivation was only attempted in AD 350 in the Byzantine Empire under Emperor Justinian who established an imperial monopoly in silk manufacture. China, however, remained the main source of raw silk for the west until the tenth century when sericulture began to flourish in Spain.

About AD 300, the Japanese sent Koreans to engage experienced silk weavers in China. The four girls they brought back to Japan taught the court the arts of plain and figured weaving and the Japanese built a temple in their honour at Settsu. Men in Egypt and the Near East took on the occupation of silk weaving. Everywhere they turned to the cultivation of mulberry groves and of worms, but men never undertook the highly skilled reeling and spinning. In Rome and in Egypt, women slaves were set to silk weaving and there was also a domestic industry in private homes and manufacturing in small workshops. But in the Far East, the tradition of the Empress Si Ling Chi lingered and the production of silk was considered genteel work, fit for ladies.[16]

Within the settled agricultural and urban communities that were dominating civilization, women's work did not alter so greatly as their status. Class and caste divisions modified the division of labour on lines of sex, the continuing sub-division of society creating an ever-greater complexity. No princess of the new civilizations would have beaten out bark cloth as the Polynesian princesses did, or gone to work on her taro patch. The new rich woman looked as slightingly on male and female manual workers as prince or noble did.

The poorer the family, the more self-sufficient they had to be. Women were not therefore excluded from the new family enterprises providing livelihoods through specialized craft working, although they were relegated to ancillary processes.

NOTES

1 Marco Polo, *The Travels*, 180, 186–7; Mumford, *The City in History*, chs. 4 and 5; Boserup, *Woman's Role in Economic Development*, 157ff.
2 Greenidge, *Slavery*, 16; Gordon Childe, *What Happened in History*, 97, 155, 158, 200, 241; R. J. Forbes, *Hist. of Technology*, C. Singer and others,

eds., i, 591–2; *Studies in Ancient Technology*, ii, 160ff; Wallon, *L'histoire de l'esclavage dans l'antiquité*, 182; Lyon, *Anglo-Saxon England*, 87–8; M. Rowley, *Everyday Life in Medieval Times*, 66, 68; George Holmes, *Europe: Hierarchy and Revolt*, 112.

3 Gordon Childe, 254, 278; Webbs, *History of Trade Unionism*, 2; Sullerot, *L'histoire et sociologie du travail féminin*, 46.

4 *Athenaeus*, xiii, 24, 28–9, 37, 50, 56, 63; Plutarch, *Pericles*, 24; Plautus, *Mostelleria*, i.3.71 and see I. L. Bishop, *Korea and her Neighbours*, ii, 153f.

5 Xenophon, *Oeconomic*, vii, 6–14; cf. I. T. Headland, *The Chinese Recorder*, January 1897, 16; G. Schlegel, *La Prostitution en Chine*, 13.

6 Homer, *Odyssey*, W. Cowper trans., xx, 129–31, pp. 142–3; Moritz, *Grain Mills and Flour in Classical Antiquity*, 33, 35, 67, 74, 97, 159.

7 *Anthologia Graeca*, ix, No. 418 (Loeb) 232; Moritz, 97, 140. He ascribes this poem to Vitruvius.

8 Moritz, 34, 99, 140; R. J. Forbes, *Hist. of Technology*, C. Singer and others, eds., vol. i, 264, 273–4, figs. 173, 174, 175; *1 Samuel*, ch. 8, 13.

9 Forbes, *Studies in Ancient Technology*, v, 83ff; *Hist. of Technology*, i, 265–6; Elderkin, *Amer. J. of Philology*, vol. 60, 1939, 293ff; A. B. Cook, *J. of Hellenic Studies*, xv, 3ff; for men gathering honey, Hemmings, *Red Gold*, 393; van der Post, *Lost World of the Kalahari*, 23; Spencer, *Native Tribes of Northern Australia*, 27.

10 H. Dussauce, *A new Treatise ... on the Arts of Tanning, Currying and Leather Dressing*, 323, 327, 335–7, 353, 360. According to Dussauce, only with the adoption of V. E. Rusco's tanning wheel introduced in Chicago, 1863, was machine leather processing really speeded up. Halle, 107; *Forbes, Studies in Ancient Technology*, v, 60.

11 ibid., vi, 150–2; Mason, *Woman's Share in Primitive Culture*, 99–100, 113; Johnston, *George Grenfell and the Congo*, 812; *Hist. of Technology*, C. Singer and others, eds., i, Gordon Childe, 195–6, 199ff, 203, 270–2; Lindsay Scott, 407; ii, Jope, 289, fig. 271; Atkinson, *J. Anthrop. Inst.*, xxiii, 90; Wesley Perrins, retd. Birmingham and W. Midlands Dis. Sec., Nat. Un. of Gen. and Municipal Workers.

12 Forbes, *Studies in Ancient Technology*, vol. iii, 1, 5, 21–2, 41; Singer, *Hist. of Technology*, vol. i, 292; Rockhill, *Land of the Lamas*, 339ff (men servants in the Kingdom of women, making up women) Mason, 181–7; *The Satires of Decimus Junius Juvenalis*, No. vi, 83–7, ls. 473–93.

13 Forbes, *Studies in Ancient Technology*, viii, 53–4, 57, 80; *Hist. of Technology*; i, Forbes, 572–6; Bromehead, 563–5, ii, 9–10; i, Gordon Childe, 46; *What Happened in History*, 194; Diodorus Siculus, vol. 11, Bk. iii, 11.2, 113.3; Ardaillon, *Les Mines de Laurion*, 48; B. Davidson, *Old Africa Rediscovered*, 57–8, 71–5; Graves, *The Greek Myths* (Pelican), i, 87–8, ch. 23, n. 1; Czaplicka, *Aboriginal Siberia*, 199, 211, 247, 285; Kuntz, *Man*, December 1935, 186, No. 203; Hollis, *The Nandi*, 35ff; Hutton, *The Angamdi Nagas*, 64n; Burton, *First Footsteps in E. Africa*, 240; John C. Allan, *Mining in Turditania, Occ. Pap. No. 27, Anthrop. Inst.*, 11–12; Musters, *J. Anthrop. Inst.*, i, 197; Strabo, i, 73, 1.2–9; iv, 169; Junod, *Life*

of a South African Tribe, ii, 96ff; Grinnell, *The Cheyenne Indians*, i, 159ff.
14 Halle, 39–46; Diodorus Siculus, ii, 45; iii, 52; Strabo, xi, 503f; Herodotus, iv, 110ff; Kowlewski, *Folk-lore*, i, 470; von Klaproth, *Reise nach den Caucasus*, i, 635; Hemming, 392; J. Gray, *China*, ii, 307; B. Davidson, 50–1; *Prayer to Ishtar*, Brit. Mus., 26.187; L. W. King, *The Seven Tablets of Creation*, App. v; R. W. Rogers, *Cuneiform Parallels in the Old Testament*, 152ff: Spencer and Gillen, *Native Tribes of North West Australia*, 44; Arcangelo Lamberti, *Rélation de la Colchide ou Mingrélie*, p. xxx; Cable and French, 17–18, 21–2, 52, 108–9, 130–1; Dyer Ball, *Things Chinese*, 424, 428ff; Rockhill, 339ff.
15 Murdoch, *Ninth Ann. Rep., Bur. of Ethol.*, p. xxx; Mason op. cit., 92; Leith Ross, *African Women*, 91; Forbes, *Studies in Ancient Technology*, vi, 122, 124–6, 128.
16 ibid., iv, 52–7; J. Needham, *Science and Civilisation in China*, iv, 103, 105, 107, 110, 168, 233, 236, 245, 296; Gordon Childe, *What Happened in History*, 240; J. Gordon Cooke, *Handbook of Textile Fibres*, 143; Aristotle, *Hist. Amin.*, v. 19, 6; Pliny, *Nat. Hist.*, xi, 75–8; Ghosh, *The Silk Industry of Japan*, 11, 117 and Figs. 12–15; P. Dickinson in *Women in the New Asia*, B. E. Ward ed.; Poiré, *La France Industrielle*, 382–3; R. Patterson in *Hist. of Technology*, C. Singer and others, eds., ii, 198.

Chapter 6

FEUDALISM AND SELF-EMPLOYMENT

The growth of the male domination of work, the increase in specialization, in guilds, the advent of the family as a specialist productive unit and of the 'family wage' are developments particularly well documented in west Europe from the time of the Roman occupation. When all due allowance has been made for differences caused by climate in crops and work-methods, the striking fact is the similarity between peoples going through a similar technological and social development. It is with the similarities that we are here concerned since it is these that throw light on the degradation of women as a world-wide feature. One of the great under-lying economic factors in feudalism as this whole development is called is that it was based upon self-employment. The self-employed peasant or artisan superseded the employed slave as the basis of production. In this way the responsibility for feeding and clothing the work force was lifted from the owner-employer to the workers themselves. They had something in return for the goods and services they rendered to their superiors, a plot of land or a price for their goods. Furthermore the self-employed if lucky or clever had scope to increase his or her own wealth. The system had four main aspects: agriculture, trade, urban crafts and the rural domestic or putting-out system of industrial production. The only reason for looking at west Europe particularly is that it gives a very clear view of how within the system women's economic status deteriorated so that we may the better understand it elsewhere and sense the trans-national similarities. At the same time it was in later feudalism that the Women's Emancipation Movement began, in west Europe ahead of anywhere else. Given slavery as the lowest of all human conditions since it is completely rightless, yet as humanity began to struggle out of this pit, women remained in it because they became legally rightless simply on account of their sex. Yet even so, through the necessities of work, they kept a freedom of movement and equality in earnings which they lost in later social forms. In the history of feudalism in west Europe we can see how these advantages slipped slowly from them.

In terms of economic development Europe became backward.

The early Christians who reached Ireland found a society still matriarchal like that in other pagan areas of north Europe. Here personal military service for women was not abolished until AD 590. This was the land of Queen Medb, of the Princess Aife who in fair fight shattered the chariot of the warrior, Cuchulainn, and broke his sword at the hilt, of the savage Geraldine Desmond who 'killed all who opposed her and took possession of their property', of the Norwegian 'Red Maiden' who led an Irish army in the tenth century.[1]

In mainland Britain, new Anglo-Saxon and Jutish invaders, descendants of Cimric and Teuton women whose aggressiveness had horrified Roman troops, strengthened the remains of Celtic matriarchy after the Roman withdrawal in the middle of the fifth century AD. Because of this, respect for women and their high social status were given a new lease of life.

WOMEN IN FEUDAL FARMING

In feudal society the military aristocracy, supported by the rest of the people, was institutionalized. The social fabric was held together by a web of rents, usually paid in labour service or in goods. Increasingly the nobility, female as well as male, was marked off from the rest of the population, less by warlike proficiency and duty to provide troops than by its power to command services. The vast majority of men and women alike became peasants, trapped in varying degrees of servitude. Both women and men cultivated the estates on which they had their rented lands. Women worked at weeding and harvesting crops belonging to their land-lords, wielding their hoes or bending over their hand sickles while men came behind to stook the grain they cut. In the northern area with its cold, wet climate, farming was more unpleasant and harder than further south. Men worked at forestry, lumbering and plough-ing, and on feudal estates most specialists were men. But women and girls too pastured cattle, pigs and especially sheep which they sheared. Helped by her children, a woman peasant did most, some-times all the work on the family holding, the men being too much taken up with work for the estate owner. She grew inferior kinds of grain such as rye and sorghum, root vegetables, herbs and vines.

She reared poultry and gathered firewood. From the wool off the backs of her own sheep, or from flax which she grew, she span and wove cloth and made all the family's clothing and linen. She kept the hearth, cooked and brewed ale. Sometimes she kept bees and she helped with making the family's shoes. Besides all this, a woman serf, like her husband, paid the lord or lady of the estate a rent in kind from her own produce, such as poultry and eggs, and of her manufactures, in addition to her work-rent of weeding and harvesting.

Among the great underlying mass of peasants, the joint role of female and male in winning a livelihood was recognized. Male peasants, when they broke the first furrow in a field, would lay in it a little cake baked by their wives and would sing over it the old pagan fertility spell:

Earth, Earth, Earth! O Earth, our mother!
May the All-Wielder, Ever-Lord grant thee
Acres a-waxing, upwards a-growing,
Pregnant with corn and plenteous in strength! ...
And the God who wrought with earth grant us gift
   of growing
That each of all the grains may come unto our need![2]

In the 1970s male peasants in feudal Arab countries similarly treated women in a more kindly, egalitarian way than aristocrats, merchants and other townsmen did.[3]

The Greeks had exported the science of viticulture westwards by 600 BC through their great colonial entrepôt of Massilia and eastwards two centuries later in the wake of Alexander's armies. They had a huge export trade all the way to the Scythians of South Russia and west to the Celts. This enterprise had two results. The inhabitants of the countries to which they exported took up wine production themselves and put the Greek women and men who lived by it out of work. Small-scale home production has never ceased. But also professional wine merchants turned viticulture from a branch of agriculture into an industry. Women along with men engaged in it as full-time workers.[4]

But in the main agriculture remained non-specialized. The work of a peasant woman of the early sixteenth century was little different from that of a woman seven or eight hundred years earlier, although the feudal structure by then was breaking down in West Europe. The long-handled scythe replaced the small hand sickle so that by the fifteenth century work roles of the two sexes in harvesting were reversed: the men now cut the grain in long swathes much more quickly than the women with their hand sickles and the women followed them, stooking it.[5] A woman married to a peasant farmer had to work extremely hard. Compared with Mi Mi Gyi of Burma, she bore a far heavier work-load and there was little time to chat and gossip out-of-doors of an evening. Her crucial importance not only to her family, but to the national economy as a whole was attested by the Englishman, Anthony Fitzherbert, in the sixteenth century when manorial service had ended and she did not have that extra work-rent to discharge. In a book about estate management he wrote:

> It is a wyves occupation to wynowe all maner of cornes ... to make heye, shere corne, and in tyme of nede to helpe her husbande to fyll the muck-wayne or dounge-carte, dryve the ploughe, to loode heye, corne and such other ...[6]

And all this on top of raising vegetables, poultry, animals, dairying, making cloth and clothes. She was the true inheritor of the hunter gatherer and hoe farmer in terms of work, but not in terms of status. She worked now mainly for her husband, not directly for a feudal estate owner.

European women, like those in Moslem countries, could inherit and manage land, which, in early feudal societies, was the main form of property. For the Roman Catholic church kept alive Roman law including not only its emphasis on women's inferiority but also the loopholes which it had provided to enable women to hold property (see p. 86). It applied to peasants as well as to the nobility. In manorial courts, claims were recognized showing that women inherited land under the same titles as men and that sisters had equality with brothers in the sharing out of family goods. It followed that women on their own were responsible for paying customary rents in services and kind. If they were unwilling or physically unable to perform these, the most noteworthy example being military service, they could hire someone to work for them, or they could pay the cash value of the service instead, a practice increasingly adopted as the Middle Ages progressed. Titles to land conferred on women the right to dispense justice in their own manorial courts.[7] Noble women had the same pastimes as noble men. They kept up the traditions of women's skill as riders and as hunters. They shot with bow and arrow and used birds of prey. They faintly echoed the military exploits of the warrior queens. It was less lack of practice that kept them out of warfare than inclination and social conventions.[8]

Women's property, whether inherited, dowry, or even widow's dower or maintenance, created the exceedingly active medieval marriage market. For once married a woman lost control of her property to her husband while he assumed full responsibility for all her actions and debts. Women's accumulation of property was provoking men into finding ways of excluding them from holding land and buildings, and in general down-grading their status. A Frankish law-book, the Salic law, expressly excluded women from inheritance. However, all over the European continent, the Roman practice was maintained of regarding dowries and other property a woman might own as hers exclusively. Income from such property was seen as a contribution towards defraying her new family's expenses and over this income a husband had complete rights, but theoretically, not over the capital. Male superiority, however, weakened the strict application of those aspects of Roman law which favoured women. Among the propertied classes the giving of a girl in marriage was increasingly seen as a means of conveying property from one family to another and of building territorial or trading alliances.[9]

CRAFTS AND GUILDS

While by far the most important class numerically in feudal societies were the peasants, the pace-setters in technological innovation and ultimately in social changes were the specialist craft-workers. They were often landless, wandering, sometimes oppressed and depressed conquered peoples whose influence eventually transcended that of the settled farmers for whom at first many of them worked.

Farmers had to stay on their land but artisans were mobile. They were drawn to the centres of government and trade where demands for their wares were greatest and where families could work together. And so great polytechnical cities arose. In these, craft-workers were no longer isolated as in villages. They formed communities with others in the same line of business, grouping in a single street, a district. Community was thrust on them also, especially in the case of the conquered, because they constituted castes socially inferior to their conquerors. Their very degradation forced them to co-operate, and inspired them to form craft guilds. Marriages were and still are arranged within guilds to prevent secrets of manufacture leaking out to the unqualified, and to keep out interlopers. Like men, women obtained entry into guilds by inheritance, not only as daughters, but in some male-dominated crafts as widows. They did not always gain the right to membership through marriage, but in some cases it descended to them when their husbands died. When they monopolized trades, they formed and ran their own all-female guilds, just as women hoe farmers ran their own societies. Whether all-male, all-female or with both sexes mixed, guilds reflected the societies from which they sprang. They were hierarchical and eventually oligarchical. This movement of self-help by the oppressed, this spirit of union among trades is said to have been carried from Egypt and Asia to Europe. Syrian and Hebrew craft-workers from Egypt emigrated to Italy, Spain, Gaul and the Rhineland until the Islamic conquest of Syria stopped the flow.[10]

As in the case of feudal farming, so also crafts and craft organizations developed much later in Europe than in the Nile and Indus basins, in Mesopotamia and China. There they had appeared by the second millennium BC, but in backward Europe they only reached their zenith from the thirteenth to the fifteenth century AD. The story of their development gives us some inkling of what happened thousands of years earlier further east and south. On feudal estates, in manor houses, castles or convents there were women servants who 'lived in'. The Franks of western Europe followed oriental custom and kept bond and household women segregated from men. Charlemagne (AD 742–814) was very precise about the conditions in which they worked, issuing instructions to his stewards:

For our women's work, they (the stewards) are to give at the proper time the materials, that is linen, wool, woad, vermilion, madder, wool combs, teasels, soap, grease, vessels, and other objects that are necessary. And let our women's quarters be well looked after, furnished with houses and rooms with stoves and cellars, and let them be surrounded by a good strong hedge, and let the doors be strong so that the women can do their work properly.[11]

Each week women bondservants were given raw materials for their work, and the work they had already completed was taken away. Whatever their jobs, domestic work or manufacturing, they worked from dawn till night, closely supervised, sometimes by the lady of the domain herself. They worked only for their food, having no land and no pay. Those who specialized in textile manufacture span and wove non-stop in work-rooms that were virtually factories. Some of them who reeled silk in France had a bitter little song:

> Always we reel the silk,
> Although we'll never be well-dressed
> We'll always be poor and naked,
> Always hungry and thirsty.
> They give us little bread
> Little in the morning and still less at night.

There were also bands of women acrobats, singers and musicians who roamed the country. Others followed armies. Squads of them foraged for food and straw and provided labour for procuring timber and firewood. Disciplined and courageous, they ran the army camps as they might have done farms. They filled in holes, dug trenches and ditches, helped to fill in ditches with faggots during sieges in preparation for assaults, and hauled pieces of artillery into place and cleaned them.[12]

In Europe, as in parts of the East where feudalism developed earlier, the range of women's crafts remained very wide for centuries. It narrowed in Europe only as feudalism started to decline. In thirteenth-century Paris, for example, as well as dominating the primary processes in the textile trades and clothing manufacture, women were also locksmiths, makers of sheaths, scabbards and needles, plumbers and smiths. Some of the most lucrative trades of all, the manufacturing of silk and of cloth and clothing in which gold was used, were entirely in women's hands.[13] François Villon saluted women craft-workers in his poems, *The Lament of the Fair Armouress At Having Grown Old* and *Ballade to the Filles de Joie.* The girls were not true professional prostitutes, however, but tradeswomen, a glove-maker, a sausage-maker, a hood-maker and Kate the Spurrier, the maker of Spurs.

WOMEN IN GUILDS

In all-female trades, the guilds were run by women in exactly the same way as those of men, regulating apprenticeship, working conditions and entry to the trade. Guild officials judged the quality of work and laid down demarcation lines between processes. Thus most of the guilds in the luxury silk trades in any country were women's organizations. In France they were powerful enough to be able gradually to improve working conditions, yet male local authorities did not consider that they were able to function on their own and so appointed men to supervise their councils.

But in 'mixed' guilds such as those of wool-combers and carders, weavers, dyers, tanners and parchment-makers, increasingly guild regulations were used to stop independent women practising the craft. In some a widow lost her right to be a guild member if she re-married, her new husband taking over his predecessor's membership. In France a guild might insist that she should remarry only a member of the craft on penalty of losing her own right to practise it. The trend was to keep craftswomen wives as family helpers. But this was long-term. There was considerable variation in the degree of independence of medieval women workers both between different guilds and countries. In England women appear to have maintained a better status than in Latin countries since here there were few all-female guilds and so less segregation. In the 'mixed' guilds with men and women members, the perpetual refrain was not keeping *women* out of trades, but keeping out *interlopers*: unlicensed, unapprenticed, practitioners of 'mysteries' ('masteries', i.e. crafts).[14]

Trades became increasingly sub-divided into ever narrower specialities. Consequently there were demarcation disputes, often because distinctions between one kind of work and another were unclear, women ribbon-makers attacking their fellow-women embroiderers, for example.

Some skills were so universal that it was quite impossible to operate a 'closed shop'. Spinning of wool and flax and sewing were those most common among women. The Parisians tried to limit entry to sewing. For three centuries, from 1200 to 1500, seamstresses were controlled by statute. Those recognized, along with men linen drapers, were allowed to have stalls in the famous market of Les Halles along the Rue de Lingerie But there was no limit on the number of apprentices they could employ.[15] Girls not completely dependent on their own earnings came into the trade, sewing and embroidery being jobs they did in their own homes unpaid. They competed with poor girls who lived on their earnings, forcing down prices for work fixed by the organized workers. Because of competition for work most seamstresses but also girls in other trades combined their crafts with prostitution. They were Villon's 'filles de joie'. There was no clear dividing line between poor tradeswomen and harlots.

PAY

By the thirteenth century statistics from some important European towns suggest a tendency for women to outnumber men.[16] The slow growth in population interrupted in the middle of the four-teenth century by the bubonic plague – the Black Death – resumed in the first half of the fifteenth century. There were therefore more women workers than men and rising population by increasing com-petition for work helped to depress women's earnings. In west Europe at the end of the fourteenth century, women on average earned three-quarters of men's wages. By the fifteenth their wages had dropped to half those of men. By the sixteenth century, a journeywoman who had served an apprenticeship earned only two-fifths of the wages of a journeyman.[17]

The expectation that a married woman would work unpaid for her husband was also undermining levels of women's earnings. Women's inability to protect themselves against male competition created a vicious circle. Men took work from them, so in order to live, women undercut men's earnings and turned against their one hope of improving their earnings – guild organization. The more they did this, the more men despised them. So a pattern was set that still exists. There grew up the notion that on marriage an employed woman 'retired' into her home. It was based on the unacknowledged fact that she merely exchanged an outside em-ployer for another in the home, her husband.

Women's work helped male craft-workers to accumulate wealth with which they bought their way to freedom, for like peasants they were subservient to the feudal nobility. Some small advantages

accrued to the womenfolk in families of freemen. Yet in France
and Italy, despite the renown of some categories of women workers,
women were excluded from any part in town government. In
England, however, they had to pay the feudal tax conferring the
right to trade and sometimes abused the tax collectors. It was
generally not they, but their husbands who were called to answer
for their violence.[18]

INTELLECTUAL AND MEDICAL WORK FOR WOMEN
Some women continued to specialize in intellectual work throughout the development of feudalism in western Europe. Class
rather than sex determined a person's status for hundreds of years
after the collapse of the Roman empire. Aristocratic women were
accepted as leaders of early Christian communities in which they
had opportunities to practise the arts and other intellectual pursuits.
Among the most celebrated was St Hilda, born 614, a member
of the Northumbrian royal house. At the age of 43 she founded
the large double monastery for men and women at Whitby in
modern Yorkshire. There she developed a famous school, running
it according to the rule of peace, love and equality of the early
Church. Accordingly she took an interest in fostering the talents
of labouring people on the Abbey estates. One whom she brought
into her school was a gardener, Caedmon, whom some people think
was the author of *Beowulf*, the first great epic Anglo-Saxon poem.
Her school produced five bishops and, most renowned of all Anglo-
Saxon scholars, the Venerable Bede. He wrote of her rule that
'all had all things in common, for nothing seemed to belong to
any individual.'

The more egalitarian Celtic Church was overtaken by the hierarchical and patriarchal Roman Church which had a monopoly
of learning.[19] Church scholars throughout Christendom continued
to provide education for upper-class women some of whom headed
religious establishments. They were not all well-suited to the work.
There was a world of difference between the romantic silliness
illustrated in Chaucer's Prioress in *The Canterbury Tales* and the
wide and welcoming intellectuality of St Hilda.

In France women earned a living as scribes. They particularly
continued to work in the field of medicine which they dominated
in Stone Age cultures. The prescribing of cures was one of the
great areas of women's work which men took over. But there were

some women students at the celebrated medical school at Bologna. At Frankfurt in the fifteenth century fifteen women had qualified and were practising medicine. In 1276 the officers of the great leper house of St Leonard's at York in England, included a Brother Gamelde, who was a nurse, and a sister, Ann, who was a doctor. The Ordinances of the Barbers' Guild of York, two centuries later, laid down that 'no man nor any woman could practise the surgical art nor extract teeth nor carry on any part of the barber's art', unless they had been approved as proficient by the masters of the guild. Midwifery remained virtually a female monopoly.

Care of the infirm was largely, though not exclusively in women's hands. While rich men, to safeguard their immortal souls, founded hospitals and provided financially for the infirm, rich women went further and actually nursed them. For instance, Queen Maud, wife of Henry I of England, made lepers her charge founded a hospital for them near London and nursed them herself. In the main these institutions were directed by the upper clergy who usually came from the upper ranks of society. Poor lay men and women were brought in to do some of the manual domestic jobs, but those being treated were also expected to turn to and do some work. They were even taken on to the permanent staff, heads of hospitals sometimes being elected from among them. The staff were known as 'brethren' and 'sisters'; the term 'brother' is no longer used in modern medical institutions, though 'sister' is.[20]

THE SPREAD OF FEUDALISM

By the middle of the eleventh century AD down the African coasts and over large parts of north and west Africa, a series of feudal states had emerged not too different from those in Normandy, England, France and northern Europe. Round the Mediterranean, north and south through Africa, however, slaves remained an important article of commerce. The African states were also distinguished from those in the north in that south of the Sahara, because of the vast amount of land in proportion to population and its richness, cultivation remained almost entirely in the hands of women hoe farmers until the twentieth century. Matriarchal power was much less undermined than in Europe.[21]

The territories we now call Russia were more backward than these African feudal states. In 1500 this area had still not turned wholly to feudalism. But by that date, because of attacks by

Teutons in the west and Tartars in the east, the necessities of military specialization were thrusting the farming people into subjection. Ivan the Terrible, Tsar of Muscovy (1538–84), sacrificed their freedom in order to maintain the support of his nobility. The explicit subjection of women followed. The Russian Orthodox Church, as the ideological arm of the nascent state, became strong enough in the sixteenth century to claim to be the arbiter of individual human relationships. One of its tracts laid down the patriarchal authoritarian structure of the family and gave men the right to beat women 'as an act of love'. In parts of west Russia and the Caucasus a whip was habitually given to a man on his wedding day and hung above the couple's bed for a husband's use.

It was not, however, until the year 1649 that the Tsar Alexis Mikhailovitch decreed that landowners had the right to pursue and reclaim runaway serfs. In order further to strengthen authority, ten years later, together with Patriarch Nicon, Head of the Russian Church, he introduced a strict Greek Christian orthodoxy in place of primitive Christian forms interlaced with pagan beliefs rooted among the peasants. The result of popular indignation was the great uprising known as the Rascol. Beginning as a purely religious movement in defence of traditional beliefs and out of respect to holy men of the past, the movement under severe repression swiftly developed into a vast peasant rebellion involving between ten and fifteen million women and men. Women peasants played a major part in it, preaching non-co-operation with the authorities and founding new religious sects. In one of them a daughter in each generation was specifically trained to act as religious guide to the whole family. The Rascolniks fled to found new communities in empty, uninhabited places, to forests or south to join the Cossacks, still ferociously independent of the central authority. In the Rascol communities women maintained an honoured place and co-operation remained the basis of life in face of persecution. Peasant revolts became endemic in Russia as the feudal grip tightened, corresponding to the despairing uprisings in France known as the Jacqueries.

The majority of peasants, however, submitted to the new state religion. Many men among them treated wives and children with great brutality. But the village council or *mir* to some extent ignored official laws that limited women's inheritance. In some, women were treated equally, the criterion in the division of property following a peasant's death being the amount of work any member of a family put in on the family holding. If a woman had contributed equally with her husband in terms of work, then she had a right to inherit. Even among the Russian nobles, the concept of matriarchy was still so far alive that they accepted a Polish peasant woman as Empress. Catherine the Great's abilities as a ruler transcended her lowly birth and the patriarchal state religion.[22]

Similarly in the German states the depression of a free peasantry into servitude occurred later than in the west and south of Europe, provoking a series of revolts in the early sixteenth century.[23]

In Japan, feudalism was also slow in touching a free peasantry. Women farmed and harvested the staple crop, rice, on the terraces constructed up the hill and mountain sides, and carried out most of the tasks that followed harvests. Adult men helped them in tilling the fields, planting and bringing in the rice crop. And old men helped the women harvest beans, red beans, wheat and other crops. Women produced silk as part of the peasant round of work, a by-industry, carrying on the whole process from gathering live cocoons to finished material.

In coastal villages women helped men to prepare boats and tackle for fishing; they unloaded the catch, dried the nets and coiled away the ropes. They also fished themselves and worked as *amas* or divers for shell fish and seaweed, another of the staples of Japanese diet. On the coasts farming was a subsidiary occupation entirely carried on by women who grew sweet potatoes, barley and vegetables on family plots.

Women also worked at forestry which was chiefly 'men's work'. The men cut down trees and made charcoal. The women stripped the trees and transported them. Only in the seventeenth century was a rigid feudal caste system imposed on this society. The Tokugawa Shogunate, the family of hereditary viceroys who ruled for the Emperor, then clearly defined the status of farmers as secondary to that of their protectors, or alleged protectors, the samurai or military. The rest of the people were expected to copy samurai habits and thought which were absolutely in conformity with the Confucian concept that women were 'nothing'. Hence men's superiority to women was virtually part of the governmental system. As well as being followers of Confucius, the Japanese, like the Chinese, adopted Buddhism so that men's higher status was reinforced through the Buddhist temple schools which admitted only boys. Upper-class girls like many of those in Europe received instruction only inside their homes.

But the uneducated country people, about 80 per cent of the population, continued to live a much more egalitarian family life. For them hierarchy and status, whether determined by sex or anything else, was not of great importance. The two chief rules of their existence were family solidarity, and then community solidarity hammered home by the fact that half a peasant family's crop was levied in tribute each year. Feudal clan government also restricted the free planting and free sale of crops to prevent the commercialization of farming.[24] Only trade and the production of certain goods were outside the feudal system. This feudal structure remained unchanged until the mid-nineteenth century.

It was mainly the young men who left the rural routine of the seasons for the free, humming life of the towns. There they helped to overstock the labour market and were one of the groups ousting women from jobs. At the same time they created work for women as landladies, maid-servants, laundresses and seamstresses, women paid for services which usually no rural husbandman could obtain save through a female member of his own family.

Townswomen themselves reduced the desirability of marriage by providing such services. They required pay, but not the continual upkeep of wives and daughters. If a man prospered and established himself in some craft, then he might have some interest in acquiring a wife and family. Age too made a settled home and hearth more attractive. But above all poverty undermined patriarchy, for a poor man had no property to bequeath and so no need of heirs.

A woman's low pay and loss of work to men meant increasingly that she sought security in a liaison with some man who was, in the main, her only source of legal standing and her chief, maybe her only source of income. By the sixteenth century in France it was not considered proper for a man to work alongside a woman in a workroom. By the seventeenth, women's work was frankly labelled infamous and dishonest, i.e. not respectable. Besides the woman worker herself, the men in her family and the men who worked with her were shamed. It appeared to be the female sex that was stigmatized, but in fact to a large extent it was poverty. For a man to be able to keep his wife idle was a sign of genteel status. If he could not do so, he was a failure in the commercially competitive new style of life. Consequently more women took to working in their own homes. Apart from the fact that homework raised no problems of working with men, they could try to conceal their work from their neighbours. They were casual workers, who did not require any large-scale equipment since most made clothing or trimmings like lace.[25] It was a means of encouraging 'sweating'. Thus as centuries earlier in the East, West European women were beginning to be shut in their homes. They clung to the institution of patriarchal marriage when men were abandoning it. They would trade any vestiges of freedom for security.

NOTES

1 D. Hyde, *A Literary History of Ireland*, 234; J. McCulloch, *Religion of the Ancient Celts*, 72; *Táin Bó Cuálnge*, Jubainville trans., 46, 242ff; E. Hull, *The Cuchullin Saga in Irish Literature*, 77f; Lageniensis, *Irish Local Legends*, 25; Knut Gjerset, *Hist. of the Norwegian Peoples*, i, 76.
2 *Rectitudines Singularum Personarum*, in Bland, Brown and Tawney, *Sel. Docs. of English Economic Hist.*, 5–9; Stopford Brooke, *English Literature from the Beginning to the Norman Conquest*, 43, given in Powers, *Medieval People*, 22, see also 13ff, 17–19.
3 Minority Rights Group *Rep. no. 27, Arab Women*.
4 R. J. Forbes, *Studies in Ancient Technology*, iii, 106–7, 109, 113–15.
5 *Hist. of Technology*, C. Singer and others, eds.: S. M. Cole, i, 514, 541; Jope, ii, 95.
6 Anthony Fitzherbert, *The Boke of Husbandry*, 1568 ed., fols. lv–lvi.
7 Bland, Brown and Tawney, 11, No. 4, 23, No. 6, 25, No. 4, 27, No. 7, 28–30, Nos. 10–11, 34, No. 18; Whitelock, *Beginnings of English Society*, 152; H. N. Mozley, 1870 *Rep. of the Nat. Ass. for the Promotion of Social Science*, 13–16; Alfred Marshall, *Principles of Economics*, vi, x, 3, modern Indian land tenure cfd with that of medieval Europe; Bateson, *Recs. of the Borough of Leicester*, 382–3, paras vii–ix; Stenton, *English Woman in History*, 78–9.
8 M. Rowley, *Everyday Life in Medieval Times*, 92.
9 Mozley loc. cit.
10 Birdwood, *The Industrial Arts of India*, 131–40; R. J. Forbes, *Studies in Ancient Technology*, iv, 49–50: viii, 53, *Hist. of Technology*, C. Singer and others, eds., i, 292; Gordon Childe, *What Happened in History*, 122; Mortimer Wheeler, *Early India and Pakistan*, 127; Cable and French, *Through the Jade Gate*, 98–9; Marco Polo, *Travels*, 308–9; H. Greeley and others, eds., *Great Industries of the United States*, 965; A. P. L. Bazin, *Théâtre Chinois* ... Introduction, xxiv; M. Gehrts, *A Camera Actress in the Wilds of Togoland*, 93f; T. C. Hodson, *The Naga Tribes of Manipur*, 47; Lockyer, *All the Trades and Occupations of the Bible*, 286.

11 Power, 19, 24.
12 Sullerot, *L'histoire et sociologie du travail féminin*, 55, quoting Chrétien de Troyes, 61–2.
13 G. Fagniez, *Etudes sur l'industrie et la classe industrielle à Paris au 13e et au 14e siècle*, 7; Ouin-Lacroix, *Histoire des anciennes corporations d'arts et métiers et des confréries réligieuses des capitales de la Normandie*; Etienne Boyleau, *Les métiers et les corporations de la ville de Paris*.
14 M. Guilbert, *Les femmes dans les syndicats*, 21–4; Sullerot, 56–8, 60; Maud Sellers, *York Mercers and Merchant Adventurers*, Surtees Soc., No. 129, 39, 40, 56; *York Memorandum Book*, No. 120, lx, lxi, 77, 209, 243; No. 124, 112–14, 160; M. Harris ed., *Coventry Leet Book*, p. xxx.
15 Sullerot, 58.
16 ibid., 61; Braudel, *Capitalism and Material Life*, 54.
17 ibid., 62; Bland, Brown and Tawney, 173, 175, cf. *Statute of Labourers* 1388 c. 4 with a *Bill presented to Parliament*, 1444–5.
18 Bateson, i, 309: ii, 172–83.
19 Bede, *Hist. Eccles*, 111, 21: Stenton, 13ff; H. R. Loyn, *Anglo-Saxon England*, 225–30; Whitelock, 158–61.
20 Rotha Mary Clay, *The Medieval Hospitals of England*, 39, 50, 71–4, 152–7, 173; E. McInnes, *St Thomas's Hospital*, 17; Braudel, 38–40, 43–51; Sellers, *York Memorandum Book*, Surtees No. 120, 209, Barbers.
21 Basil Davidson, *Old Africa Rediscovered*, 47, 55–6, 62, 67–8, 72–6, 84, 119–20, 124, 138, 146, 151, 193–4, 196 etc.; Rowley, 68; Mackenzie Wallace, *Russia*, (1912 ed.) 233–5.
22 ibid., 232, 274–6; Symons, *Russian Agriculture*, 23–4; Halle, *Woman in Soviet Russia*, 15–16; Stepniak, *The Russian Peasantry*, i, 129–30; ii, 388–9, 396–7, 410, 423–6, 430–1, 433–4, 468, 470.
23 George Holmes, *Europe: Hierarchy and Revolt*, 1320–1450, 260.
24 Koyama, *The Changing Social Position of Women in Japan*, 8, 10, 77–80; Thomas C. Smith, *The Agrarian Origins of Modern Japan*, ix–xx, 1, 4, 6, 51, 208–10.
25 Sullerot, 69.

Chapter 7

WOMEN AND TRADE

In the growth of trade and the merchant capitalism that arose from it to become the predominant economic power in many parts of Europe in the later Middle Ages, continuity and similiarities can be seen over four millennia from 2500 BC to the eighteenth century AD. Practices connected with work and trade in north Africa and Asia were being adopted in Europe, and women's work was of crucial importance. As people became more settled in tribal territories and urban states, they produced more surpluses of food and goods and these in turn stimulated trade. Their economies were increasingly held together by a network of merchandizing as well as by leases of land. The modest social exchanges of aboriginal peoples burgeoned into a massive, local, inter-tribal and finally international trade.

Besides surpluses for exchange, the other prerequisites of trade are carriers and the means of transportation.

After slavery developed, the usual division of labour between the sexes in the matter of carrying was that men carried adults and continued to do so in sedan chairs until the twentieth century. Women continued to carry small children and all goods or freight until fortified towns ended the need for constant guard duty by men. This in turn reduced the need for military specialists so that men from the unfree mass of the population could be pressed into the regular carrying service.

One of the commonest methods of carrying remained on the crown of the head. It has been used in Europe to the present day by women for carrying milk pails and loads of washing. Sometimes they put ring pads under the pitchers or loads to reduce the discomfort. For carrying huge bundles of grain or firewood, women used their backs. The Apache and other Arizona Indians made water vessels which they placed when filled on their backs, supporting them by straps round their heads, carrying them from the river valleys to their camps. In the Caucasus there was a peculiar

load. High in the hills the topsoil was thin, so for their orchards
and plots, the women brought up rich soil from the valley bottoms
in baskets on their backs, again supported by head-bands, driving
loaded donkeys along the precipitous paths. An Eskimo woman
has been known to carry a boulder on her back weighing not less
than 300 lbs for the foundation of a house. European men found
that Eskimo women could carry far heavier loads than they themselves could.[1] Kurdish women commonly carried huge loads. In
a Presbyterian missionary journal, in November 1888, a Mrs
Shedds described their work:

> Soon we came to a place where the road was washed away,
> and we were obliged to go around ... We saw a woman there
> with a loaded donkey; the donkey could not pass with its load.
> The woman took the load on her own back and carried it over
> and led the donkey over. She also carried a load of her own
> weighing at least 100 lbs and she had a spindle in her hands
> ... when they (the women) lie down they place under their heads
> the ropes used in binding the heavy loads of grass and wood
> which they bring down from the mountains. A little after mid-
> night they go out to get great loads ... In the early morning
> I often saw the women looking like loaded beasts, coming down
> the precipitous mountain path, one after the other, singing and
> spinning as they came.... I saw women with great panniers on
> their backs and babies on top of these or in their arms, going
> four days over that fearful Ishtazin pass, carrying grapes for
> sale and bringing back grain.[2]

Women therefore came to specialize in porterage. For example
Tibetan nuns carried all travellers' baggage[3] and women in various
parts of China also did this work. Han Suyin, the writer, and her
officer husband, journeying in 1937 to catch up Chiang Kai-shek's
headquarters in the retreat from Japanese bombing, met them at
Kweilin in south central China. She relates how, on descending
from the train

> We were at once beset by porters, mostly women, with raucous
> voices, but among them a few timid men. The women were
> astonishing, almost as tall as the men, and their equal for
> strength – heavy-set, deep-bosomed, muscular, bare-foot, free-

standing ... They carry loads, till the fields, and contribute their share to public works, repairing roads, breaking stone for the railway. They wear short coats and trousers, the usual peasant dress with a distinctive blue cloth apron, fastened at the neck with silver chains. A tall, gaunt Amazon of forty took charge of our things, wresting them forcibly from men carriers and scornfully saying, 'We'll do this work, you go away and fight.'[4]

In the mid-1970s Japanese women were still working as railway station porters.[5] One tall old lady in blue cotton trouser suit and head scarf was seen at the Tokyo central station resting the luggage she carried on her back on a railing. It was a huge load and evidently caused her some distress.

Women also transported goods by water. The distinction in the building and operating of Eskimo boats was that men made kayaks, from skins prepared by women, for hunting and fighting, but women made uniaks for carrying passengers and freight. They propelled these with oars, not paddles as the men did, three or four women to each oar, using their oars to steer. Sometimes in a fair wind they set a sail made from the intestines of seals. They used these boats to move their families and goods as the needs of hunting required.

Sioux women towed canoes made of buffalo hide stretched over a frame of willow boughs across rivers by swimming with them. When ignorant Europeans came and asked to be ferried across, they applied to the local chief, partly because he too was a male, and partly because in their own countries males were the disposers and lords of all things. The chief spoke to a woman, who carried a canoe on her head to the water's edge, floated it, then, after the passengers were seated aboard, she pulled it through the shallows to deeper water, pulled off her skin dress and flung it on the shore and plunged naked into the water towing the canoe, her long, black hair floating in the water around her. In mid-stream she was met by another woman who had been told of the crossing. The pair of them then had a habit of amusing themselves by twirling the canoe round and round in mid-stream until the passengers agreed to raise the payment for their services. The woman who had brought the boat out then swam back, and the other one towed the boat the other half of the journey to the opposite shore.[6]

Women participated in trade from its earliest beginnings as we
have seen (page 32). When they made most of the articles of trade,
they were the best placed to exchange them. In some places like
Nicaragua, women did not merely carry on trade, they absolutely
controlled it. The Spanish and Portuguese found that there 'the
women wore gorgets and shoes and went to market; the men swept
the house and did other such service, and in some places they spin'.
In Tibet trade was regulated by a council of women who conferred
the right to trade, for in central Asia, trade was entirely in women's
hands. The North American fur trade until the nineteenth century
was entirely in the hands of women tanners and leather workers.
In Melanesia, in New Britain and New Hanover, trade was in
women's hands. In Assam, in Manipur in India, in the Malay
Peninsula at Tranganore, in the Luchu Islands and Timor women
carried on all trade. Some made a special profession of it. When
a Japanese merchant arrived at Luchu, his first act was to engage
a professional saleswoman and to hand over to her all his
merchandise. He then left her to sell it and received when he
returned a strict account of all transactions and the profits she
had made for him. In Burma women carried on most of the retail
trade and a good deal of the wholesaling even in the 1960s. Wives,
as well as marketing their own produce, kept all the accounts of
their husbands' sales and earnings. A woman like Mi Mi Gyi not
only sold her products in her own village but went down-river by
boat to the nearest town to sell at the market. In the Congo and
Cameroons in Africa, women were in charge of the trading stations
and markets. The markets of the Nigerian Ibo were run by a
women's council presided over by a 'queen', a terminological relic
from the days of the Motherhood. This council fixed prices, the
cowrie shell being the unit of exchange value. Its local branches
decided what markets women from their district should visit and
with which towns they should establish and maintain trading
relations.[7] All over Africa, women like Kengeran had the right
to sell because they owned the products they grew and manufactured and so had the right to dispose of surpluses after their
primary duty of providing for their families had been met. Sylvia
Leith Ross has given a marvellous description of the excitement
of these gatherings in Eziama in south-western Nigeria in the 1930s.

Women, youngsters and some men set out carrying their produce on their heads, and in their arms, along the narrow paths from their farms. The ways were as familiar to them as city streets to townspeople. They plunged 'silent-footed' into what seemed to be dense jungle, the girth and height of the trees increasing and the roof of branches thickening until the path was 'a dark tunnel'. As they walked there came to them 'a murmur as of the far-off approach of wind or rain'

> the path suddenly flung us out on to the edge of an immense open space ringed with forest, the huge drum of Iyeke uplifted beneath its thatched shelter on the farther side, and filled with clamour, as of a stormy sea beating against the banked trees, which rose from a crowd so dense that it seemed only able to sway and ripple where it stood. Every moment fresh buyers and sellers poured in from numerous side paths, so that it was impossible to guess at the number ...

Yet all the goods for sale were set out in appointed places and sections and lanes somehow kept open. These markets were held two or three times a week and at any time of day, the women always spending the previous twelve hours preparing. Here they met friends and relations, visitors from other villages whom they had not seen for months; they heard the news and gossip of the whole area and in their turn sent messages passed from one woman to another as safely as a letter through the post, accepted with the phrase 'I will speak of it in the market.' It was at the markets that they could show off their ability to bargain hard and to calculate quickly, exulting over any advantage they obtained, however small. No matter that the palm-oil they bartered for yams, the yams for peppers, peppers for fowls could all have been exchanged within their own villages, and that they only really needed to go to market intermittently to obtain non-local products such as salt, iron, pottery, tobacco or dried fish. Here there were none of the constraints of their camps and villages. They could laugh and shout and gossip to their hearts' content.[8]

Where barter was replaced by money as a common medium of exchange, women often used the proceeds of their sales to buy goods cheaply in one market and sell at a profit at another, using their detailed knowledge of local market rates.

As well as marketing their own and their family's produce at
local fixed markets, women had charge of barter trade with passing
caravans, for example among the Kikuyu of Kenya and the Masai.
All over north-east Africa caravans carried on a trade in salt. At
their approach, the men fled into the hills in order not to be in
the way while the women conducted the barter.

Because they dominated trade women must have been associated
with the development of currencies. The block salt of the north-east
African caravans was used as currency, and block tea on the
Chinese and Russian routes, as well as cowrie shells and coconuts
on the coasts. To avoid 'breaking bulk' at each halt, portable
commodities of small bulk were used, essences, incense for fire
rituals, precious stones, and, above all, gold. But even before the
introduction of metal currency, the establishment of units of
exchange helped men to economic supremacy. For among herding
peoples the unit of value was cattle against which weapons, slaves
and marriageable women were bartered. This applied only where,
as among the Masai, men nominally at least had charge of the
animals.[9]

Men encroached on women's trading rights as they asserted
authority over them and claimed that their products, food, pottery
and cloth in Africa, for example, belonged to them as fathers and
husbands. When a woman grew yams on her husband's land, the
yams and any payment from their sale belonged to him. A woman
collected palm-wine, but only her husband had the right to sell
it along with any he had collected himself, if the plantation was
his. Men's take-over of all the profits of trade has been a feature
of all the areas in which feudalism has developed throughout Asia.
In some European countries it occurred before the end of the
Middle Ages. Peasants' wives still had to carry out the marketing
but even if the goods were their own, like poultry and dairy
products, all the proceeds of sales went to their husbands. Anthony
Fitzherbert's sixteenth-century peasant wife had also 'to bye all
maner of necessary thynges belongynge to houssolde and to make
a trewe rekenynge and a-compte to her housbande, what she hath
payed'.[10]

Even when mere girls, wives of wealthy sheepfarmers like the
fifteenth-century Pastons of Norfolk in England had a great deal
of responsibility for trade. They ran family estates and saw to local
sales of wool, their menfolk spending most of their time in London

or at overseas trading centres. Some traders sent their daughters to live in the households of competent business women to serve a kind of apprenticeship.

The English had a special law allowing the wife of a freeman to trade on her own. Instead of the law of the *femme couverte* by which a wife was subject to her husband and he was responsible for all her actions, a trader's wife could sue and be sued at law as a *femme sole*. Her husband was not allowed to intermeddle in her business affairs. But if a legal judgement went against her, she was punished, a provision which provoked some of these women, when it suited them, to try to wriggle out of their *femme sole* status. For example, Mabel, the wife of John the Haymonger of London who kept an inn and traded in hay and oats was summoned by Gilbert the Brazier for a debt for beer about which her husband knew nothing. In August 1305 the case came before a jury which held that she must accept judgement.[11]

WOMEN AS OVERSEAS TRADERS

In contrast to inland trade, most seaborne trade seems to have been carried on by men. However, women played some part in it. Queens of the Balkan countries and of the Caucasus where, it will be remembered, there were 'women's realms', queens like Dynamia who ruled the Bosporus at the start of the Christian era and queens of Egypt, sent forth cargoes for exchange. Reliefs and inscriptions at the temple of Bahri in Egypt record Queen Hatsheput's trading expedition down the Red Sea to the land of Punt (Ethiopia) in 1460 BC. It brought back

> all goodly fragrant woods ... heaps of myrrh-resin, with fresh myrrh-trees, with ebony and pure ivory, with green gold of Emu, with cinammon wood ... incenses ... eye-cosmetic, with apes, monkeys, dogs and skins of the southern panther and with natives and their children (i.e. slaves).[12]

Plebeian women also traded overseas. The most famous of Biblical women traders was Lydia who ran a prosperous business in the precious purple dye made by the Phoenicians from a small mollusc. She must have been a member of the guild of importers of the 'royal purple'. She employed a staff of female slaves and freed women at her depot at Thyatira in Greece. She became St

Paul's first European convert to Christianity. Wealthy, generous and hospitable, she offered her large house to his little band for their meetings so that it became a centre for the church at Philippi.

In feudal Europe similarly women overseas traders were not unknown although some groups of women including the famous Italian silk weavers came to be prohibited from selling and exporting their products. For instance, Johanna, wife of Admar of Lile (Lille), imported wine into England. And in 1420–1, Nell Bartholomiexdoghte was bringing in spice cakes and paten cakes. In England women were enrolled by their husbands as members – 'sisters' – in their merchant venturers' guilds and gave proof of amicable and mutually beneficial business partnerships. Women continued freely to carry on family trading businesses if their husbands pre-deceased them. One at least rose to be a member of the Council of a guild, the York Merchant Adventurers, Mariona Kent, mentioned in the Ordinances of 1474–5. Customs accounts of the reign of Edward IV name seven women overseas merchants and eight others who did small-scale importing. Overseas traders sometimes lived far from ports. Margery Russell of Coventry in the heart of the Midlands was robbed of export goods to the tune of £800 by the men of Santander in north-west Spain on one of her ventures.[13]

On a fresh morning in 1473, Alice Chester stepped out of the front door of her house in the High Street in Bristol. She sniffed the sea on the wind and looked upwards complacently for this was her own house which she had had built to her own design after being widowed two and a half years earlier. No other house in the street had oriole windows. Alice made her money exporting English woollen cloth to Flanders and to Spain, and importing iron and probably wine and oil too, her son, John, managing the overseas end of the business. This morning she was dressed in her best, for she was going with her workpeople and many more besides including the town worthies to see the final erection of her crane at the Back by the Marsh Gate on the low-lying, boggy ground between the Rivers Avon and Frome. It was a gift from her to the citizens of Bristol 'for the saving of merchants' goods of the town and of straungers' and it had cost her three times as much as her fine, new house. No longer would they have to rely on people to load and unload their cargoes. At the quayside she stood with her skirts and wimple fluttering in the wind. The two men operating the crane pushed on the treadmill and the wheel began creakily to turn as the hawsers were wound on to it and the first bale of cloth swung through the air and was deposited in the hold of the waiting ship. Seven years later she donated to the church of All Saints a new rood loft in the latest highly ornate carved style and, before she died in 1485, had wealth enough to provide a new carved front for one of the altars, various other decorations, altar cloths and vestments, and, in her thrifty way, a cross of silver gilt as a substitute for the church's 'best cross'. It was all proof not merely of her business acumen, but also of the freedom with which she operated as a merchant, whatever the law said. No feudal economy could run without women workers of all sorts, nor could they be kept out of merchant capitalism.

THE DOMESTIC OR PUTTING-OUT SYSTEM OF INDUSTRY
The manufactured goods in which the merchants dealt were made by small craft-workers and increasingly by peasants for whom they were by-industries. The textile manufactories of the landed classes in which women serfs worked full-time began to disappear. Instead, in addition to what their peasant tenantry supplied as part of their rent, they bought in luxury goods from urban craft-workers, while their tenants, women and men, for their part established the right to sell their surpluses at local markets. Each charged a price for goods he or she had made. As we have seen, when a whole family was engaged in the manufacture of an article, more and more it was the male head of the household who was paid the total price.

The prices country people charged for their products were lower than those of urban workers and merchants naturally stepped in to take advantage of this. Among rural workers there were no craft guilds to fix minimum prices below which members would not sell. For peasants, manufactures did not represent their total livelihood but a supplementary income to food they produced and the fuel they gathered. Whereas town dwellers, cut off even from food sources available to the poorest country folk, were totally dependent on their earnings. And peasants were content with lower living standards. There was a further advantage to merchants in obtaining goods from rural producers in that more of them used their own equipment. Although too poor to afford them when they first appeared, spinning wheels for example became part of the utensils of all but the poorest cottagers' homes. Whereas in towns the trend was for women *not* to own the tools of their trades. Many of the merchants for whom they worked lent them scissors, spinning equipment and looms. The rare urban women who owned their looms were well-off town notables.[15]

On the other hand the manufacturing equipment supplied by merchant capital in towns was more up-to-date and the product of a better quality. Urban labour could be more closely supervised and standards of yarn and cloth more easily maintained. There was a constant war waged by cloth-dealers against spinners and weavers, especially in the countryside, who tried to make their production seem greater than it was, and by the spinners and weavers on their side against dealers' tricks to make them do more work than they realized so that they lost pay.[16] This created a deep conflict between urban and rural workers. Since all country-women worked at some by-industry or another, the charge was made that the cheap rates they accepted were due to the weakness of their sex, and not, as in the case of men, to the fact that they already had other means of gaining a basic livelihood. When the balance began to shift away from farming and towards industrial work in the second half of the sixteenth century, the low pattern of prices had already been set in the days of cottage industry.

This so-called system of domestic industry was an adaptation and expansion of the practice of giving out raw materials and collecting finished work from bondservants in workrooms and from individual tenants on feudal estates. Merchants and their agents took over the functions of stewards.

Merchants operating on this system included women as well as men. Besides exporting merchants like Alice Chester, there were dealers, the links between the big exporting merchants and those making goods in their own homes. They have been called 'middle-men'; among them there were also 'middlewomen'. Women dealers were the rule in all needlework trades and lace-making, and were common in the nail, chain and other small metal trades and in hosiery. The merchants entrusted these dealers with giving out raw materials and especially with collecting finished goods, paying for them when they were delivered.[17] The dealers took a 'cut' from this price of, say, 25 per cent, passing on the rest of the money to the actual makers. In time chains of these middle dealers developed so that there might be two or three of them between the producer and the merchant, each taking a cut from the price the merchant paid. The growth in numbers of dealers was one reason for the increasing impoverishment of those who made the goods. As non-productive 'foggers' (dealers), they reduced rates of prices paid to the producers.

In addition women carried on retail businesses and, stemming from their ale-making activities, some ran inns which, as communications improved, became large coaching establishments.[18]

As merchants accumulated wealth they took on the provision of hospitals and provision for the poor. But, when it came to the poor their philanthropy was tempered by their commercial instincts. The new poor houses which they helped into being were sources of cheap labour where the destitute of both sexes earned shelter and a bare subsistence by their work. Similarly townswomen, spinners and seamstresses, working in their own houses, dependent on their earnings, made up a large proportion of those for whom merchants contributed alms. In place of the direct compulsion of serfdom which kept girls working from dawn until late at night, there was the indirect but equally effective compulsion of poverty because of the very low rates they were paid for work. This 'sweated' homeworker emerged in Europe by the later Middle Ages.[19]

The range of by-industries for women and children widened. From the late fifteenth century, lace-making spread north from Venice all over Europe and ornamental crochet work was developed from the late Stone Age technique of net-making. During the sixteenth century pin-making came to England from France. Lace, crochet, embroidery, all non-essentials, became female monopolies as influence spread. They were lighter and less hard on the body than farm labour and some other by-industries like metal-working, and more refined, but much harder on the workers' eyes as they laboured away on winter nights by the light of feeble rush-lamps and tallow candles: blindness caused by close work was one of the commonest fates of women.[20]

Lace-making and sewing, like weaving, required more intellect; inventing new patterns and variations exercised the mind more than hoeing endless rows of turnips and harvesting maize. It encouraged the idea of 'light work' as 'women's work'. In France women cottagers' concentration on lace-making is said to have created a local shortage of domestic servants in Velay in the Puy and in Aquitaine, for example. In 1640 the Parlement of Toulouse banned women from making lace. The lace-makers found an advocate in Father François Régis with whose help they re-established their right to go on working.[21]

Countrywomen were not necessarily tied to their homes. At harvest times in some places more labour was needed than could be found locally. So in France girls and women were annually recruited in their villages by agents of farmers and habitually travelled two or three hundred kilometres to help gather in olives, grain or grapes. The authorities were forewarned of their coming and they were always under strict surveillance.

In England agents were not required. Women of their own free will made long journeys to obtain work or to escape from disagreeable jobs. Irish and Welsh peasant women and specialist domestic industrial workers, such as women pin-makers from the Birmingham district and women from the Shropshire mines, all came to work in the market gardens growing up round London and to sell the vegetables they grew in Covent Garden, the central market. They slept rough in sheds and huts, often women and men together, conditions that persisted for itinerant agricultural labour until the twentieth century. London women went to cultivate the hop fields of Kent and were paid more for harvesting than men because they were quicker and more expert at it.[22]

Subsidiary cottage industries included not only handicrafts like making baskets and brooms and knitting, but also work that proved to be the foundation of vast modern industries, coal mining for instance. Families took to gathering coal for fuel, as an alternative to firewood. When the coal on the surface of the ground near their homes was used up, they began to dig it out of the ground – open-cast mining we call it today – and finally to burrowing under the ground for it. Families in the pottery trade would dig coal as well as clay from the 'banks' in their smallholdings which were too small to sustain them merely through farming.[23] Women worked not only in coal, but also in limestone and ironstone mining, some being sub-contractors employing girls to help them, and supplying ore to foundries by the ton. As 'pilers' they carried on exclusively one of the processes in manufacturing bar-iron.

Women, men and children shared the work just as they did agricultural jobs, and they carried on their manufacturing and mining as they had done from primeval times in conjunction with obtaining food by working on their smallholdings. Further, they might carry on more than one industrial job. This kind of half-industrial, half-agricultural life characterized Welsh mining, for example, until the mid-twentieth century, just as people elsewhere grew oats and rye, dug peat for fuel and span and wove, not specializing in any of these activities but doing each of them according to the season, the weather and their own inclinations.

Only when, in the second half of the sixteenth century, coal was replacing timber as fuel on a scale large enough to be profitable, did landowners start to exploit deposits and require their tenants to spend far more time getting the coal than in supplying their own wants. So the men, women and children in the country as in the towns began to merge into an industrial labour force.

Thus as merchant capitalism developed, there were echoes of ancient precedents, of Egyptian town governors who made free people work on buildings. In the same way the practice of putting male slaves on 'women's work' was adapted and perpetuated as poor boys and men took over cookery and domestic work in the households of the rich just as they ousted women from crafts. But thanks to the profits of trade the numbers of households which could afford servants was increasing.

Although the growth of merchant capitalism to the point where it became a political force developed first in west Europe, there were parallels in the ancient feudal areas. Marco Polo described the wealth of Chinese merchants in the early fourteenth century and in India they formed the third estate below the Brahmin and military castes. There, too, women lost jobs to men, and had to live off a narrowing range of trades. They were forced to accept a lower women's wage, compelled to take up prostitution on a mass scale and above all had to work as unpaid family helpers in the shops of artisans. In India on the coast north and west of Bombay, where trade was the most important means of gaining a livelihood, and there was little work for women, girls' dowries became larger and larger. Overseas trade was 'men's work', so their value to husbands lay in the wealth they brought with them on marriage. The result was that to avoid the high dowries, parents increasingly resorted to killing their female babies.[24]

Along with the persistence and greater use of ancient practices, however, there were also signs of future developments. By the 1370s in west Europe, political disruptions to overseas trade played havoc with crafts and domestic industries and led to uprisings of working people in the main manufacturing and trading centres, north Italy, Flanders and England. There in 1538, cloth-makers petitioned Parliament to intervene in order to help them improve the prices they were paid for their products because 'the rich men, the clothiers, be concluded and agreed among themselves to hold and pay one price for weaving the said cloths.' The struggle between labour represented in this case by self-employed home weavers, and capital represented by the big overseas cloth merchants, had begun. Industrial organization and protest pre-dated factories and it was community, not just male activity, in which women and children as well as men were involved. There was no talk of excluding women from protests as there was of putting them out of crafts. Protests with a serious economic aim, as opposed to the riots of over-exuberant urban craft apprentices, were a feature of the country, industry as all united against a common threat to their livelihoods.

It was in Italy, the first hub of west European merchant capitalism, that the Renaissance began. At the same time a more settled existence led to a softening in relationships between women and men of the aristocracy. High medieval 'courts of love' left commercial marriage intact, but spread the notion of extra-marital 'spiritual love' expressed in songs composed by women as well as men. Their outpourings merged into the artistic Renaissance. In this context women began to rebel against their inferior status. In the middle of the Hundred Years War, Christine de Pisan, an Italian widow living in France and obliged to make her own living and keep her family by her writing, took as her theme women's loss of status. She exposed men's use of women's emotions and advised women that they were no longer on a pedestal and had better come to terms with reality. Her main contribution to feminism was the *Book of the City of Women* (1405) in which she glorified women's past achievements.[25] Women's degradation at law increased. By 1500 women university students, let alone teachers, were a thing of the past. Yet women's emancipation had begun. For from the fifteenth century a trickle of women artists, starting in Italy,[26] and of women writers in England and Germany, continued. And the paradox arose that while girls were kept out of public institutions of learning, in respectable and wealthy families they were taught privately. To be at all considered at home or abroad girls had to master foreign tongues and ancient languages as well as musical instruments.[27] As wealth from merchandizing spread into the new middle class that was being created, so did girls' chances of education.

NOTES

1 Mason, *Women's Share in Primitive Culture*, 118ff, 123, 125, 178–9; Heckewelder, *History, Manners and Customs of the Indian Nations ...* vol. xii, 155; Werner, *Natives of British Central Africa*, 135; Hearne, *Journey from the Prince of Wales Fort ...* 55; W. M. Thomson, *The Land and the Book*, vol. i, 80: *British New Guinea*, 121; J. Collinson, *Roy. Geog. Soc. Jour.*, xxv, 201; Halle, *Women in the Soviet East*, 107; F. V. Coville, *Amer. Anthropologist*, 1892, v, 354; Pelleschi, *Eight Months on the Gran Chaco ...* 64; Dodge, *Our Wild Indians*, 186; Murdoch, *Ninth Ann. Rep. But. of Ethnol.*, 38; Robert Wallace, *J. Soc. of Arts*, xl, 599 & etc.
2 Mrs Shedds, *Woman's Work for Women*, Nov. 1888, 295–7.
3 Briffault, *The Mothers*, vol. i, 661, n. 1.
4 Han Suyin, *Destination Chungking*, (Panther), 131.
5 Information from Japanese Embassy, Lond. and personal observations in Japan, 1974.
6 Mason, 126, 128.
7 Wollaston, *Pygmies and Papuans*, 130; Chalmers and Gill, *Work and Adventure in New Guinea*, 76, 95, 99; Basden, *Among the Ibos of Nigeria*, 90, 195; Bancroft, *Native Races of the Pacific States ...* vol. iii, 145; de Herrera, *History of the West Indies*, vol. iii, 297; Bandelier, *Rep. of an Archaeological Tour in Mexico*, 138; A. Fytch, *Burma, Past and Present*, ii, 72; Gurdon, *J. Asiatic Soc.*, lxxiii, pt. iii, 60; *Voyage d'Abd'allah ben Abd al Kader*, 43; B. H. Chamberlain, *The Geog. J.*, v, 448f; J. Thomson, *Through Masai Land*, 308, 312; J. Richardson, *Travels in the Great Sahara*, vol. ii, 346; Büchner, *Kamerun*, 33; Mi Mi Khaing, in B. E. Ward ed., *Women in the New Asia*, 126–7; *The Chinese Repository*, 1840, 40; Marco Polo, *Travels*, 67; Heckewelder, 158; Schoolcraft, *Indian Tribes*, v, 176; Gurdon, *J. of the Asiatic Soc. of Bengal*, lxxiii, pt. iii, 60: *Voyage d'Abd'allah ...* 48; *J. Anthrop. Inst.*, H. H. Johnston, xiii, 474; J. H. Weeks, xxxix, 118.
8 Leith Ross, *African Women*, 75–6, 86–8, 92, 138–9, 245. Iyeke was the husband of Ajala the Earth Spirit; his priest organized the market.
9 Myres in G. Elliott-Smith ed., *Early Man*, 146–7.
10 Leith Ross, 91; Kaberry, *Women of the Grasslands*, 23, 27, 95, 101–2, 111, 118, 121; *Rep. of the Status of Women Committee of India*, 1974, 181, paras 5.130–5.132; *Sacred Books of the East*, vi, *Koran*, Intro., Mohammed's wife; French and Cable, *Through the Jade Gate*, 129; L. M. Hanks Jnr and J. R. Hanks in Ward ed., *Women in the New Asia*, 444; Halle, 108; Anthony Fitzherbert, *The Boke of Husbandry*, 1568 ed., foll. lvj.
11 *Paston Letters*, J. Fenn ed., Archer-Hind, re-ed.; E. Power, *Medieval People*, 138–9; M. Rowley, *Everyday Life in Medieval Times*, 84; *Early*

Mayors' Court Rolls of the City of London, Roll, G, A. H. Thomas ed., 214–1215 and n. 4; Collins, *Freemen of York*, Surtees Soc., No. 96, i, p. xiii.

12 B. Davidson, *Old Africa Rediscovered*, 40.

13 Lockyer, *All the Trades and Occupations of the Bible*, 286–7; *St Paul's Epistle to the Philippians*, Ch. 4; *Acts of the Apostles*, Ch. 16, vs 14, 17; *St Luke*, Ch. 24, v. 45; *Psalm* 119, vs 18, 130; Gras, *Early English Customs System*, 401, 500; Maud Sellers, *York Memorandum Book*, Surtees Soc., No. 120, 77, 82, 112, 180, 198, 201, 221, 243; No. 124, 50, 122–3, 160–1, 166, 191–2, 243, 279, 291 etc.; *York Merchant Adventurers*, No. 129, 52–3, 60, 64; *Ordinances of the Tanners' Guild of Gloucester*, 1541/2, No. 4; Bland, Brown and Tawney, *Sel. Docs. of English Econ. Hist.*, 141–2; G. des Marez, *L'Organisation du Travail à Bruxelles, au xve siècle*, 107–15.

14 Carus Wilson, *Medieval Merchant Venturers*, 76, 93–4.

15 Sullerot, *L'histoire et sociologie du travail féminin*, 58.

16 Langland, *Piers the Ploughman*, Goodridge trans, (Penguin), 105.

17 Bateson, *Records of the Borough of Leicester*, iii, 147, item clxxxix, 1575.

18 Pinchbeck, *Women Workers in the Industrial Revolution*, 296–7.

19 Tawney and Power, *Tudor Econ. Docs.*, ii, 313–16, 326–8; Braudel, *Capitalism and Material Life*, 40–1.

20 *Rules and Orders of a Woman's Benefit Society at the House of Mary Adam, Sign of the White Lion, Litchfield Street, Birmingham*, 12 Jan, 1795.

21 Sullerot, 70–1.

22 A. Young, *Northern Tour*, 1771 ed., iii, 312, 361–2; *B. of Agri. Surveys*, Middleton, *Middlesex*, 323–5, 497–8; Foot, *Middlesex*, 29.

23 Warburton, *Hist. of Trade Unionism in the North Staffordshire Potteries*, 35–8, 43–4.

24 Mrs Krishna Swami, Commonwealth Secretariat, Lond.; Majumdar, 59, 62–3.

25 Rabaut, *Histoire des féminismes français*, 6–21.

26 P. and L. Murray, *A Dictionary of Art and Artists*; E. Tufts, *Our Hidden Heritage*.

27 Stenton, *The Englishwoman in History*, 32ff; Rabaut, 22–3; Sullerot, 66–7.

Chapter 8

COLONIES, POPULATION AND PROFESSIONAL WORK

Before trade had become established as a secure source of wealth, people came to regard the accumulation of bullion as a most desirable end. They hoped that a way lay westward to the riches of the Orient. So west European fortune hunters were exploring this route from the late fifteenth century. The Spanish and Portuguese who established themselves first in the West Indies killed off the indigenous people at such a rate that they had to look elsewhere for a labour force.

First Portuguese and Spaniards, then English, Dutch and French arrived at the west African slaving ports. The traditional African slavers who supplied the markets south and north of the Mediterranean, roped or shackled together the slaves they bought in the hinterland villages. The slaves were then obliged to walk to their destinations for sale in a single file. The women particularly had a dual usefulness since, in their role as burden-bearers, they transported other goods as they walked. Usually women made up about a third of the transatlantic cargoes. There was a thorough cost analysis on the part of both shippers and colonists in respect of cargo space per slave. Some thought it cheaper to import slaves afresh as required rather than support them through childhood until they could work. In that case women slaves were less required for breeding purposes.

The ill-treatment of slaves must be seen against the misery of the colonists' home populations and the draconian punishments which were then conventional. Those men and women who accepted the rack and the screws would not be too squeamish about the branding and beating of slaves. Still less did they care about the shock to societies still partly matriarchal, in which women were held in high esteem, of their own patriarchal system in which women counted for much less than men. In their plantations they violated deeply held religious beliefs of both indigenous Indians and Africans by requiring men to cultivate plants that were considered female.[1]

Almost from the first, colonists included women as well as men. As Lord Francis Bacon, a member of the English Royal Council for Virginia, put it, women should go to the colonies as well as men 'that the plantations may spread into generations and not be ever pieced from without.'[2]

Many young women were willing enough, for the life that faced them was little worse than that at home, often better. Turned out of landholdings, women in the same way as men caught wandering away from their home parishes in search of work were whipped from parish to parish and returned to their places of origin. Those of both sexes who were unemployed in towns were consigned to the new municipal Poor Houses and there 'set on work' of a hard and monotonous kind under the rod of overseers. In the colonies on the other hand they had scarcity value, and their farming and craft skills were in demand. In order to attract poor men, the promoters of Georgia, for example, dangled the bait of gainful employment for their wives and children including 'feeding and nursing silkworms, winding off the silk or gathering Olives...'

For the past two centuries, moreover, population had been rising slowly in Europe and people were dispatched across the Atlantic to relieve the pressure in towns. So to diminish the numbers of the destitute at home, to establish settlements in America and to provide men with worker wives, white European girls were sent out for sale. Four years after Virginia was settled, in 1619, 'ninety young persons, young and incorrupt', were sent out from England on a marriage speculation and bought by the male colonists for 120 lbs of tobacco each. Two years later another batch of sixty went for 150 lbs each.

People of both sexes were lured to the colonies by grants of land. For instance Lord Baltimore offered 100 acres apiece to a man and his wife, with a further 100 acres for each manservant, 60 for each maidservant the couple employed, and 50 acres for each of their children. Thus for all the shortage of women, maids were valued at less than men.

Several women adventurers in the late seventeenth and early eighteenth centuries obtained large grants of land, brought in servants and set up plantations. One of the richest women planters in the seventeenth century was Elizabeth Digges, widow of a governor of Virginia, who owned one hundred and eight slaves, more than anyone else in the colony.

But unmarried women would not help the plantations to 'spread into generations'. The Maryland Assembly in 1634 passed a Bill requiring a woman to marry within seven years

> after land shall fall to hir, [or] she must either dispose away hir land or else she shall forfeite it to the nexte of kinne and if she have but one Mannor, whereas she canne not alienate it, it is gone unlesse she git a husband.

Once the initial desire for wives had been met to some extent, women came to the colonies mainly as indentured servants. Women and men too poor to buy their own passages contracted with a merchant company or ship owner to pay for their passages by a voluntary period of bondage over years, in place of the yearly bond system used in Europe.

This indentured white labour system was, however, paralleled by a more sinister supply of labour. Not all the slaves sent to the Americas were Africans. Seeing the profitability of indentured labour, sea captains and ship owners began to employ British agents to induce their own nationals to bond themselves. This developed into kidnapping or 'trapanning'. Conditions on the ships conveying the whites were sometimes worse than for Africans, since Africans were accounted more valuable merchandise. Usually men, women and children were simply battened down under hatches. When the ship anchored, the hatches were opened under armed guard and the living allowed to go ashore for purchase while the dead were thrown into the sea. A Charleston slave dealer observed that the Irish were even worse treated than the Africans.

Whites were offered for sale along with Negroes as, for instance, in an advertisement in the *Boston News Letter* of 3 May, 1714

> Several Irish Maid Servants time most of them for Five Years and one Irish man servant ... also Four or Five Likely Negro Boys...

Much wonder has been expressed at the work these women emigrants did. But many were of peasant and small farmer stock, women like Anthony Fitzherbert's housewife, a lot of them Dutch or German. They simply did the same work in the new country that they had been doing in the old. The more enterprising were often adventuresses escaping from the urban half-life of service and prostitution. It was in the colonial trade, too, that the tradition of women overseas merchants was kept alive.[3]

PROFESSIONAL NURSING

One of the main groups of colonists were religious Dissenters, women as well as men. In addition to carving out homesteads in North America, Puritan women in England made some practical contributions towards extending women's work at home. Mrs Hannah Woolley, self-taught, wrote not only a volume on the conduct of gentlewomen, but also a cookery book and instructed herself in nursing. Women served in the Puritan armies in the English Civil War as commanders, but they also made a great contribution to the victory of the Parliamentary side by their nursing. Two centuries before Florence Nightingale lived, an organized nursing service was briefly set up and seems to have had a very high recovery rate. In 1644 at St Bartholomew's, one of the four great London Parliamentary hospitals, while 152 men died, 1,122 maimed soldiers and others pulled through, cleanliness and rest being major factors in their recovery. Women also nursed in military hospitals abroad. It was generally recognized that soldiers' wives and widows made the best army nurses, so many of the troops took their wives with them on the West Indian campaign in 1655 when the Commonwealth seized Jamaica from the Dutch. A considerable number of these women succumbed to fevers while carrying out their nursing duties.[4]

With the Restoration and persecution of Dissenters, there was a general deterioration in standards of nursing care. Troops were left once more to the mercies of peasants in areas surrounding battlefields, or to women camp followers. In the cities nurses could always be recruited from the poor, but as Daniel Defoe described in his *Journal of the Plague Year*, 1665, it was not always pity or a vocation that moved them:

> It is indeed to be observed that the women ... committed a great many petty thieveries ... and some of them were publicly whipped for it, when perhaps they ought rather to have been hanged for examples ... till at length the parish officers were

sent to recommend nurses to the sick, and always took an account whom they sent...

The growth of girls' education revived women's work as teachers and fed the nascent Women's Emancipation Movement. A homily written under the patronage of the extreme Protestant Edward VI of England summed up a growing feeling that husbands should use 'moderation and not tyranny'. Many Protestant artisans shared this view because of the work of their womenfolk and their staunchness under persecution.

The strongest statement in England in support of women's rights was the anonymous seventeenth-century *The Lawes Resolution of Women's Rights* published in 1632. It seems to have been partly a riposte to legal conveyances or transfers of property intended to bar a wife's right to maintenance in widowhood, which was a device increasingly used. Thought to have been written by two common lawyers at the end of the sixteenth century, its purpose was to warn wives of their very weak economic status at law, because they were dependent on their husbands' affections which were likely to diminish sooner or later. They therefore believed it a necessity for women 'to have when they are widdowes a coach, or at least an ambler, and some money in their purses'. They noted that a wife who committed adultery lost all her worldly goods and if she killed her husband, she did not commit simple murder but treason for which the penalty was burning at the stake.

In the seventeenth-century Quaker sect, women were regarded as completely equal to men. Quakerism was inspired and founded by George Fox (1624–91), but it was sustained from its inception by the lady who became his wife, Margaret Fell of Swarthmore Hall at Ulverstone in Lancashire. As rebels against the State Church, i.e. non-conformists, Quakers were excluded from universities and their abilities diverted into commerce, industry and welfare. Women were expected to earn acknowledgement as peers of men in all these spheres and in preaching the Ministry.[5]

Half a century later gentler manners were a theme of the Anglican religious revival led by John Wesley. He set out to preach the gospel and Christian conduct to the rough peasant-industrial communities where blood sports flourished and strong liquor was a solace. He condemned wife- and child-beating still prevalent at all social levels and reluctantly accepted women preachers as an interim measure. In however small a way, here was an intellectual outlet for working women and a stimulus to female literacy.[6]

The spread and improvement of girls' education made of teaching a mass paid occupation for women. At the beginning of the eighteenth century, Charity Schools were providing education for the poor beyond craft training gained in their families, and with these schools, women really came into the teaching profession. Already in the seventeenth century private schools were being set up for upper-class girls. Poor genteel girls began to replace duennas with their purely watchdog functions in the new occupation of governess. Notwithstanding low pay, long hours and the domestic work expected of them, their teaching duties gave them a little extra status.

Middle-class girls swelled the trickle of women writers who included Margaret Lucas, Duchess of Newcastle (1617–73). Her works inspired the new Royal Society to hold a reception for her. Educated upper-class women found an outlet for their wit and intellect in their salons, at their best in pre-Revolutionary France, to which they attracted male writers, artists and musicians. The general spirit of scientific enquiry brought women back into scientific medicine. Mademoiselle Biheron (1719–86), a friend of the philosopher Denis Diderot, developed gynaecology in the teeth of male medical opposition. Madame de Coudray (1712–89) campaigned for improved midwifery with the blessing of the French authorities. They paid her 300 livres and more for each of her courses, double the amount paid a Soeur de Charité for a whole year's work. Her book on midwifery published in 1759 went into six editions.[7]

Behind the release of wealthy women for intellectual pursuits was the take-over by the poor of wet-nursing. In the past wet-nurses were a luxury for only the very wealthy, but the custom spread. Increasing numbers of children were simply abandoned by the poor. In and around Paris their collection and delivery to Hôtels Dieu became an occupation in itself.[8] Infanticide was still practised among the poor. The most acceptable form carried on in Britain into the twentieth century was 'overlaying' by a mother of a baby placed in the same bed with her as it could be classed as mere accident that the infant was suffocated. Rich women were tending more to abortion and to birth control measures used in the oldest civilizations.

WOMEN'S PLACE IS IN THE HOME

Reaction to women's increasing freedom and attainments gathered momentum from the middle of the eighteenth century. One of its early exponents was Jean Jacques Rousseau. He called on women to exert influence not directly, by meeting and speaking out but only through their activities in their homes. Among the wealthy in England a new all-male institution developed, the club. It was adopted by the French in the 1780s and killed the salons. Well-to-do women working for emancipation claimed the same right as men to set up clubs and to enter and speak in those of men. They had some powerful male supporters including Mirabeau and the mathematician, the Marquis de Condorcet.

At first they were admitted, but finally their claims were resisted. In the meantime, the club fashion spread down through the social hierarchy and womenfolk in the families of artisans and shop-keepers were admitted. The opponents of women's clubs and of women in men's clubs were of a divided mind, for many were also opponents of the *ancien régime* and wanted to use the hatred of poor working women for the aristocracy. Thus at one and the same time Prudhomme's anti-feminist journal, *Révolutions de Paris*, was proclaiming 'women's place is in the home', and inciting women to take to the streets and undertake violent action against the enemies of the Revolution that had broken out.

Working women were concerned to stop the male take-over of their jobs. The women of the 'third estate' petitioned the helpless king in 1789:

> We ask, Sire, that men may not be able to exercise under any pretext crafts which belong rightly to women.... Leave us the needle and bobbin.

A handbill entitled *The Griefs of Poor Jarotte*, insisted 'We want an occupation, not to usurp our husbands' and fathers' authority, but to be able to live.'

Laundresses, tired of trailing round male clubs to find spokes-men to put their case against monopolists raising prices of raw materials for their trade, sent a deputation to the Convention in 1792 and demanded arms. On 10 May 1793 they and other women formed the Société des Citoyennes Révolutionnaires, devoted to the ideals of Marat. Lyon women established two clubs and gained admittance to the central men's club. In September 1792, extreme Revolutionary Lyon women took over the city and ran it for three days, their aim being to stop profiteering. The new constitution made no reference to women's rights in spite of the claims of the Société des Citoyennes Révolutionnaires that 'the Declaration of Rights applies to both sexes. The only difference consists in duties...'[9] 'Liberty, Equality, Fraternity' were not to be extended to women. In the imperial France of Napoleon, 'women's place is in the home' prevailed to a great extent among both the upper and middle classes. Women once married were expected to stay in their homes and attend to the feeding and upbringing of their children in contrast to their old free life in pre-Revolutionary days. In so far as children benefited, the movement was progressive, but as in Eastern countries shutting women up in their homes tended to stultify them. There was moreover an economic motive behind the authorities' sudden desire to bring down infant mortality especially among the poorer classes. New industrial developments and the growth of demand called for more 'hands' to work.

THE WORLD POPULATION RISE

A generally-rising living standard in many countries led to a sudden speed-up in the rate of increase of their populations. In the two continents of Asia and Europe, including Russian Europe, from 1650 to 1850, population went up about one and a half times. In America, much of the Mexican lowlands on both the Gulf and Pacific coasts had been emptied of human beings by the Spanish and Portuguese. The Mexican and Central American Highlands had continued to lose population heavily. The decline continued until about 1750 but in the next century it rose about five times, although it was still much lower than in any area other than Oceania. The population of the whole world has been estimated at about 500 million in 1650; about 700 million a century later; and, in 1850, at about 1000 million; so that in two centuries it approximately doubled.[10]

The essential basis for this growth was increasing food supplies. In China, India, Europe and North America this increase came in part from new crops, for example the potato introduced into Europe, and maize introduced by the Portuguese into China in the sixteenth century. It also proceeded from the internal colonization of wastelands, the races of plough cultivators pushing into the uncultivated lands of the races of nomads or more primitive agriculturalists.[11]

In China a similar situation developed. From 1740, land development and food production were not keeping pace with the population rise. Great natural disasters retarded but did not halt this growth. Peasant poverty increased. The institution of the *mui t'sai* – 'little sisters' – the unwanted girl children sold into slavery – was strengthened. Infanticide also increased. In some places hollow towers were built into which unwanted infants, mainly girls, were cast to rot, their stench wafting over the countryside. Capitalist syndicates paid people to grow cash crops like reeds and cotton on reclaimed land and rich landowners hired poor peasants. But whatever work was going mainly went to men. In the foot-binding northern regions, women on their three-inch stumps could move only with painful slowness. They had to kneel on the ground when helping to bring in the annual harvests. They were useless for bringing crops in quickly. One great by-industry helped these foot-bound peasant women to maintain a place in the market economy and that was the sewing of cotton shoes. As with other clothing, they sold any surplus not required by their own families. Demand was high because cotton shoes wore out every three months.[12]

In Britain already by the fifteenth century a high demand for wool had led estate owners to throw peasants off their land in order to increase sheep farming. So capitalist farming had already begun, closely linked to the wool export trade. The growth of numbers of people who contributed nothing to food production and whom the surrounding countryside had to feed, along with rising population constituted a rising market for food and encouraged these enclosures of peasant land. These capitalist farmers had every incentive to experiment and to innovate in order to increase yields. A number of them were well-to-do women as enthusiastic about the new 'improved' farming as men. They sent accounts of their experiments to agricultural journals. Landowners had taken on men as directly-employed cultivators since traditionally they had done most of the work on estates and manors. But their wives and families, though still required to help at seasonal work and in domestic work in landowners' homes, less and less had their own family holdings to farm while the men worked for landlords. So women were ousted from their age-old work of farming.

However, capitalist landlords in Britain rediscovered their use-fulness as directly-employed labour, in planting sets for peas, beans, potatoes and wheat, and in transplanting cabbages, madder, rape and other crops. In the late eighteenth century agricultural wages were higher than in many trades. In Worcestershire in 1794, for example, a good female hand could earn 14d to 20d and a quart of cider a day. In addition to harvesting roots in winter, they gathered hay, grain, fruit and hops.[13]

The British women who worked in agriculture in the nineteenth century were sometimes organized in gangs by men who contracted for work with farmers. These gang-women along with children were set to remove stones from fields and to weed and harvest crops. Others carried on in the non-specialized tradition combining farmwork with part-time and seasonal work in small manufacturing trades.

Single women were the worst off, since some concern at least was felt for mothers and widows. It was the single girls and women who provided the constant supply of cheap domestic servants, undermining the standards of the aristocrats of that occupation, the cocky, sharp maids and cooks in the wealthier houses who forced up wages and who, on at least one occasion, set up a trade union.[14]

Single countrywomen were also used as nurses, sent locally to the homes of the sick, and so they helped to hold down the status of nursing and to pauperize it too. Some of them were paid by the parish authorities for nursing members of their own families, for example in the parish of Yattendon in Berkshire:[15]

	s.	d.
To Elizabeth W., a present for her kindness to her father...	5	0
Lucy A., for looking after her mother when ill	3	6
Mary B., for sitting up at nights with her father...	2	0

But industrialists particularly were not in favour of paying rates to subsidize such unproductive work. Besides, the vast majority of women and girls were expected to do it unpaid, and payments lapsed. Only now, nearly two centuries later, are women themselves demanding payment from governments for looking after invalid relatives on the grounds that this is paid work in institutions and hospitals and that it prevents them from going out to do other paid work.

In the eighteenth century industrialists who had risen on the profits from trade and from overseas colonies, were poised to profit from the rising population and the dispossessed peasants.

NOTES

1 Mannix and Cowley, *Black Cargoes*, 1–2, 41, 52, 60, 106–7, 250–1; Löven, *Origins of the Tainan Culture*, 370 and n. 2, 516, 673; Basil Davidson, *Africa: Misery of a Continent*, 221; Carsten, *The Civilisation of the South American Indians*, 307, 322–3.

2 Alexander Brown ed., *The Genesis of the United States*, vol. ii, 799–801.

3 Spruill, *Women's Life and Work in the Southern Colonies*, 5, 8, 11, 16–17, 64, 278–9, 288–9, 305–7; H. Greeley and others, eds., *Great Industries of the United States*, 245; Mannix and Cowley, 56ff; Burlingame, 165–6.

4 Firth, *Cromwell's armies*, 262–6.

5 Suenton, *The English Woman in History*, 45, 61–6, 76–82, 102ff, 120ff, 146–9, 152–5, 176–80, 222, 226, 242.

6 A. B. Lawson, *John Wesley and the Christian Ministry*, 176–81.

7 McCloy, *French Inventions of the Eighteenth Century*, 163–5.

8 Braudel, *Capitalism and Material Life, 1400–1800*, 381, 417; Sullerot, *L'histoire et sociologie du travil féminin*, 36 quoting Camille Bloch, 76, 80–2.

9 De Villiers, *Histoire des clubs des femmes etc.*, 1–8, 10, 19–21, 43–5, 224–5, 233, 236–9, 243, 250ff, 265–6; Sullerot, 75–6.

10 Braudel, 11–14; S. Karnow, *Mao and China*, 12–13; Lossing Buck, *Agrarian China*, 35, 47; Cipolla, *Economic History of World Population*, (Pelican), 84–5, Table 14.

11 Sauer in W. H. Thomas ed., *The Agency of Man on Earth*, 60; only in the British and French West Indies were rural populations rebuilt fairly quickly; Burlingame, 166–8.

12 Braudel, 13–14, 17, 248; Greenidge, *Slavery*, 106–8; Lossing Buck, 42–3, 47; Davin, *Woman–Work*, 119; Somerset Maugham, *On A Chinese Screen*, 180–8; baby towers were also used in India; Cable and French, *Through the Jade Gate*, 91.

13 Pinchbeck, *Women Workers in the Industrial Revolution*, 19ff.

14 Defoe, *Everybody's Business and Nobody's Business*, 1725, *Coll. Works*, vol. ii, 445–508; *Strike Notice*, Edinburgh Domestic Servants' Un, 1825, Nat. Lib. of Scotland.

15 PP *Rep. of the Poor Law Commissioners*, 1835, No. 3, H o C Paper No. 500, App. b, 225, Rep. on Haddenham; Pinchbeck, 79ff.

Chapter 9

THE INDUSTRIAL REVOLUTION

In Europe the demand for the manufactures of country workers increased so much that people began to specialize in them. They became less and less peasants and more and more industrial workers. Such were the people engaged in the small metal trades that developed in the English West Midlands from the end of the seventeenth century. They were described by William Hutton on his approach to Birmingham from Walsall in 1741. He was surprised by the number of smithies on the road:

> In some of these shops I observed one or more females, stripped of their upper garments and not overcharged with their lower wielding the hammer with all the grace of their sex. The beauties of their faces were rather eclipsed by the smut of the anvil...

Struck with the novelty he enquired if they shod horses, but was answered with a smile, 'They are nailers'. At the forges they worked a 15- or 16-hour day, and, as in all family trades, all hours on Fridays, sometimes right through the night to complete orders of nails in time to take to the factors or dealers. But they habitually took Mondays off. While, however, men did no work at the weekends, girls and women attended to household chores. People blistered their hands badly and were burnt in various parts of their bodies by flying sparks. Mothers had young infants with them, breast-feeding them at forges, letting them crawl in the mud amid showers of fiery sparks. A few worked on their own, their babes sometimes hanging in little swing chairs from poles so that while working the hammers, they could rock the infants. It was the custom in most forms of work, including coal mining, for them to work to within an hour or two of childbirth, and miscarriages and stillbirths were frequent. William Hutton, however, considered them poor in goods but prolific in children. 'Plenty', he said, 'is unknown among them except in rags and children.'

As in any other job, their well-being depended on their natural physique and temperament. Those strong enough for the work and untroubled by poverty and worries over whether their earnings would provide enough food for the week were well set up and jolly. A century after Hutton saw them, a Parliamentary Commissioner reported that 'They often enter beer shops, call for their pints, and smoke their pipes like men.' Some of them supported three or four illegitimate children and worked for them uncomplainingly. Others married into the trade at 16 or 17 years of age and went on working.[1]

At the same time the numbers employed, as opposed to the self-employed domestic-industrial workers, increased as a result of two developments. Manufacturers used the tradition of migrant farming labour to meet new demands for labour in the luxury trades. For example growing prosperity and the development of overseas trade and colonies increased the demand for silk and so for silk workers in Lyon, the European centre of the trade. To provide the extra labour, manufacturers embarked on a system of industrial recruitment of countrywomen and girls in the poor mountain villages of Savoy, very similar to that used in the recruitment of men for the armed forces. Recruiters went round the villages, beating drums, asking girls to sign up. They were signed on a yearly bond and, like seasonal agricultural workers, were marched down under supervision to work for the small weaving masters and mistresses in Lyon. They were employed as drawers, working under the looms, bent double, pulling together the very heavy warp threads. They also made bobbins and cleaned workrooms, working an 18-hour day and 'living-in' with their employers. Not surprisingly, they filled large numbers of sick beds in the Hôtel-Dieu. If trade was depressed, employers did not honour the yearly bond, but sent them back to their homes. In the recovery that followed a slump in 1751, Lyon town council sent messengers to compel them to come back and bring other girls with them.[2]

But there was another reason for the growth of directly employed labour. Already by the late fifteenth and early sixteenth centuries, a few west European merchant capitalists had turned from the putting-out system of manufacture to investing in large workplaces in which they concentrated their labour forces under one roof as in pre-Christian, Egyptian workrooms. Here the workpeople were set to carry out all the operations of producing finished cloth, for example, whereas in the domestic system families specialized in each process and the material had to be fetched from spinners and given out to weavers, and then taken from them to fullers and so to dyers and shearers. One of the most famous of these early industrial capitalists was John Winchcombe, Jack of Newbury, whose apparently idyllic early sixteenth century establishment with four hundred men as well as women workers was celebrated in a poem:

> A hundred women merrily
> Were carding hard with joyful cheere
> Who singing sate with voyces cleere,
> And in a chamber close beside
> Two hundred maidens did abide...
> These pretty maids did never lin
> But in that place all did spin...

He had in addition a large number of children in his workforce, most of them boys helping the men, but also 150 wool-pickers, 'children of poore silly men', working for a penny a day 'Which was to them a wondrous stay' and who included girls.[3] However, two hundred years later factories were still unusual.

WOMEN WORKERS AND THE NEW TECHNOLOGIES

The change from paying people for their products to paying them for their labour was proceeding slowly until in a short space of time in the eighteenth century a number of technological innovations forced the pace. It was at this point that women's work in Europe began to develop on a different pattern to that elsewhere in the world. At one and the same time the new industry both stimulated women's retreat into their homes and blocked that retreat by requiring their labour.

The simple fact was that the Industrial Revolution could not have taken place without women and girl workers. It depended as much on female as on male labour. For, after mining and metals the trades most affected were textiles. A simple list of the main new textile machines is proof of the impact of the Industrial Revolution on women workers, and of their importance in carrying it through:

1733 – Kay's flying shuttle
1767 – Hargreaves' 'spinning jenny'
1769 – Arkwright's water-frame
　　　　water-powered factories
　　　　cotton thread strong enough for warp
1776 – Crompton's 'mule' combined the advantages of 'jenny'
　　　　and water-frame
1785 – Cartwright's power loom

The flying shuttle and hand-cranked spinning jenny people could use in their own homes. Even when water-power stimulated the opening of factories, women still worked jennies and a new spinning machine called a 'throstle' at home. When in Britain mass-production methods in textiles began to make the concentration of labour in factories more desirable than the putting-out system, entrepreneurs did not immediately try to bring independent family workers from their homes into direct employment in factories. Instead they obtained the cheapest of all kinds of labour, pauper children of both sexes from poorhouses. Independent women and men workers also made use of this labour supply. In the nineteenth century parents were still working their children as hard as ever. The mistress of a plaiting school in Hemel Hempstead in 1843 told the Children's Employment Commission: 'I think the mothers task the children too much; the mistress is obliged to make them perform it, otherwise they would put them to other schools...' Children were set to compete with one another: 'We knit as hard as we cud drive, striving whilk (who) cud knit t'hardest yarn (one) again anudder ... that 'at knit slawest ... get weel thumpt.' So little Bettsy Yewsdale, a Yorkshire girl aged 12, explained life in one of these dame schools to which working-class mothers sent their children.[4]

In 1660, the men, women and children going down the ever-deepening coal mines in north-east England were driven to protest about their conditions. Nearly two hundred years later going down the pit was simply accepted: 'I went to the pit myself when I was five years old,' one Yorkshire mother told the Royal Commission on Mines, 'and two of my daughters go. It does them no harm. It never did me none.' Most of the evidence of pit women, however, was a tale of strained backs and legs, distorted bodies and miscarriages.[5]

The standard of treatment shown to children by employers of all classes, along with the long-standing tradition of low prices paid to rural textile workers, set a pattern of behaviour towards girls and women when, unable to find enough paupers to meet their demands for staff, employers turned to female labour instead.

The division of labour had a good deal to do with wars and in eighteenth-century Europe there was a succession of them. In textiles and the clothing trades as in metals, wars meant work. When men enlisted or were press-ganged into the forces, there was more work for women. When peace was made and many of the men returned, there was heightened competition for work. It was in 1776, between the end of the American War of Secession, when the colony broke from Britain, and the start of the wars with France that Samuel Crompton's 'mule' was put on the market and finally broke European women's age-old monopoly of spinning. That is, its advent coincided with a time of peace when men were at home and looking for work. It was a big, heavy machine that could only be operated in a factory. It was said that it was difficult for women to follow the 'mule' as it slid along rails set in the floor because of their long skirts. But they could have dressed for the job and worn trousers as women mineworkers did, for instance. Women were largely, though not completely relegated to an auxiliary capacity in mule-spinning. Along with boys, most of them were 'piecers', tying together the broken ends of yarn, while men did the main job. Women's specialization in spinning was thus broken, first by children in factories using 'jennies' and then by men using the 'mule'.

However, what women lost in spinning, they gained in weaving because along with a minority of boys they ousted men from the new power looms. Men tried to keep them out of processes they then monopolized. For instance they tried to prevent modifications to powered knitting machines which would have allowed women and boys to operate them. This was one of the reasons for the outbreak of machine-wrecking known as Luddism.

More than ever men proclaimed their prior right to work not only to escape unemployment, but also because they wanted to maintain wage differentials in their favour, or to increase their earnings. Those who went off to the wars tended to come home more aggressive and ruthless. This was particularly so from 1815 after the lengthy wars with France.

PRICES AND WAGES

Factory employers were nearly all men. Their interest was not the sex of labour but whether it was the cheapest available that could reasonably do the job. Apprenticeship regulations and price-fixing agreements of the old craft guilds broke down before water- and steam-powered mass production methods. Boys as well as girls undercut adult rates. Masters in 'sweated' trades undercut each others' rates. It was no worse and no better for women to undercut men's rates of pay than for men to take work from women without thought of the consequences. Employers tried to fix each employee's wages separately since they could then more easily play one worker off against another. So obtaining an agreed list of prices for work for all workers in a district or factory was the first step towards establishing a stable trade union.[6] But the negotiators were usually men who either accepted a lower women's rate, or, if they felt threatened by cheap female competition, asked for the 'rate for the job' for women, assured that employers would take men instead. Even in power-loom weaving where the old 'rate for the job' tradition held, women were put on lower-paid, lower-graded work, weaving narrower materials.[7]

Employers also seized on the 'women's place is in the home' theory to hold down women's pay. Their policy was not that women should leave work on pregnancy or to look after small children, but because they married. When employers needed a lot of 'hands' no 'marriage bar' was introduced; when they did not it was implemented. So less was heard about it in cotton textiles, clothing, the potteries, brickyards and metal trades than in lighter, more genteel trades. The 'marriage bar' coalesced with the old 'family wage' precept. The idea that a 'bread-winner' should earn enough to keep a family did not, however, apply when the 'bread-winner' was female, although men with no families nevertheless received the 'family wage'. It was a rough and ready rule based on the average life cycle of a man, rather than a logical policy. But it helped to increase cheap female labour.

Men were both fearful of this competition which they themselves helped to create and eager to proclaim their superiority to which a servant wife bore witness. Some became strong supporters of the 'women's place is in the home' campaign. Among the most virulent was Proudhon (1807–63), a French compositor and politi-

cal theorist whose influence on European radicals was far-reaching.
On the one hand he declared: 'What is property? Property is theft.'
On the other he denied to half the human race any rights at all.
A woman, he held, must on no account earn, as she must not
be independent and self-supporting. The only role open to her other
than that of housewife, child-bearer and family servant was that
of prostitute. He wanted legislation that would broadly give a
husband the right of life or death over his wife – death for 'dis-
obedience' or 'bad conduct'. He cannot be dismissed as a freak,
a pathological misogynist, for he was expressing views that were
prevalent among men at all social levels, although the majority
were less extreme. For instance in Germany the free labourers were
the working-class élite in which men were visibly losing ground.
Women in 1816 made up 18 per cent of free, non-feudal, non-guild
labour. Thirty years later in 1848, they accounted for 25 per cent.
The general reaction of the nascent German trade unions was to
forbid their male members to co-operate with women workers, a
policy also followed by an increasing number of British unions,
especially those set up in craft trades.[9]

THE PHILANTHROPIC INTEREST

By the second half of the eighteenth century some of the leisured
and employing classes were initiating moves to help first child and
then women workers. They were appalled by the life-styles, coarse-
ness and brutality of those who worked for a living. They did not
properly consider the effects of abruptly breaking up the traditional
family economy in which women and children not only had a
recognized work function, but in which they could support themselves if need be. They did not see that the evils lay less in women
and children going out to work than in the greed and exploitation
on the part of employers and sub-contractors, for after all they
themselves depended on a growing army of low-paid women
domestic servants.

At first they too advocated 'woman's place is in the home'. They
succeeded in passing through the British Parliament legislation
removing women and children from underground work in mines.
There is no doubt that most women wanted to leave the pits, but
:hey did not want to exchange even this work for unemployment.
When the Act excluding them from underground work was passed
in 1842 and they found no other work provided for them, the

women were bitterly resentful. As in the case of peasants who lost their holdings because of enclosures, it was the single women who suffered most. Some of them were reported to be making 3d a day hawking and collecting manure on roads. Many women continued to work underground until the visit of a Commissioner two years later to see the Act enforced. Six years later still, in 1850, the same Commissioner found at least 200 of them working underground in Welsh pits, some of them dressed as men.

There were instances of women circumventing prohibitions on female labour elsewhere. The late nineteenth-century Russian press published several accounts of women who passed themselves off as men or who had male identity papers in order to earn a living. The best known was Ouliana of Kamychine who called herself Egot, and disguised herself as a man for ten years, working as a porter. Questioned as to her motives, she said she did it for the higher pay. The woman who started the Paris Flea Market had earlier dressed herself as a man to dodge the rule of the French typographers' society forbidding women from working in their trade. She penetrated that fortress of male exclusiveness, the composing room, where her pay was four times higher than before.

The 1842 Act did not stop women doing very heavy work. They continued to work above ground at collieries. In the Bilston district of south Staffordshire, for instance, nearly a thousand were employed. As well as sorting, picking and cleaning the coal, they wound both coal and men up from the pit bottom by windlass, weighed coals and loaded them on to canal boats. Unguarded pit mouths and defective winding gear produced such a high rate of fatal accidents among them that one observer compared the prevailing atmosphere to that of a battlefield. It was many years before there were suggestions that they should abandon this work.[10]

FACTORY LEGISLATION

Some English factory owners were responsible for the start of legal restrictions on the employment of children and women, starting with the 1802 Act forbidding the employment of child apprentices for more than 12 hours a day and prohibiting their working overnight. The 1844 British Factory Act was the world's first law to improve working conditions for adults. It also imposed a 12-hour working day for adult women and in 1847 was followed by another Act stipulating a 10-hour day. Country after country adopted similar restrictions on women's hours of work. If there was no threat to women's jobs from male competition, such restrictions were pure gain. Where there was such a threat, they tended like equal pay to increase the chances of men taking over work from women. Dr Mitchell, one of the Parliamentary Commissioners in the 1844 Commission on Mines, remarked:

> When we consider how many employments men have engrossed to themselves, and how few ways there are for women to gain a living, we must be cautious not to attempt to narrow what is already so limited...

The philanthropists were prompted to reconsider their absolute opposition to women working by the growth of 'sweating' and prostitution, and by lack of work for needy, genteel girls, some of them unfortunates from their own social class.

EMIGRATION

The late sixteenth and early seventeenth century remedy of emigration was proposed. In the expanding west European colonies girls found opportunities for working as teachers and as domestic servants often with a much better status than in Europe. They also found better chances of matrimony than at home, indeed many went overseas for that express purpose and were nicknamed 'the fishing fleet'. There was also emigration within Europe itself for dressmakers and milliners from Paris, the capital of fashion. They were in demand in east European capitals and, since their work was relatively well-paid because they had scarcity value, they could more quickly save for their dowries.

Those women and girls who joined the great trek west in the United States, or went out with husbands to the back blocks in Australia were returning to subsistence economies. There is some evidence that so long as they remained in short supply co-operation was re-established between wife and husband and the bitter competition over work and earnings subsided. Reporting on the condition of women in the early twentieth century in Australia, Jessie Ackermann, a church worker, noted that the hard life on the plots of land in the rigorous climate inland made for family solidarity and sometimes deep love and appreciation on the part of a man for his wife. She also reported that parents 'were quite as willing to agree to the criminal sweating of their children as the (fruit) growers were to avail themselves of the advantage of child-labour.' She found the same appreciation in the élite of the working class, men understanding that success or ruin depended on their wives' skilful housekeeping.[11]

WOMEN'S ATTITUDES TO WITHDRAWAL FROM WORK

With a total lack of labour-saving devices for work in the home, it was not surprising that women who felt their husbands could support them should see withdrawal from paid work as an escape from many hardships. Payments for child-minders could cancel out her earnings, as a Scottish woman coal-bearer explained;

> While working in the pit, I was worth to my husband 7s. a week, out of which we had to pay 2s. 6d. to a woman for looking after the younger bairns ... Then there was 1s. a week for washing; besides there was mending to pay for, and other things. The house was not guided. The other children broke things...[12]

There was a further disincentive to women to work in the mid-nineteenth century in most of west Europe and in the United States. A married woman's earnings belonged to her husband. Her economic independence was contingent upon her husband's affection for her, on whether he permitted her to keep her earnings.[13] In many cases a wife's wages simply went into the pool of housekeeping money, spent on keeping home and family going when a man might spend most of his money, his 'family wage', on drink, betting and other pleasures.

Women also wanted to leave off paid work and concentrate on keeping their homes because of rising living standards. Cottages of peasants engaged in the domestic industrial system had been bare of all but necessities. When trade was good, as with the hand-loom weavers before the powerloom overtook them their houses were

> well furnished with a clock in elegant mahogany or fancy case, – handsome tea services in Staffordshire ware, with silver or plated sugar tongs and spoons – Birmingham, Potteries and Sheffield wares ... wherever a corner cupboard or shelf could be placed to shew them off.[14]

Mass consumerism had begun and wives wanted time to look after their possessions.

But as upper- and middle-class women had long since found in North Africa and the East, however hard a woman worked in maintaining home and family, such work did not enter directly into the market economy. She might subsidize outside employers by caring for her husband and male relatives, but they did not pay her a price for this. Whereas when she herself worked for pay, in a market economy her work had a recognized economic role, an objective value. Moreover cheap domestic help became available even to the upper ranks of the working classes. Employing a maid was another status symbol and, as in the case of the wealthy, helped to reduce the value of a wife as worker.

The female labour aristocracy now included not only sub-contractors but also the new female factory élite in the textile trades. Like unmarried men of the same class, they paid others to make and mend their clothes, to launder, cook and brew for them. Cooked meat shops and pastry shops had always been a feature of cities. Now they appeared in the textile districts, selling pies, peas, tripe or cooked cow-heel.

As much as men these relatively well-off working women supported a sub-proletariat. The Rev. G. S. Bull in 1832 attested to a Parliamentary Enquiry the smartness of factory women. It might be clogs and shawls for work, but

> in many cases the young women employed in factories do not make their clothes at all; their working clothes they obtain in the slop-shops which abound in manufacturing districts ... and their Sunday dress is, of course, of a very smart description ... manufactured by some notable milliner who knows how to set these matters off to the best advantage.[15]

It was the more extraordinary that this female elite should permit the lower woman's wage to operate. They were paid relatively high prices for their work in comparison with very low rates paid in cottage industries and in the 'sweated' urban trades but, except in power-loom weaving, particularly low prices in comparison with men on comparable work. A Dr Ure philosophized in 1834 that low prices paid to female factory workers induced them the more easily to accept 'household duties' as 'the most profitable as well as agreeable occupation' and to care for children instead of going to the mill.

WOMEN AS INVESTORS IN THE NEW TECHNOLOGIES

Just as in the Agricultural Revolution, so in the Industrial Revolution women played a small part as inventors. During the shortages of the French Revolution, Citoyenne Masson was awarded 3,500 livres for inventing the best method of removing printer's ink from newspapers so that they could be reprocessed. A number of American girls and women found new materials and new methods of making straw hats.[16]

The bottleneck in preparing raw cotton was picking the black seeds out of the cotton wool, one of the most laborious of women's jobs. The invention that picked the seeds out twenty times as quickly as a female hand-picker, and which finally made cotton 'king', was the cotton-gin. It was Mrs Catherine Littlefield Green, a general's widow, who herself ran a cotton plantation, who thought of substituting wire for wooden teeth, the key adjustment. Her lodger, Eli Whitney, who actually made the machine in consultation with her claimed the patent rights which she was too genteel to claim herself. The cotton gin is known to posterity as his invention.[17]

Colonization, population growth and the Industrial Revolution all swung work women's way and prevented their being shut away in their homes. The need for female labour outweighed the closing of occupations to women. Women also benefited through inheritance and wealth which enabled them to invest in new enterprises and as shareholders, to become economically independent. Faced with women's growing economic importance men insisted on female inferiority. Male workers thus helped to perpetuate cheap female labour which became a threat to their own jobs.

NOTES

1 Hutton, *History of Birmingham*, 1783 ed., 84: Pinchbeck, *Women Workers in the Industrial Revolution* ..., 274–5, 277–80; Sherard, *The White Slaves of England*, 215ff; Lloyd, *Cutlery Trades*, 402; Mackenzie Wallace, *Russia*, 108.
2 Sullerot, Le féminisme dans le socialisme français, 73–4.
3 Power, *Medieval People*, 79, 170–2. Morris and Wood, *The Golden Fleece*, 73ff.

4 Southey, *The Doctor*, 1847 ed., vol. vii, 79–80, 'A True Story of the Terrible Knitters of Dent'; *Victoria County History., Rutland*, 225.

5 1842 *Rep. of the Roy. Comm. on Mines*, xv, 186–8, 194; 1844 *Rep. of the Roy. Comm. on Mines*, xvi, 178, 214, 276, 387, 422, 456, 458, 460, 479, 793; 1845 *Rep. of the Roy. Comm. on Mines*, xvii, 75, 123, 165–6, 215, 217 & etc.

6 *Trade Societies and Strikes, Rep. of the Committee on Trade Societies of the Nat. Ass. for the Promotion of Social Science*, 1859, 433, lists for spinners, 1 Oct., 1852; for weavers, July and Aug., 1853.

7 For women with near equal or higher rates than men: Young, *Northern Tour*, 1771 ed., vol. i, 137–8; vol. iii, 187–8; *Thoughts on the Use of Machines in the Cotton Manufacture by a Friend of the Poor*, Manchester, 1780; high spinners' rates: Hammonds, *Skilled Labourer*, 222; *Parliamentary Papers*: 1818, ix, 90–2, 98, Rep. on Ribbon Weavers' Petitions, 1830, x, 221; 1834, x, 279–80, Rep. on Handloom Weavers; xix, 33, Factory Comm. Rep.; for lower rates cf.: Clark, *Working Life of Women in the Seventeenth Century*, 226–7; George, *London Life in the Eighteenth Century*, 182: Macdonald ed., *Women in the Printing Trades*, 30ff; *Parliamentary Papers*: 1818, ix, 117 Rep. on Ribbon Weavers' Petitions, 1833, vi, 323 Sel. Comm. on Manufactures; 1834, vii, qq, 1341–2 J. McNish; 1840, xxiii, 442; xiv, 33, Reps ... on the ... Handloom Weavers *Rep. of the Proceedings of a Delegate meeting of the Operative Spinners of England, Ireland and Scotland*, 50–1, Resolutions 18 and 24; *The Pioneer*, 15 Mar., 1834, Initiated Weaver's Wife; 12 April, 1834; 5, 31 Mar., 1834; Sullerot, 103:

	Women's Rates	Men's Rates
Amiens factories on same work	1·25–2·0 frs	2·5–3·5 frs
Fourmies, women spinners on work only slightly different from that of a man	1	4
Average wages all trades, Paris, 1870	2·14	4

Doran, *A Lady of the Last Century*, 139–40, 184–5, 199–202. Sholl, *A Short Historical Account of the Silk Manufacture*, 1811, 39.

8 Thibert, *Le féminisme dans le socialisme français de 1830 a 1850*, 171–3, 185–92. Sullerot, op. cit., 86–7. But cf. Engels, *Condition of the Working Class in England*, (Panther, 1969), 'The employment of the wife dissolves the family utterly ...' He blamed the factory system and economic role of marriage.

9 Thönnessen, *Emancipation of Women*, 13, 15–16, 20, 28–9; *PP Rep. of the Factory Inspectors*, 1844, xxvii, p. xxx, L. Horne Horner; Bradley and Black, *Econ. Jour.*, 1899, 61ff; E. Faithful, 1860 *Trans. of the NAPSS*, 819–22; E. Paterson, *Lab. Rev.*, Apr. 1874, reprinted in *The Englishwoman's Rev.*, New Ser., Oct. 1874, 215–16.

10 *PP Rep. ... Midland Mining Comm.*, 1843, xii, 136; *PP Rep. of the Commissioner ... to Inquire into ... Mining Districts*, 1844, xvi, 4, 461: 1850,

xxiii, 59, 63. *PP Factory Inspectors' Reps.*, 1846, xx, 574–7; 1847, xv, App. 3, 31; Hodder, *Life of the Seventh Earl of Shaftesbury*, (1887 ed.), 228; Sullerot, op. cit., 106.

11 Hammerton, *Emigrant Gentlewomen*; Ackermann, *Australia from a Woman's Point of View*, 66–7, 72, 80.

12 *PP Rep. of the Commissioner . . . to Inquire into . . . Mining Districts* 1844, xvi, 4. See also *PP Rep. on Women and Children in Agriculture*, 1843, xii, 67–8.

13 Eden, *Observations on Friendly Societies & etc.*, 21–2. In Britain it was not until 1870 that an Act gave married women rights in their own earnings. Flexner, *Century of Struggle*, 7–8, 62–3.

14 Radcliffe, *Origin of the New System of Manufacture*, p. 67 *PP First Rep. . . . on Mines*, 1842, Pt. 11, App. 11, xvii, 92.

15 *PP Sel. Committee on the Factory Bill*, 1831–2, 423. The Rev. G. S. Bull, vicar of Bierley near Bradford, was a leader of the 10-Hours Day Movement. *PP 1833 Fact. Comm. Rep.*, xx, p. Dl, 34–5. PP *1840 Handloom Weavers' Rep.*, xxiv, 44; Burlingame, op. cit., 162, quoting Charles Dickens, *American Notes*, Ch. iv and Lucy Larcom, one of the girls from the U.S. Lowell mills.

16 McCloy, *French Inventions of the Eighteenth Century*, 67.

17 Burlingame, 169–73, 176–7; Matilda Joslyn Gage, *North American Rev.*, May 1883, 482–3, given in E. F. Baker, *Technology and Woman's Work*, 4, n.4.

Chapter 10

THE SPREAD OF THE INDUSTRIAL REVOLUTION
WORLDWIDE

In addition to the adoption of mechanical power on an unheard-of scale, the technological changes that began in the eighteenth century were only the start of a series of radical technical innovations which followed one another with great speed and which are still going on. As they succeeded one another with furious rapidity the allocation of work between women and men switched back and forth.

It was not really until after the end of the Napoleonic wars, in 1814, that the centralization of work in factories away from homes, requiring large amounts of capital expenditure, began to spread from Britain to the rest of the world. In the next half-century it took root in France, Belgium, central Holland, part of Germany and, above all, in the United States of America. This industrial capitalist system created the same products in all the countries where it evolved so that it kept in being and intensified the competition which was a feature of mercantile capitalism. There was rivalry both in marketing products and for sources of raw materials which were necessary to an ever more complex technology and which the industrializing countries of the northern hemisphere lacked.

The United States outdistanced Europe in this new system, partly because its population in relation to its size was much smaller than that of Western European countries. Labour in the States was therefore scarcer and more expensive so that there was an extra incentive to invent labour-saving machinery, to adopt the new kinds of power – advanced hydraulics, steam or electricity – and develop mass factory production methods. By 1824 the connection between a mass of urban labour which did not produce its own food and prosperous farmers was understood. General Jackson wrote to Dr Coleman in that year:

Withdraw six hundred thousand of our people from agriculture to employ them in manufactures and you give to our farmers a larger and better market than all of Europe now affords them.[1]

Home production in the United States, already stimulated by shortages caused by the revolt of the colonies followed by the French wars, was now further boosted by protectionism. Northern farmers believed that if cheap European manufactures had been let in – cheap because European wages were lower – their home customers would prefer European goods. Consequently, United States manufactures would decrease, unemployment would rise and they, in turn, would have to lower food prices to their home customers. It was a policy directly opposed to that of the southern slave states whose interest lay in the mass export of raw materials to European markets. The import of slaves grew along with European demand for their products, particularly cotton, just when European states, starting with Britain in 1807, were abolishing the slave trade.[2]

Some of the early American industrialists were immigrant Europeans, like Samuel Slater, a mechanic skilled in textile machinery, who in 1789 crossed the Atlantic bringing with him the knowledge which the British were vainly trying to monopolize. He not only built the first United States water-powered plant for carding and spinning yarn, but also reproduced the traditional British method of organizing work by employing families of women, children and men.[3] It was the template for numerous other cotton-spinning factories in the north-eastern states. The Americans welcomed factory work for women since fewer men had to leave off farming.

In 1790, Thomas Clifford in the United States was granted a patent to mass-produce nails and the hand-made nailing trade of the English West Midlands was doomed. (see page 130). Similarly in the United States 41 years later, a Dr J. I. Howe invented a pin-making machine and a decade after that, Sam Slocum produced a machine for sticking pins in papers, dealing a deathblow to the hand-made domestic family pin trade.[4]

In 1814, Francis Cabot Lowell, a Boston merchant, pirated designs of British textile machinery as Slater had done, and with some associates, formed the Boston Manufacturing Company. This company deliberately designed mills for the use of female labour using, for instance, 'frame' and not 'mule' spinning. They built a model mill named after Lowell himself near Waltham,

Massachusetts. To avoid the child labour adopted in the New England mills, they recruited daughters of farmers, for whom almost the only choice of work away from their homes was as private domestic servants or as teachers on about a quarter of servants' pay. At Lowell there was something more than pay. The girls were given all sorts of opportunities for education in line with the New England belief in self-help – evening schools, lectures, concerts, above all a circulating library. The girls themselves paid something towards these amenities to ensure their interest in them. When they returned to their homes, they were admired and envied for to be employed at Lowell was an education.

Outsiders criticized their housing because in the company boarding houses they lived sometimes eight to a room and two or three to a bed. But in their own large families, it is questionable how much better off they might have been in the 1820s. Their standards were not yet those of middle-class critics like Harriet Martineau.[5]

It was the American, Elias J. Howe Jnr., who finally perfected the sewing machine in 1848[6] and mechanized the clothing trades. In the same way knitting moved into the factories in the 1830s when the power-loom was applied to the process and in 1861 the sewing machine was introduced in the manufacture of shoes. Steam power brought other family trades such as brush-making, pottery, printing, compositing, the whole process of making books, and the women's by-industry of cigar-making into centralized manufacture. New industries began in the factories: the production of paper goods, such as doylies, paper collars, cuffs, shirt-fronts for men and paper 'bosoms' for women, the papier-maché trade, the making of matches, pencils, watches, clocks and rubber goods. The rising standard of living among the mass of the people in the countries affected created a complex network of industries supplying other industries – bristle manufacture for brushes, screws, nuts and bolts not only for the new engines but for homely brass bedsteads, japanning of tin trays – industries supplying the myriads of new articles that then came into common use. In most of these trades women worked, often constituting the vast majority of operatives.[7]

In addition there was a great growth in white-collar work. The really important invention for women was the typewriter in 1867, although a few women in the United States were employed as telegraphists from 1844 when Samuel B. Morse's machine came on to the market. They became not merely shop assistants, but book-keepers. The need for staff for new industries and processes as well as a great public appetite for education led to an expansion of demand for teachers.[8]

The labour shortage from which the United States all along was suffering was aggravated by three events. In 1848–9 the Californian gold discoveries drew women as well as men from the eastern manufacturing states. The 1862 Homestead Act giving small farming a new lease of life exerted a similar westward pull. Women went not only as farmers' wives and homesteaders but as nurses, servants, adventuresses, entertainers. There was also the short-term labour shortage created by the Civil War of 1860–5 when women and girls replaced the men who went to fight. The southern states, still agricultural and with an abundance of slaves, witnessed less of this substitution. It was in the manufacturing north that the great growth in women's employment occurred.

Technical innovations succeeded one another so quickly during the nineteenth century, that within a single trade there was a considerable switching back and forth of work between males and females. For example in the boot and shoe industry in the 1820s women and children worked as stitchers and binders and by 1830, with the development of ladies' lightweight footwear on a large scale, more women were coming into the trade. In 1845 a leather rolling machine, and then the introduction of the Singer shoe-stitching machine in 1852 both put men out of work. Prosperity, however, brought footwear within reach of poorer people, the new mass demand being not for fine soft leather, but for hard-wearing, serviceable boots and shoes made of thick leather. To sew this material in the 1850s a heavy sewing machine was introduced, too heavy, it was said, for women to operate. Thick thread was needed for this heavier leather, waxed to make it easier to pull it through. Where hand-sewing was still used, people were apt to cut their hands on it. So men took over stitching and sewing and continued to work in these processes when they were further mechanized by the introduction of the Goodyear welt machine for part of the sewing. In 1862 the introduction of a sole-sewing machine, and the Civil War, enabled women to maintain their place in the trade. Nevertheless they lost work to men in ladies' and children's shoe manufacture. The sort of effect on the workforce is visible in figures for Lynn, Massachusetts, a great centre for women's and children's shoes:

	male operatives	*female operatives*
1855	4,515	11,021
1865	6,984	4,489

The labour force overall declined in the ten years from 1855 to 1865 by about 30 per cent, but the decline was entirely in numbers of female operatives. During this decade their numbers *dropped* by well over half, whereas numbers of men employed *rose* by over half.[10]

Again in the tobacco trade, cigar-making was a traditional female subsidiary industry for farmers' wives. But in 1860, it was hit by a federal tax and moved into factories, where, however, male labour was preferred to female. By the end of the decade, however, a landless female labour force arrived, experienced Bohemian women cigar-makers, refugees from the war between Prussia and Austria. At the same time the German wooden mould simplified and mechanized the work, so women staffed a new cheap cigar trade which moved from small into large factories. The result was that in the USA by the end of the century, cigar-making employed more married women than any other occupation except that of seamstress. In the meantime, however, the cigarette trade developed as new machine-rolling equipment made mass production possible; women then continually gained work at the expense of males. From 11 per cent in 1870, the total numbers of women employees rose so that by 1900 they made up 36 per cent of all those in the tobacco trades.[11]

The same kind of switches occurred in printing and compositing which had been old, family craft trades. In 1810 König applied steam-power to the roller and as a result the formes holding the print were increased in size and weight, giving the advantage to men. This was the start of a bitter battle, in every country apparently, between women and men in the printing trades which is not yet resolved.[12]

The picture that emerges in the United States is in many respects different to the conventional European notion of women's work in the nineteenth century. In the main, they lost ground in their traditional manufacturing work such as textiles. In 1848–9 women and girls accounted for 69 per cent of the total labour force in cotton weaving; in 1900 for only 42 per cent.[13] To balance this decline in traditional work, the proportion of women in a number of newer trades was rising, for example in watch and clock manufacture, glass-making, food production and confectionery. Seventy-three per cent of all teachers in 1900 were women, 30 per cent of typists, 29 per cent of bookkeepers, but only 13 per cent of clerks and copyists. We are here talking of proportions employed, not absolute numbers. There were in fact nearly as many female clerks and copyists as there were typists, 81,000 to 85,000; but males made up a much larger percentage of the clerks than of the typists.[14]

There was, of course, immense variation in trends in women's employment throughout the revolutions in industry. In contrast to the United States, in France, for example, there were marked rises in percentages of women employed in banking and commerce and in the food trades, but in the liberal professions, mainly teaching, there was only a small proportional increase. In agriculture and especially in textiles between 1866 and 1901, there were increases with textiles retaining its traditional place as the greatest manufacturing occupation for women.[15]

Table 3   Percentages of Economically Active Women in Various Occupational Groups in France

YEAR	Book Trades	Textiles	Upholstery	Leather & Tanning	Metallurgy	Precious Metals	Banking & Commerce	Personal & Domestic Service	Liberal Professions	Public Service & Administration
1866	18·91	45·14	78·00	18·42	8·47	20·09	25·56	79·90	40·96*	11·11
1901	20·99	53·70	88·63	15·14	0·93	32·26	37·85	77·94	43·29	16·27
1906	21·41	55·88	88·97	16·22	1·04	32·00	38·49	77·15	41·62	18·03

* Figure is for 1896; no figures available for 1866.
Source: M. Guilbert, *Les femmes et l'organisation syndicate avant 1914*, pp. 13–14 From 5-yearly census figures.

French demands for coal and iron during the Napoleonic occupation turned the valley of the River Ruhr into an industrial zone. In the German mines, long after they had been excluded officially from underground work in Britain, women pushed the cars loaded with ore. Four girls hoisted 80 tubs containing 1 to $1\frac{1}{2}$ hundredweights of ore to the surface per 8-hour shift.[16] It was lighter than the work of the British women 'drawers' and 'hurriers', some of whom in the West Riding of Yorkshire carried corves (baskets) weighing $2\frac{1}{2}$–3 hundredweights so that in a single day they raised $1\frac{1}{2}$–2 tons to the surface (miners were paid by the weight of usable coal delivered at the pit-head). German women worked in foundries, steel works and rolling mills as day labourers.[17] They tapped zinc furnaces pouring off the molten metal and the separated slag. They tended the ovens in the mornings when the foundries were full of dust and zinc vapours. Girls and women preferred the freer atmosphere in mines and foundries to the restrictions and long hours of domestic service. Their working conditions in factories and furnaces were not so deplorable as those of sweated urban manual labour.

The new industrialism spread to Asia when, in 1868, the Meiji dynasty replaced the Tokugawa in Japan. Three years later silk-reeling machinery was imported from France and this staple peasant industry of women moved into factories. Here there was a conjunction of feudal autocracy with modern factory methods. By the 1880s the large-scale development of the silk industry had started, strictly controlled – from mulberry seed to the finished bolts of cloth – by the government, which represented the wealthy nationalist entrepreneurial class. Some of the big Japanese silk factories were even more thorough-going than the New England Lowell mills in their control of their girl workers and provisions for their welfare. At the Gunze factories there was not only a training school for all employees, but a hospital which ran training courses for nurses. There were arrangements for regular physical exercise long before the Chinese People's Republic instituted this. The general and moral education of the factory hands was of the best standard – the girls, selected by the larger employers and taken on in the silk-reeling mills when they left school, were not expected to stay after they were about twenty years old. It was anticipated that by that age marriages would have been arranged for them. Sixty per cent stayed only three years, but a few continued to work for thirty years and were given rewards or gratuities. The élite among the girls were the examiners at the government stations where the moths were checked to ensure they were not diseased. But this work was highly seasonal and when one season's girls were paid off, a new lot were sought for the following season. Girls never reached the high schools and university faculties of agriculture.

PERSISTENCE OF THE DOMESTIC INDUSTRIAL SYSTEM
Perhaps the most extraordinary aspect of women's work in the second half of the nineteenth century and until after the First World War was the toughness and survival-power of the old domestic industrial tradition. The Japanese peasant women continued to manufacture silk in their homes. Usually together with men, but sometimes on their own they created co-operatives which began as marketing societies for home-reeled silk. They adapted to the new industrial methods. They bought equipment and sold it to members, along with other co-operatively produced necessities like fertilizers and implements. 'Mixed' co-operatives provided cash through loans, savings deposits and credit societies. They also had vast interests other than silk, such as rope and mat manufacture, irrigation, drainage, machines for preparing barley, the marketing of any and every kind of agricultural produce, livestock farming and forestry, all providing work for women as well as men.

Paralleling the development of co-operatives, in Japan there was a development of guilds whose aims were identical with those of European craft guilds. In these also women workers played a part, for under the authoritarian Japanese regime, once a guild was sanctioned, everyone in the occupation it covered had to join.[18]

As in Japan, the domestic industrial system survived in Continental Europe and in North America largely because independent small farming had been given a new lease of life. On the Continent a pattern was set in which the ending of feudalism was marked by the break-up of big estates into smallholdings which were given to the erstwhile serfs. The military successes of the French under Napoleon started the process. The defeated nations were persuaded that military service ought to be a specialized profession paid for by taxes. In the 1840s, the Rhineland feudal landowners preferred to acquiesce in laws granting peasants free status and ownership of land they farmed, as a way of shifting on to them liability for the new land tax imposed to raise funds for the new-type army. So agriculture, and with it, by-industries flourished. The old forms of peasant 'women's work' were strengthened just when the new factory industry was beginning to develop.

William Howitt, an English traveller, in 1841 described these German women peasants:

> They reap, thrash, mow, work on fallows, do anything. In summer without shoes and stockings, clad in a dark blue petticoat and body [bodice] of the same, or in other colours, according to the costume of the neighbourhood, and with their white chemise sleeves in contrast with their dresses, and with their hair burnt to a singed brown ... with the sun, they are out in the hot fields. Nay, you may even see women driving a wagon, in which two or three men are sitting at ease smoking ...

The great crops of tobacco were weeded and kept clean by women wearing huge straw hats and wielding the ubiquitous hoe. The distinctive dress of each different village had enabled feudal landowners immediately to identify their own tenants and to check on their movements if they left their own area. Howitt observed that the hard life made people bent and wizened with rheumatism. In spite of this, he described the old women as quite jolly and cheerful. Life expectancy in Europe at this time was about 35 to 50 years for a working person.[19] These nineteenth-century German women farmers had much in common as far as work was concerned with Kengeran the African hoe farmer. For both, health and life expectancy were better than for 'sweated' urban workers. But the German women had long lost the economic independence of the Africans.

When the choice was between factory work and the old peasant life divided between farming and domestic industries, except in the case of a few enlightened employers who made factory conditions exceptionally good, women preferred the old life. The German women fought specially hard to retain it, not surprisingly since, when landless and homeless, they were apt to end up in cities as street sweepers, porters, or, at best, street traders.[20]

In England people from workhouses were coerced into factories as cheap labour. Cartloads of miserable girls and women arrived in factory areas. They also went voluntarily, however, because wages in farmwork had dropped by the mid-nineteenth century and factory wages were higher. But it took this sort of pressure to force them from their homes.[21]

In 1840 Villermé described country women who went into factory work in the French industrial districts, for example in the east at Mulhouse. They came from neighbouring Germany and German Switzerland as well as France. Many were too poor to pay the rents for lodgings in the town, so they found places in the country. He described them coming into Mulhouse every morning to work in the factories, 'pale, thin, walking with bare feet in the midst of the mud and who, lacking umbrellas, put over their heads aprons or skirts to protect their faces and necks.' They rose about 4 am, worked a 15-hour day in unhealthy workshops and walked miles bringing their children with them to work at auxiliary jobs.[22]

At an International Labour Congress called by the Swiss Workers' League in Zurich in August, 1897, the British delegation, concerned particularly about urban sweated workers, with the support of Lily Braun of Berlin moved a resolution for the abolition of homework. But it failed because, as the German Social Democrat, Georg Heinrich von Vollmar, said, voicing the views of many continental delegates, large districts were absolutely dependent on home industry.[23]

Moreover the new technology encouraged home industry, especially in the United States. The Lamb knitting machine and Howe's sewing machine, which brought clothing into factories, not only enabled urban manufacturers to make use of urban homeworkers who rented machines, but also took garments cut in the cities to be sewn by women and girls in the families of farmers and labourers in the countryside. It was a system virtually no different to that of the woollen cloth trade in England and the Netherlands in the fifteenth century.

But the railways, urbanization, mass production and the flow of European immigrants to the factories in the east enabled the North American housewife in the town to cease contributing directly to her family's livelihood. Like an old homesteader, as suburbs grew, she was marooned in her home. But unlike her, she was utterly dependent on her husband, and like the growing number of non-working wives in Europe, she was supported by the labour of many other men and women.[24]

THE LOW POINT FOR WOMEN WORKERS

In spite of rising living standards for some working women and the widening range of work, world-wide, the middle of the nineteenth century from about 1830 to 1870 was probably the lowest point for women workers numerically. Greater numbers of them were 'sweated', lost their occupations because of the population rise in the industrializing countries, or were made wretched because of those countries' demands for cheap raw materials and cheap labour in other parts of the world. Colonists and settlers were increasingly disrupting Stone Age economies in which women were dominant or had a status nearly equal to that of men and imposing on them the inferior status of women in their own economies.

By the mid-nineteenth century, as we have seen, there was much more concern about women's and children's working conditions. Philanthropists and journalists like Charles Dickens and Henry Mayhew in England publicized the lives of 'sweated' workers. One woman, a maker of rowing shirts, told Mayhew:

> I often gets up at two and three in the morning and carries on till the evening of the following day, merely lying down in my clothes to take a nap of five to ten minutes. The agitation of mind never lets one lie longer ... I clears about 2s. 6d. a week ... it's so little I can't get a rag on my back ...

The foremen at the large shops, she stated, generally married shirt-makers, 'or someone in the line of business'. They took work home to their wives, who gave it out, or sub-contracted it to agents, who in turn gave it out to poor people like her. The agents, she said, 'take one-fourth part of the price, be what it will ...' It seemed that a 25 per cent commission was still general.

Desperation increased parental callousness and, as a consequence, the numbers of destitute girls. 'Five years ago my father turned me out of doors. The shoe-binding is so low [so poorly paid] that I wasn't able to pay 1s a week for my lodging ...' one girl told Mayhew.[25] Prostitution continued to be a mass occupation.

Philanthropists were also increasingly concerned about slavery, which persisted in the United States alongside modern factory industry. It could be argued that the life of a 'sweated' urban European worker was not much better than that of a plantation slave. Conditions varied enormously, being determined by the personal characters of owners, by the kind of work and by the local climate. Household slaves were usually considered the best off, being merely domestic servants. The southern cotton plantations of mainland America were among the worst climatically, being situated in fever-ridden swamps, and masters were apt to be cruel.

Recently a centenarian ex-slave from one of the Cuban sugar estates recounted life at first hand. They worked a 12-hour day, the women as hard as the men, and they suffered the same punishments: a woman knew how the whip thongs bit when the overseers cracked her over the shoulders. Grown slave women suffered additionally the indignity of being beaten on the buttocks when they were pregnant. A hole was dug for a woman's distended belly, she was made to lie face downwards over it and whipped carefully so as not to damage her baby. As the English cracked down on the slave-ships, the value of slave children rose. But how much worse were conditions than in English workhouses where women and men were segregated and subject to beatings?

An American negro woman slave had advantages, firstly of climate, for the plantations were in warm latitudes, not all of them unhealthy. Not all slave babies were the result of forced breeding at the orders of their owners. She could make love when she chose. And slave women like men had their own vegetable plots. They had a personal income from sales of their produce which enabled them to save up to buy finery, or even their way to freedom. They had clubs through which they saved funds for revolution. Freedom, however, meant the responsibility for keeping oneself and, in an increasingly competitive economy, that meant insecurity. Yet the slave's view of slavery ultimately was shown by her decision to opt for that insecurity since it brought a chance of human dignity.[26]

In 1811, the Spanish abolished personal slavery – the assigning of individual men, women and children to colonists. They then converted the slaves into feudal serfs. Women continued to work to a large extent as 'unpaid family labour'. In our own times, although no longer under Spanish rule, many in Central and South America still work in both communal and family fields and orchards, as well as at their traditional poultry breeding. Like the medieval serf, the peon was obliged to pay a labour-rent for his plot. In addition he and his family might be sold with the land. They were deliberately kept in debt through the 'tommy shop', that is the only shop within reach, which was often owned by the proprietor of the land, just as British and North American industrial workers were. If the peon, unlike his Indian forebears, was harsh to women as were serfs the world over, his own life was harsh enough.[27]

The mid-nineteenth century marked the low point for women workers as a whole. Yet it also marked the turn of the tide. There was greater concern to end slavery. Some colonists tackled cruel practices such as suttee (see page 83) and tried to improve the health of those whom they oppressed in other ways. There was greater concern for women workers' welfare and a stronger appreciation of work they did unpaid in homes. But more than all this it was the time when women really started to fight their way out of their inferiority in an organized way.

NOTES

1 *Great Industries of the United States*, eds. Horace Greeley and others, 870.

2 ibid., 870–2; Mannix and Cowley, *Black Cargoes*, 188, 196; R. Burlingame, *March of the Iron Men*, 177.

3 ibid., 158, 161–2; Elizabeth F. Baker, *Technology and Women's Work*, 5, 10, n. 9.

4 *Great Industries of the United States*, 1072, 1287.

5 Benita Eisler, *The Lowell Offering*, 13ff, 24–5, 56–60; E. F. Baker, op. cit., 9–14.

6 ibid., 25; Burlingame, op. cit., 362, 364, 371, 373–4.

7 *Great Industries of the United States*, 203, 206–7, 735, 973–4, 1124–5, 1143, 1145–7, 1229; G. C. Allen, *Industrial Development of Birmingham and the Black Country, 1860–1927*, 166–71, 226–7, 274–5, 294–5; M. J. Wise, *Birmingham and its Regional Setting*; E. Cadbury and Others, *Women's Work and Wages*, see Tables, 309ff; Elihu Burrit, *Walks in the Black Country*, 62–3, 66–7, 116–23 & etc.

8 E. F. Baker, op. cit., 70–3.

9 See the documentary novels of Conrad Richter e.g. *The Fields*, the character of Sayward Wheeler (Corgi ed.) 31, 103, 116–18; O. Coolidge, *Women's Rights, The Suffrage Movement in America, 1848–1920*, 13–14, Lucy Stone's mother. Note also the hard creed for Quaker women, Lucy Anthony, 18–19.

10 ibid., 28–30, 156–8; *Great Industries of the United States*, 1255–7, 1261–2.

11 E. F. Baker, op. cit., 31–7.

12 ibid., 37ff.: Sullerot, *L'histoire et sociologie du travail féminin*, 106; M. Guilbert, *Les femmes et l'organisation syndicale*, 48.

13 E. F. Baker, op. cit., 17, 113–14; Janet M. Hooks, *Women's Occupation Throughout Seven Decades*, 105–6.

14 E. F. Baker, op. cit., 48–51, 73; *Great Industries of the United States*, 77, 79. Women made the minute screws required for watches.

15 M. Guilbert, *Les fonctions des femmes dans l'industrie*, 33, 41; also in *Les femmes et lorganisation syndicale*, 13–15. For Dutch women workers see W. N. Schlistra, *Vrouwen Arbeid in Landbouwen Industrie in Nederland in de Tweede Helft der 19a E. Eiuw*, 8, 14ff.

16 O. T. Mason, *Women's Share in Primitive Culture*, 131 quoting Rep. of U S Consul Dithmar, March 1889, No. 103, 431 and British Blue Book on women's work.

17 *P P Roy Comm. on Mines*, App. to first Rep, pt. i, 1842, xvi, 182, 252, 280, 464; pt. ii, 1842, xvii, 165–6; R. Bald, *A General View of the Coal Trade of Scotland*, 134.

18 C. C. Ghosh, *The Silk Industry of Japan*, 21–6, 31–4, 56–7, 65, 81–4, 93–6, 103, 106–9, 113: By 1927 silk reeling factories employed 462,594 women and girls; 33,335 males; Nobuko Takahashi 'Women's Wages in Japan', ILO *Women Workers and Society*, 111.

19 W. Howitt, *The Rural and Domestic Life of Germany*, 40–1, 44–5, 50–1: See also T. C. Banfield, *Agriculture on the Rhine*, 9–10, 37, 58, 60, 90, 157–9.

20 O. T. Mason, *Woman's Share in Primitive Culture*, 134–8.

21 G. Unwin, *Samuel Oldknow and the Arkwrights*, 118, quoting *Manchester Mercury*, 6 Feb., 1787; Hammonds op. cit., 25–6; *Annals of Agriculture*, vol. 15, 564.

22 Villermé, *Tableau de l'état physique et moral des ouvriers employés dans les manufactures de coton, de laine et de soie* vol. 1, 27.

23 *Women't Trade Union Review*, Oct. 1897, 11, 13: '... the advanced proposals of the English were several times defeated by a combined Catholic and Continental Socialist vote.'

24 *Great Industries of the United States*, 588, 592; E. F. Baker, op. cit., 20–1; Burlingame, op. cit., 376.

25 E. P. Thompson and E. Yeo, eds., *The Unknown Mayhew*, 145–6, 329–32 (an account of 'sweating' in Germany), 239, 351–3.

26 *The Autobiography of a Runaway Slave*, Esteban Montejo of Cuba, M. Barnet ed., trans Jocasta Innes, 21–4, 27, 31, 38–40, 69, 71–2, 74–5, 90, 102, 105.

27 Oscar Lewis, *Pedro Martinez*, 463, 497–8; C. Greenidge, *Slavery*, 75–6.

Chapter 11

WOMEN'S INDUSTRIAL ORGANIZATION

Since Britain had a head start in the Industrial Revolution, it was inevitable that trade unionism should develop early there, including the industrial organization of women. Women continued to participate in sporadic protests which had begun by the sixteenth century at lack of work or at merchants' fixing of prices paid to them for work. Or, like men they built on the craft guild traditions. In the same way as there had been all-female guilds, so they set up trade societies on their own initiative or sometimes with male help. There was a good deal of activity during the first half of the eighteenth century among men and women weavers in the West of England woollen trades. By 1747 a 'mixed' male and female society was functioning among the Small-Ware Worsted Weavers in Manchester. By the 1790s a very powerful 'mixed' society of spinners had been established in Lancashire. Women were specifically mentioned on equal terms in its rules governing apprentices. There was an all-female Leicester Sisterhood of worsted spinners and some sort of organization among Derbyshire silk weavers and Nottingham lace-makers.

It was on the basis of new industrial growth that all-female friendly and benefit societies were set up among West Country weavers and – for any working woman of the necessary standard of respectability and prosperity – others in Birmingham and especially in Manchester, where there were at least four. In addition women joined with men in 'mixed' Friendly societies. Just as in the case of men, these organizations institutionalized hierarchy within the labouring classes. For they were set up by the élite.[1]

British women's industrial organization was not obliterated by the Acts of 1799–1800 proscribing trade unions. It merged with a movement to keep down food prices which was backed by the new manufacturing interests who saw no reason to subsidize the poor, especially the rural poor. Thus early on working men and women entered into an alliance with some of the manufacturing employers.

From the end of the Napoleonic wars in 1814, strikes and protests about cuts in the prices paid for work gathered momentum. They could not have taken place without women's support, and often not without their active participation, for they occurred in trades in which the female labour force predominated or was of considerable importance, that is in all kinds of textile trades, among market gardeners, maids and charwomen and among some of the clothing trades.[2] The movement amounted to a great demonstration of unity by a mass of labouring people still held together in small communities by the proximity of home and workplace, for even the new factories were mostly near where the workforce lived. Quite frequently protests involved confrontations with army and police. Even when, over two or three generations, women's physique might have been weakened by long hours of factory work, their spirit remained intact. Women 'sweated' homeworkers were trying to organize at various times throughout the nineteenth century in Britain; for example, Nottingham lace-embroiderers, Northampton shoe-binders and Birmingham tailoresses.[3]

But by the late 1820s, the determination of men to take over women's work or to hold on to their own work against women's competition was already fracturing unity. Craft practices of excluding women from membership simply on grounds of their sex were carried over into trade unionism. Men retained some interest in their organization, however. Both in John Doherty's Grand General Union of Spinners in 1829 and in the Grand National Consolidated Trades Union women were encouraged to form their own separate societies on the lines of all-female friendly and benefit societies.

After the collapse of the Grand National Consolidated Trades Union in 1834 in Britain the trade union movement was split. The pace was set by workers in the more prosperous trades, largely men, except in the case of textiles. Unlike Continental workers they made purely industrial demands over hours and wages. They did not support revolutionary political change, not even the reforms proposed in the great Charter, except temporarily when their trades were depressed. They were doing well out of capitalism which, with Britain's industrial lead and second wave of colonialism, was raising living standards.

Women were also involved to a considerable extent in another form of working class self-help, the co-operative movement. One of the movement's leaders was Robert Owen, the philanthropic industrialist and one of the champions of the 1802 Child Apprentices' Act. Although his cotton spinning mills both at New Lanark in Scotland and at New Harmony in the United States both eventually failed as experiments in co-operative industrial communities, he upheld in these enterprises, a woman's right to work and to equal dignity with men. The Owen mills were organized on a basis of family labour. He educated and gave confidence to a number of women outside his own workforce, among them Charlotte Elizabeth Tonna, whose book, *The Wrongs of Women* (1843–4) was among those works that changed the philanthropists' thinking about women's lives. Owen, in his turn, studied women workers in France, Belgium and Germany. He was part of the counter movement to Proudhon and all those men who were trying to maintain women's inferior status and even to worsen it.

FRANCE

Although French women and men failed to establish their right to equality during the Revolution, the women's emancipation movement did not die out. Men who respected women's work could not honestly uphold women's inequality. They included leaders of the emerging French Socialist movement, for example, Claude, Comte de St Simon (1760–1825), lover of Mme. de Stael, the novelist, Cabet, Michelet and Charles Fourrier who not only stood for the 'rate the job', but for women's right to choose their professions and to fulfil their talents and capabilities.[4]

In 1825 there was a strike of Lyon silk-workers, mainly women. The trade was organized on the sub-contracting system and it was the sub-contractors, better educated than those who worked for them who, in 1831 and again in 1834, led renewed struggles. There on 9–12 April 1834 there took place what Lefebure has called 'the first purely workers' insurrection in modern times.' It was also hailed as 'the first visible link between the workers' aspirations and the republican ideal'. It sparked off a revolt in Paris, and was the prelude to the rebellions of 1848.[5]

To a much greater extent than in the Revolution of 1789, women workers in France during the 1830s and 1840s were putting forward demands and programmes to improve their lot. A growing number did not accept the prior rights of men, but claimed equality. They took up the idea of 'union' as the sole means working people had of pulling themselves out of their miseries. Among them was the half-Peruvian, half-Spanish Flora Tristan, who wrote articles and books including *Working Peoples' Union*, (*L'union ouvrière*) in which she cried:

> Workmen, workwomen, count yourselves; taken one by one you are no more than a grain of dust ground under the big wheel. But assemble together, unite together. You are five millions, and five million people is a force.

If each contributed a few sous to their association, they would build up funds and add the power of money to that of numbers. She exhorted them to form consciously a 'working class'. But it could only exist if it was a union of women as well as men. She died in 1844, no political revolutionary, but a believer in industrial union and education and greatly loved by working people.

1848 was a year of Continental revolutions and there were other Frenchwomen who also saw political action as necessary to progress towards equality. On 20 March that year, some of them launched a journal, *La Voix des Femmes*, whose policy was embodied in the old republican slogan: Liberty, Equality, Fraternity. They formed one of the earliest Frenchwomen's emancipation associations. The best mind among them was that of Jeanne Deroin, (1805–95), a seamstress and disciple of Robert Owen. With great difficulty she educated herself into becoming a teacher, and in 1834 she had answered Proudhon. Maternity, she pointed out, did not confer freedom on a woman since she was not free in the first instance to choose whether or not she would be a mother. How many, she asked became courtesans out of disgust at housework? 'It's not right, as you say, to get women out of workshops, but instead it's necessary to transform the workshops.' With Desirée Gay, another seamstress who had worked for a time in Owen's factories, in August 1848 she started the journal *La Politique des Femmes*, more political even than *La Voix des Femmes*.

La Voix des Femmes sent workwomen's delegates to the Commission of the 1848 revolutionaries in session at the Luxembourg Palace where they were segregated from the men to Desirée Gay's annoyance. The Commission set up national workshops for women as well as men. The workwomen proposed 'people's houses' containing public laundries, restaurants, amusements and meeting-places for the use of men and women as a means of combating both alcoholism and cabarets, which were closely linked with prostitution. They asked for a National Institute to sort out social labour problems. *La Voix des Femmes* found that the two main causes of workwomen's hardships were competition from prisoners' manufactures, sold to the public at very low prices which undercut those of free labourers, and middlemen and women. The State, it suggested, by raising prices of articles made by prisoners, would increase its revenues. To obviate agents between those who manufactured and those who sold, their proposed remedy was co-operatives of production and national workshops such as were being set up. Crêches for working mothers were already being advocated in the mid-1840s in Charles Dickens' magazine, *Household Words*. One was actually run by Miss Mary Merryweather at the Courtauld powerloom silk mill at Halstead in Essex in 1847–50. The French midwives in 1848 called for them, along with halls of refuge for women. They also asked that they themselves be employed as what today we call social workers so that needy women would not have to attend the humiliating Offices of Charity. Associations were formed of dressmakers, midwives, milliners and teachers. Elise Lemonnier, who ran a dressmaking establishment, founded a united working women's society which provided education for its members. She also opened a proper school and other Elise Lemonnier schools followed. Others of these women worked to open the professions to women. All believed that by increasing women's competence at work they would materially improve their economic situation.

When the 1848 French revolt foundered, the women leaders were tracked down and exiled. Jeanne Deroin, along with Pauline Roland, another of the group, was sent to St Lazare prison accused of conspiracy. The police report credits her with having been the moving spirit behind the idea of Union, for she brought the small craft associations of workwomen into a sort of large federation. She was apparently the first promoter of 'mixed' male and female trades unions in France, finally bringing together one hundred and four associations. On her release from prison she came to London and, widowed, she followed her original trade of seamstress to keep her children, still, however, working for 'Union'.[7] It was only in

1864 that the French trade unions obtained the legal recognition which the British had gained forty years earlier. By that time, however, women's presence in the French Labour and Trade Union Movement was established.

THE UNITED STATES OF AMERICA

American women, too, were taking part in industrial action by the 1820s, the earliest known example being in a factory strike in Pawtucket, Rhode Island in 1824, against a wage cut and an attempt to lengthen working hours. It was the girls at the Lowell mills who in 1844–5 founded the first major women's union, the Female Labor Reform Association.

Conditions at Lowell had deteriorated greatly from the initial relatively high standards. One of the main causes of the decline was the constant inflow of European immigrants. They brought with them the sub-contracting system, labour hierarchy, the inferior status, low pay and long hours of their home countries and strengthened all these tendencies already present in the United States. They undermined what was left of the pioneers' relatively greater appreciation of women's working capacities.

They increased urban populations and competition for work. Those who had fled from tyrannies, created in the United States a different tyranny. Those who employed others drove themselves relentlessly and had no time for philanthropy.

By the mid-nineteenth century, younger managers were taking over firms. They had been brought up, not to paternal interest in their employees, but in the tradition of ruthless pursuit of profit by means of the new factory division of labour and mass production methods. The distinctive feature of urban industrialism in the United States by the second half of the nineteenth century was already mass production and wholesaling, the urban workers themselves creating, as General Jackson predicted, a new mass market.

EDUCATION, EMANCIPATION AND THE PROFESSIONS

Hand in hand with the early women's trade union movement went women's emancipation which, in turn, was linked with women's determination to obtain the same education as men. As we have seen, the country 'dame' schools, often under parental pressure, were mainly 'sweated' workshops. The advances in girls' education began in the United States. In 1818, Mrs Emma Willard, an experienced and determined teacher of girls, presented to Governor Clinton of New York State her 'Plan' to put women's education 'on an equal footing with that of men'. Fifteen years later, in 1833, Oberlin College in Ohio Square opened its doors to all, irrespective of race, colour or sex. It was intended that the women students should be trained for motherhood.

In the 1830s young women were moved by revulsion at women's lives to start fighting for legal and social equality. For example, Lucy Stone, a Massachusetts farmer's daughter, was so appalled at the way her mother was overworked and taken for granted by her husband and sons acting on Biblical authority, that she asked for something to take to kill herself. But she lived to educate herself with a struggle and become a teacher. The upper-class Elizabeth Cady Stanton was moved by the stream of sad women unable to obtain redress at the law court over which her father presided. One branch of the American Women's Emancipation Movement was closely linked to the Anti-Slavery Movement since not only slaves suffered, but also plantation owners' wives who were, as one of them put it, merely the heads of harems which incorporated the women slaves.[8]

As primary education extended, women came to dominate teaching. Their special aptitude for dealing with young children was acknowledged, but not in levels of pay. In higher education where the financial rewards were greater, men still had precedence.

The movement for women's education affected all European countries. It was extremely strong in Russia in spite of the fact that serfdom was only abolished there in 1861 and 1866. The more strong-minded girls sought release from their use as merchandise in the marriage market through education. In 1859 a women's journal, *Daybreak*, appeared and St Petersburg University was opened to women. A vigorous feminist movement had built up, much influenced by socialism. Most women students were upper- and middle-class radicals, some of whom had supported an attempt to oust the Tsar in December 1825. Many spurned a life without work and opted for poverty as teachers, doctors, nurses and midwives among the peasantry. They set up communes and co-operatives of shoe-makers and book-producers and took in female students who had left families and husbands. Their male counterparts were equally heroic. To help girls escape arranged marriages, they volunteered to marry them without any thought of consummating these marriages. They left their 'wives' to live their own lives.[9]

Upper-class Russian women invaded the Sorbonne in greater numbers than the native French. A Russian, Sophie Kovalevski, was the first woman appointed to a chair of higher mathematics which she obtained at Stockholm University. Mary Somerville (1780–1872) became an eminent contributor to research in physics and chemistry. Her works included *Mechanism of the Heavens* and *Molecular and Microscopic Science*. Women fought their way into law practice. In 1869, the American, Arabella Mansfield, became the first woman to practise at the bar. Others who qualified in the 'eighties and 'nineties, Marie Popelin in Brussels, Emilie Kempin-Spyri in Switzerland and Sarmisa Bileşçu in Hungary, failed, however, to break the male monopoly and had to content themselves with jobs as assistants in solicitors' offices.[10]

The first woman doctor in modern times was Elizabeth Blackwell an Englishwoman who managed to qualify in Switzerland and to practice in the United States. She even set up a small hospital in 1857, but again only against tremendous odds.[11]

In France, from the seventeenth century onwards, the Soeurs de Charité had established a high level of professional vocational nursing. But British nursing had never recovered from the deterioration in standards after the Civil War. The rehabilitation of this occupation began towards the middle of the nineteenth century. Mrs Elizabeth Fry's Institute of Nursing was training nurses for private households from 1840 and a Protestant sisterhood was formed in 1848. St Thomas's Hospital in London was the cradle of world-wide public professional nursing. Improvements begun by Mrs Sarah Savery, matron in 1816–40, were continued by the great Mrs Sarah Wardroper who became matron in 1854. In that year the Crimean War broke out, and Florence Nightingale went to fight her epic battle, imposing cleanliness and order on filth and unnecessary disease in army nursing. She learnt from the Soeurs de Charité that good nursing was possible. When she came home she went to St Thomas's, having heard of Mrs Wardroper's work. There, with the help of funds from the public, she established a professional nursing training school, with the avowed aim of organizing similar training courses in other hospitals. Nightingale-trained nurses went all over the world, carrying with them the new high medical standards.[12] Her work inspired genteel women on both sides in the American Civil War to nurse troops at the front, those in the north having first a considerable battle with the military authorities before they were permitted to do so.

It was the educated women emancipators who pushed through the New York legislature in 1860 a bill giving women the right to sue in court, giving widows the same rights as widowers to inheritance and to the guardianship of children and, of first interest to working women, giving women the right to collect their own wages. In 1870 Congress introduced equal pay for women and men clerks in the Treasury. These were part of the female white-collar elite, positively eager for 'the rate for the job' as an affirmation of their equality with men. A generation later the Congress Industrial Commission in its final report upheld the much more far-reaching proposition, that the only 'fair basis' for the fixing of wages was 'that of the *quality* of work performed'.[13] (my italics). A standard set by quality meant that the quality of work done only by women and not by men would be recognized in pay levels. It would kill the 'lower women's wage'. It implied a recognition of the value of work.

WOMEN'S ORGANIZATION IN THE LATE NINETEENTH AND EARLY TWENTIETH CENTURIES

Throughout the nineteenth century in the industrializing countries small groups of women were setting up their own societies. The United Kingdom first Annual Trade Directory of 1861 showed a number of them: Manchester Small Ware Black Silk Weavers, Finger Warpers, Heck Warpers, Bradford Wool Sorters, Coventry Ribbon Weavers, Birmingham Burnishers, Bone Button and Metal Workers for example. They were setting up their own societies in the printing, book-binding and tobacco trades before men or philanthropists tried to recruit them. It was Mary Galway, one of the mill-women, who started organizing the Belfast linen mills.[14]

In Lyon in 1869 the women in charge of the silk cocoons carried out a successful strike and joined the International Workers' Association, in spite of the fact that a majority at the International's first conference upheld the ideas of Proudhon. Eugene Varlin in 1866 had incorporated in the rules of the Paris Bookbinders' Mutual Society, the equal rights of women and men. The Limoges

porcelain-makers decided to enrol women because they 'manufactured goods as well as men did and felt the same needs'.[15] Women
workers were at the barricades again in 1870–1 when the Socialists
overturned another Emperor as they had in 1848, and set up the
short-lived Paris Commune.[16] Small numbers of Frenchwomen
attended national inter-union Congresses in the later nineteenth
century, speaking and serving occasionally as Congress officials.

The United States followed this pattern. The secret working-
men's order, the Knights of Labour founded in 1869, in 1881 came
into the open and began to bring together men's and women's
societies. Existing women's societies which joined included the
Daughters of St Crispin (shoe-makers), St Louis stocking-knitters,
New York lead-pencil makers, San Francisco whiteware-makers,
tailoresses in Newark and Milwaukee, cloak-makers in Chicago
and Boston, organizations of cooks, washers, laundresses and
housekeepers. Many came in who had never organized before,
including clerks and teachers. The Knights, like the British Grand
National Consolidated Trades Union of 1833–4, accepted married
women and a few women went out to recruit. It was hard, heart-
breaking work. The influx of Negroes from the South after the
Civil War added to the downward pressure on wages of European
immigrants and mass production methods.

**Table 4   Growing Participation of Women in the Labour Force
Outside Their Homes in the United States of America, 1870–1940**

Year	Number of women gainfully occupied	Percent of total labour force	Increase between each census year	Percent of all Females of working age
1870	1,917,446	14·8	—	13·3
1880	2,647,157	15·2	38·1	14·7
1889	4,005,532	17·2	51·3	17·4
1900	5,319,397	18·3	32·8	20·4
1910	7,444,787	19·9	40·0	25·2
1920	8,636,512	20·4	16·0	23·3
1930*	10,752,116	22·0	24·5	23·6
1940*	13,015,000	24·4	25·2	25·7

* Persons in the Labour Force.
Source: U.S. Bureau of Labor, Women's Bureau, *Bulletin* No. 218, 1947.
Janet M. Hooks – 1870–1890 Those aged 10 years and over.
                1920–1940 Those aged 14 years and over.

Working mothers turned to this trade union work. The Irish Leonora Barry blamed those women who were earning good wages and consequently refused to support organization. She castigated their 'foolish pride, prudish modesty and religious scruples' and the expectation that 'with marriage their connection with and interest in labour methods ends ...' Living proof to the contrary was Mrs George Rodgers, Workman or head of the entire Knights' organization in Chicago except the stockyards, a mother of twelve who brought her latest infant to the Knights' 1886 Convention.

By the 1890s, the Knights were dissolving in internal strife. But in 1881 a federation of unions had been founded, the American Federation of Labor. Its constituent unions were largely those of the better-paid male craft-workers, disinclined to spend money on trying to organize the low-paid, unskilled working people.

The tendency for women to organize separately from men persisted. In 1900 small local unions of tailoresses were founded from which was to arise the International Ladies' Garment Workers' Union. The tailoresses struck in desperation, without funds or organization, as women so often did. In 1909–10 the shirtwaist makers of New York and Philadelphia came out against conditions in two large firms. Angered by the preponderance of words over suggestions for practical deeds at a meeting and unintimidated by the presence of Samuel Gompers of the AF of L, sixteen-year-old Clara Lemlich went up to the platform and spoke:

'I am a working girl, and one of those who are on strike against intolerable conditions. I am tired of listening to speakers who talk in general terms. What we are here for is to decide whether or not we shall strike. I offer a resolution that a general strike be declared – now!'

The resolution was carried. The strike not only involved large numbers of workers, but went on for some time. The organization to carry it on was built up gradually and painfully. Three-quarters of the strikers were women, but they were of different nationalities. In New York alone twenty-four halls were required for meetings with speakers at each in Yiddish, Italian and English. Hundreds of women pickets were beaten by the police and arrested. Yet more turned up to replace them, day after day for thirteen weeks. The strike failed, but it proved to the United States women's capacity for organization. It led to a great strike in the men's garment trade in Chicago as a result of which the United Garment Workers' Union obtained recognition, the right to arbitration and to an employees' grievance committee in three factories. It was the start of official acceptance. It could not have been carried out without women in the shops, who held out with the men for 14 weeks in the winter.[17]

Even in Russia, the mass of whose people were among the most miserable in the world, women workers were in revolt. At the turn of the century, Russia was not dissimilar to the Britain of three hundred years earlier. Women's life expectancy there averaged 33 years, just as it had in seventeenth-century England, but there it had risen to 55 years by this time. In 1905–6 there were nearly 1500 peasant riots. The peasants formed a union and joined the 1905 revolt against the Tsarist government. In towns the new technology was being introduced and peasant women were brought in to staff factories. They played an active part in industrial disturbances from 1872 in textile mills in Moscow and St Petersburg. It was the women leaders who forced the government to abolish night work for themselves and their children. Women factory workers in the 1890s were striking against reductions in pay and standards of working conditions. Women cigarette-makers were attacked by police and soldiers and some of them were killed. In 1913, the women at the St Petersburg spinning mills went on strike. Like the clothing workers' strikes in the USA this action grew to serious proportions. It was broken by blackleg labour brought in under armed guard.[18] There was thus a history of women's industrial activity and unrest which became part of twentieth-century revolutionary pressure.

The divisions on women's work and social status in industrializing countries were complex, but they also showed a remarkable uniformity from country to country. They cut across sex lines so that women and men were found on both sides. They also cut across political lines in that political Liberals and radicals were on the same side. It was the manufacturing employer, Moritz Müller, who at the 1865 Conference of German Workers' Associations proclaimed the connection between the growth of female factory labour and mechanization on one hand, and progress towards a higher and better form of society on the other. He was supported by some of the most advanced workers, those from

Saxony where women made up the majority of 'free' factory workers, liberated from feudal bondage and guild restrictions. English Liberals like Lady Emilia Dilke and Mrs Millicent Fawcett supported equal suffrage and legal rights for women. But they were opposed by working men who believed that within a property franchise framework such changes would strengthen the propertied against the unpropertied working people. Few working women had property. Finally all agreed on universal adult suffrage. There was, however, no conflict between working men, the majority of working women and middle and upper class campaigners for women's trade unionism on the policy of 'woman's place is in the home'.

A vast rise in numbers and proportions of women employed was noted in the second half of the nineteenth century in the United States, Japan and many European countries.[19] To some extent this increase was more apparent than real in that for the first time the taking of censuses was revealing the extent to which women worked. Evidence was flooding in from ethnographers of the skills and abilities of older mated women in earlier cultures. The presence of married women in the workforce was attested by papal denunciations of them in the 1890s.[20] Yet socialists like Jules Guesde and Paul Lafargue of France and the Germans, Marx, Engels and Clara Zetkin – most of them middle class – constantly tried without success to persuade international conferences to accept women's equal right to work and to equality of pay in spite of all this evidence.[21]

First in Britain, then in France, Australia, New Zealand, the United States and Canada small groups of middle- and upper-class women set out to foster women's trade unionism as a means of helping those worst off. The poorer women were, the less likely their sudden strikes of despair were to succeed. The United States Women's Trade Union League differed from its British forerunner initiated by Emma Paterson in 1874, in that it arose from the initiatives and industrial action of women workers. Its moving spirits included Mary E. Kenny, a bookbinder, appointed the American Federation of Labor's first woman organizer in 1892. But it was because the Federation's affiliated unions, along with other organizations, denied women the help they needed that the League was formed in 1903.[22]

It was the middle class women's Trade Union Leagues which

led the fight against industrial diseases some of which caused long drawn-out and horrible deaths. They campaigned for men as well as women against the use of white lead in the glazing of pottery and of yellow phosphorus in matches. Working people's attitude had been one of resignation. The nightmare of losing a job, the social inferiority imposed by class and, in the case of women, by their sex, and the resulting lack of confidence combined to produce in them the same sort of docile acceptance of ill-treatment evinced by many Australian aboriginal women in the nineteenth century. The policy evolved by trade unions was that any health or accident hazard would be borne in return for higher pay. Very slowly, however, women left men behind and became more insistent about working conditions as the middle-class Liberals won remedial legislation.[23]

It was the middle- and upper-class pressure groups also who obtained legislation to fix minimum standards of pay and maximum hours of work. They continued to try to encourage in women self-help and trade unionism, but began to despair of organizing 'sweated' workers unable to establish standards for themselves, some of them, like the British chain-workers, because of a history of discouragement from men in the trade. They managed, first in Australia, then in New Zealand where European workers were in short supply, to have set up Trade Boards or Minimum Wages Boards as they were sometimes called. The United Kingdom and the United States followed suit. These bodies made up of workers' and employers' representatives first of all established floors in earnings and hours of work which the middle-class leaders and workers could then together see enforced. Trade Boards also promoted organization by giving unorganized workers in the lowest graded jobs experience in negotiating with employers. So they were taken up enthusiastically by unions trying to recruit such workers although established unions were disdainful and suspicious of some support from employers for these statutory wage-fixing bodies. In Britain by the early 1920s there were a large number of Trade Boards and in nearly all of them never less than 70 per cent of those they represented in any given trade were women.[24]

By the turn of the century it was clear that industrialization, and the effects of colonialism, the growth of world trade and of new transportation methods had enabled women in the most prosperous states to stop the slide into total subjection. They avoided the fate of those who had endured millennia of feudalism and then been further crushed by the growth of population and the consequent competition for jobs. In industrializing countries most major legislative measures to give women legal equality were gained before 1900. In these countries girls' and boys' equality in elementary education was established. There were groups of women workers, mainly middle- and lower-middle-class white-collar workers, so confident that they demanded the 'rate for the job' and competition for jobs on equal terms with men. In the United States they despised trade unions,[25] but in Britain in 1913 they accounted for 59·1 per cent of membership of teaching unions and 17·1 per cent of those in unions for commerce and distribution, as compared with 49·1 per cent in the traditional women's union stronghold of textiles and 28·8 per cent in more recently organized clothing trades other than boot and shoe manufacture. But these increases were not wholly due to the women's determination, nor to support from the middle and upper class. Men trade unionists increasingly realized that because of technological changes which destroyed established skills, and permitted employers to introduce cheaper female labour in their trades, they must accept women into their unions if only to control their competition. But they also showed concern at the fate of workless women and especially the widespread recourse to prostitution.[26] For all the fears dividing men and women workers before the First World War, in the industrializing countries there were signs of a growing unity between them aimed at establishing a better standard of living and the right to work for all.

NOTES

1 Hammonds, *The Town Labourer*, vol. i, 73, 79, 148, 152, 157, 262–3; Eden, *Observations on Friendly Societies*, 15–18, 21–2; Lewenhak, *Women and Trade Unions*, 18–20.

2 Hammonds, *The Skilled Labourer*, 92, 271, 309; Webbs, *The History of Trade Unionism, 1666–1920*, 104–5.

3 *Nottingham Review*, 4, 11, 18 Dec., 1840; Corbett, *History of the Birmingham Trades Council, 1866–1966*, 172; Trade Societies and Strikes, *Rep. of the Trade Societies Committee of the Nat. Asscn for the Promotion of Social Science*, 3; See also *1861 Trans. of the NAPSS*, 634, Bessie R. Parkes.

4 Thibert, *Le Féminisme dans le socialisme française*, Chs 1 and 2; Sullerot, *L'histoire et Sociologie du travail féminin*, 88.

5 Sigmann, *1848: The Romantic and Democratic Revolutions in Europe*, 46–7.

6 Pulch, *Le socialisme français, 1803–1848*; Michaud, *Biographie Universelle, Ancienne et Moderne*, 174–5; Thibert, op. cit., 279–84.

7 ibid., 313–17; Adrien Ranvier, *Bull. de la Soc. d'histoire de la Révolution de 1848*, 5th year, 1908–9, 480–98; Sullerot, op. cit., 111–13; Thibert, op. cit., 318–26, 328, 330–4; Rabaut, *Histoire des féminismes français*, 119ff.

8 Flexner, *Century of Struggle*, 22, 25–7, 29–39, 45–52, 55–60; Baker, *Technology and Woman's Work*, 15–16, 56–8; Eisler, *The Lowell Offering*, 31–3, 38–40, 113ff, 214; Coolidge, *Women's Rights: The Suffrage Movement in America, 1848–1920*, 13–17, 22ff.

9 Halle, *Women in Soviet Russia*, 4–32, 35–45; serfdom was abolished on imperial estates in 1861 and on private estates in 1866.

10 Sullerot, op. cit., 121–5, 146; Constance Rover, *The Punch Book of Women's Rights*, 56ff, for a light-hearted view.

11 ibid., 78–85; Strachey, *The Cause*, 167ff.

12 ibid., 18–29, 85–6; McInnes, *St Thomas's Hospital*, 115–22.

13 Baker, 62, 73, 411.

14 F. Devine, *Women in the Irish Trade Unions*, Paper to the Irish Congress of Trade Unions Women's Advisory Committee Conference, May 1975; D. W. Bleakley, *Trade Union Beginnings in Belfast and District*, Queen's Univ., Dublin, Thesis.

15 Guilbert, *Les fonctions des femmes dans l'industrie*, 27; Sullerot, op. cit., 126–7.

16 Jellinek, *The Paris Commune of 1871*, 74, 112–13, 253–4, 324–5, 379–80, 400.

17 Baker, 30–1, 33–5, 39, 43, 198–204; Emma Paterson, *The Englishwoman's Rev.*, n.s., 1874, 215–16, unions of female umbrella-makers and typographers in New York; Flexner, 135–44, 200–7, 215–16, 248–51.

18 Halle, 83–5, 88–9; Sullerot, 146–8.

19 Vallentin, ILO Yearbook, vol. 25, Jan.–June 1932, 481, 488–9.

20 Sullerot, op. cit., 177.

21 Thönnessen, *The Emancipation of Women*, 16–19, 21–7, 29, 35, 39–42; Guilbert, *Les femmes et l'organisation syndicale avant 1914*, 49–51, 174–5, 186–7; Hutchins, *Women in Modern Industry*, 154–68 (German women).

22 Boone, *The Women's Trade Union Leagues in Britain and America*; Flexner, 218–19, 252–5; Barbara V. Cormack, *Perennials and Politics*, 57–8, United Farm Women of Alberta; Goldman, *Emma Paterson, Her Life and Times*; Hamilton, *Women at Work*, 51–2; Drake, *Women in Trade Unions*, 10ff, 26.

23 ILO Rep., *The International Protection of Women Workers*, ser. i, no. 1; Guilbert, *Les fonctions des femmes dans l'industrie*, 23; Baker, 88–96; Thönnessen, 43–4, 50–1; Nora Vynne and Helen Blackburn, *Women under the Factory Acts*.

24 Sells, *The British Trade Boards System; British Wages Boards*; Tawney, *The Establishment of Minimum Rates in the Chain-making Industries*. Trade

Boards were introduced in Australia in 1896. Middle- and upper-class philanthropists organized sweated trades exhibitions in Berlin in 1905 and in London, 1906.

25 Drake, op. cit., 174–6; Pierrotti, *The National Union of Women Teachers*, 1–4; Trades Union Congress, *Women in the Trade Union Movement*, 57–9; Humphries, *Clerical Unions in the Public Services*, 55, 235, chart facing p. 135.

26 Alison Neilans in R. Strachey ed., *Our Freedom and its Results*, 175–200; See also Thönnessen, 23, 51.

Chapter 12

THE FIRST WORLD WAR AND THE RUSSIAN REVOLUTION

The First World War temporarily halted the withdrawal of women from work outside their homes on marriage. It also severely limited the numbers of women and girls in private domestic service in all the countries involved. Another innovation was the sheer quantity of women who went into munitions factories, shipyards and other war production jobs, as well as those who took over from men on public transport, and in shops and offices.

Few of the kinds of work they did were totally new to women. For example, women had been engaged on munitions work in England in 1862 and in engineering even earlier. In Belgium and Silesia they had never left off working underground in mines.[1] It is not yet clear whether they ever left off working underground in British coal mines. It is not generally known that even before the war broke out, at the Carronshore ironworks' mines near Falkirk in Scotland women like Miss Mary Waugh were once more loading coal underground into wagons and seeing them to the shaft for raising to the surface. Mary Waugh married while working, left her job in 1916 for a short while to have a child and then went back to her underground work at which she remained until 1921 or 1922. The company gave her a gold watch as a token of appreciation for her work.[2]

Because so many of the women who came into war work were middle class, they were given a great deal of publicity for doing what working-class women had been doing before. First of all there was government publicity to bring them into work, and then there was publicity to keep up morale while they were working, often longer hours and certainly at lower rates of pay than men. In Britain the established 8-hour day was stretched to 10, 12 and sometimes 16 or 17 hours and the industrial accident rate shot up. Most of the women who rushed into war industries in the various belligerent states, had no trade union experience. They accepted whatever conditions they were offered out of a sense of patriotism.

They did not see that they were undermining standards of pay and conditions painfully built up over many years and through many weary struggles and privations. Employers played on women war workers' eagerness, but experienced men and women trade unionists and workers reacted with suspicion and hostility. The effect of the First World War was not to cement the growing unity both national and international of working people, but to disrupt it. Tensions and hostility between men and women workers characterized labour relations in all the main warring countries.[3]

Under the stress of war production, employers were more easily able to circumvent union objections to the sub-division of processes which, together with mechanization, reduced the level of skill required of operatives. Women were considered to have a lesser capacity for skilled work than men, even by so illustrious a member of their own sex as Beatrice Webb. They did have skills, but they were often not those required. And they were simply not given the elementary grounding for many industrial occupations that was given to boys. Because they were paid less than men and often skimped themselves so that other members of their families might not go short, they suffered to a greater extent than men from a lack of nourishing food.[4] Even so, as a United States survey showed, their performance was not always nearly so much below that of men as was alleged.

Men's fears of cheap female labour were a strong element in the revolts that broke out in Clydeside war industries at the end of 1915 and in 1916. Almost from the outbreak of hostilities the unions were demanding that all men going into the Forces should be guaranteed their jobs back at the end of the war and that their pre-war wage structures and standards should be preserved. British and many United States women trade union leaders particularly the middle-class officials of the National Federation of Women Workers, led by its Secretary, the Scottish Mary Macarthur, strongly supported the men's aims for they realized that this was the best means of ensuring continued progress in the acceptance of women in the unions. And they saw that union organization was the best hope of a better life for women.[5]

The increased wartime employment of women outside their homes in occupations in which organization was already established was accompanied by a great growth in women's trade unionism. The growing impulse of women to organize before the war was strengthened by their greater access to higher-graded jobs. At the same time, once unions won government guarantees, they intensified their campaigns to enrol women as the best way to protect their male members' standards and jobs. A number began to take women in for the first time; more began to recruit them seriously. Women were also encouraged by press and public authorities' recognition of the importance of their work. In Britain women's trade union membership rose from 437,000 in 1914 to 1,342,000 in 1920; in the United States from 76,748 in 1910 to 396,000 in 1920. There, while clothing remained the best organized female sector, white collar workers continued to make progress. Over the decade 1910–20, the percentage of women members in United States printing and publishing unions more than doubled (11·6 to 25·0 per cent of total membership) while among railway clerks the number rose from a mere 62 to 53,000. The story was repeated in many unions on the other side of the Atlantic. One result was notable gains for women in pay. The 'rate for the job' was officially accepted for women doing precisely the same work as men. More important in view of speeded-up technological changes were advances in Britain in establishing a minimum rate for women on 'women's work'. Women workers won a more important role in unions and women leaders who rose from the ranks felt strong enough to jettison their middle class helpers by the time the war was over.[6]

In Germany, however, the war halted progress towards women workers' equality. The protagonists of women's trade unionism were also the most militant and uncompromising champions of women's equality and of peace. The intellectual brilliance of the teacher, Clara Zetkin, and the Polish-born political theorist, Rosa Luxembourg, antagonized large numbers of working men, and women too. In the defeated countries the war terminated in revolutions. In Germany itself Workers' and Soldiers' Councils were set up which elected a National Council to take over from the discredited government. The rising, led by the extreme left-wing Spartacus League to which these women belonged, was put down by a combination of capitalists, militarists, moderate Social Democrats, small farmers and peasants. But before it was forced out of office, the National Council instituted universal adult suffrage. When new elections were held the new women voters, the majority of them, it will be remembered, countrywomen, helped

Table 5 Performance of United States Women Workers in the First World War

	Firms –			Firms reporting women's work –				
	substituting women for men	reporting number of women substituted	total women substituted	as satisfactory or better than men's		not so satisfactory as men's		not comparable
				number	per cent	number	per cent	
Metal working	278	257	37,683	212	82·8	44	17·2	22
Chemical working	58	50	6,935	32	66·7	16	33·3	10
Rubber working	11	10	4,959	9	100.0	–	–	2
Wood working	152	145	2,545	91	68·4	42	31·6	19
Textile making	16	13	1,589	12	80·0	3	20·0	1
Leather working	20	18	1,545	17	85·0	3	15·0	–
Electrical working	22	21	897	18	90·0	2	10·0	2
Abrasive material and glass working	14	12	730	9	75·0	3	25·0	2
Miscellaneous work on airplanes, seaplanes, ships and musical instruments	15	14	1,834	8	80·0	2	20·0	5
TOTAL	562 (1)	533 (2)	58,717	386 (3)	77·4	113 (4)	22·6	63

(1) Includes women employed only in the 533 firms which reported the number of women substituted as well as the fact of substitution.

(2) 17 firms substituting women in metal-working occupations also substituted women on chemical, electrical, wood, textile, or abrasive material and glass-working occupations; these did not report the numbers employed on either substance. Seven firms substituting women in wood-working occupations also substituted women on textile and miscellaneous work.

(3) 22 firms substituting women on two materials reported their work to be satisfactory in each group.

(4) 2 firms substituting women on two materials reported their work to be unsatisfactory in each group.

Source: *International Labour Review*, vol. 111, No. 3, Sept. 1921, p. 99.

to bring in a moderate Social Democratic government. Further, women left-wing intellectuals made a crucial mistake by failing to grasp the importance to working women of social welfare. It had become the main activity of their moderate counterparts. So whereas in Britain women trade union and Labour leaders gained influence by their concentration on industrial issues and their unity with men, in Germany they helped to divide the Labour Movement.

INTERNATIONAL PROGRESS IN WOMEN'S ECONOMIC
EQUALITY

Whatever the setbacks in individual countries in women's economic progress, internationally the value of their war work was recognized. In 1919, the Versailles Treaty officially laid down as an international goal the principle enunciated by the United States Congress Industrial Commission in 1890 – 'equal pay for work of equal value'. Thus a number of countries now accepted theoretically that the value of work to an employer was to be taken into account in settling levels of pay, and not the supply and demand for labour of a particular sort. It had in any case been already amply proved that a high demand for labour did not automatically lead to higher pay. The considerable demand for women domestic servants, tailoring and garment workers, chain-makers, ring-frame spinners, brickyard workers had still left them as the lowest paid workers. Child labour and their lack of organizations that would really bargain on their behalf with employers, their isolation and many other pressures interfered with the operation of purely market forces.

In 1919 the International Labour Organization was created to help to improve labour relations. Each country affiliating to it had representatives of its government, workers' and employers' organizations at ILO conferences. An International Labour Office was set up to carry on its work, to implement decisions and to collate information on all labour matters in the various countries. The ILO set out to build up an international code of fair labour practice. In accordance with the Versailles Treaty, its stated aim was that

> all human beings whatever their race, creed or *sex* should have the right to pursue their material progress and spiritual development in freedom and dignity in economic security and with *equal opportunities*. (my italics)

Women were to be helped to economic equality and their role as workers was recognized. The ILO has unswervingly pursued this policy, although individual member countries may have been slow in adopting agreed international conventions. In accordance with these aims, its first International Conference held in Washington in 1919 produced Conventions on Childbirth and Maternity, Children's Employment, and on Hours and Shift Work for Women.

These were matters that concerned white-collar and industrial workers. The most important fact was that in 1918, in Europe as in the rest of the world, the bulk of working women were still peasants. Only in Britain and the United States had the balance tipped decisively away from farming. Even so relics of the past in Britain such as the annual hiring fairs and the yearly bond were still a feature of some agricultural districts and women, like men, were subject to them as they always had been.

WOMEN WORKERS IN THE UNION OF SOVIET SOCIALIST REPUBLICS

Women in Russia sparked off the Revolution for the immediate cause of the violence that brought down the Tsarist regime was a demonstration to mark International Women's Day, 8 March, 1917. The Tsarist government tried to prevent it and so provoked a strike at the Putilov works in St Petersburg. Large numbers of women supported the second uprising in October which ended in the setting up of the world's first Communist government and Russia's withdrawal from the war.

Lenin followed the early nineteenth-century feminists in condemning 'woman's place is in the home' and the stultifying psychological effects of drudging housework:

It is impossible to assure liberty, it is impossible even to build democracy, still less socialism without women's participation in public life, in political life, without tearing them from the brutish atmosphere of household and kitchen.[8]

The new Soviet policies on women's work were immediately made public. Four days after the takeover of power, on 29 October 1917, decrees announced the introduction of an 8-hour day and the banning of nightwork for women and young persons and of

underground work for women. On 14 November there followed
the social insurance programme laying down paid maternity leave
of eight weeks before and eight weeks after confinement when most
advanced capitalist countries only gave four weeks in each case.
A year later, on 1 September 1918, the Soviet government enacted
equal pay: a woman's earnings were to be equal to those of a man
where she did work that was not necessarily the same, but was
identical in quantity and quality. This was not a short-term wartime measure such as had been introduced for substituted women
in Britain and the United States of America. It was the first large-
scale application of 'equal pay for work of equal value'. The quality
of a woman's work was taken into account. The same minimum
wage was fixed for adults of either sex. Article 122 of the
Constitution of the Union of Soviet Socialist Republics laid down
equal rights for men and women in all economic, cultural, social
and political spheres. But it was Article 134 of the penal code
that proved the seriousness of the government's intentions towards
women. Preventing a woman from enjoying her legal rights was
specified as a crime punishable by law. The Communist leadership
acted advisedly. Every pair of hands was needed to make the ruined
economy work. They offered women freedom and equality. In
return women gave their support to the Revolution which released
them from that bondage imposed three hundred years before. Sir
John Maynard found that:

> ... the actual reception of a solid dividend for the work done
> by the women, in solid rye and potatoes, was like the entry upon
> a new world ... the woman's dividend is one of the reasons why
> there has been acquiescence in collectivisation: because it has
> put the women on the side of the Soviets.[9]

The application of these decrees, was, however interrupted by
renewed war within and without. Women soldiers and workers
helped to pull the new Soviet state through this crisis. From 1919
women's work sections were created. Members of these 'women's
sections' saved the state in the fearful Volga famine of 1921.

When the war ended the legislation had to be renewed, sure sign
that it was not being implemented. But also it was foreseen that
demobilized troops would take work from women, unless women's
jobs were protected. This they began to do. However, the thirteenth

Party Congress in May 1924 underlined as a matter of political importance the preservation of female manual work. The drain of women from all kinds of jobs, intellectual and manual, was stopped and in the following year the female manual labour force rose by 217,000. Everybody had to work; it was an obligation, except for two categories: mothers with children under 8 years of age who had no help in caring for them, and women over 40 in the context of a society in which working women scarcely expected to reach that age.

There was one great obstacle to women's employment – illiteracy. The government launched a literacy campaign and, during 1924–25 when women's equality and rights as workers were assured, 17 million people, of whom 14 million were women, enrolled in classes. The results may be seen in the statistics below:

Percentage of literate women aged 9–49

	1897	1926	1939	1959
Urban	43·1	73·9	91·0	98·1
Rural	9·6	35·4	79·2	97·4

Source: Central Statistical Board of the USSR Council of Ministers, *Women and Children in the USSR*, Moscow 1963.

The Soviet government turned its attention to women in the Asiatic and Caucasian states, annexed by Tsarist Russia. These were sovietized and converted into 'autonomous republics'. The support of women was vital for Soviet success in breaking down the opposition of Mohammedans and Cossacks, who received help from various foreign states. Conversely, the Soviet government's support promoted women's liberation in these patriarchal societies. This liberation was dangerous work. Some of the European Russian women who went to work for women's independence and equality in Moslem communities, Arab and eastern countries were killed by enraged men. The more ancient customs, the 'shanat' and 'adat' (see page 86) had taken precedence over the humanitarian aspects of the Moslem creed. European Party activists and local Communist Party officials of both sexes encouraged the Moslem women to discard their uncomfortable clothing, some of it evolved in time long past as a protection against mosquitoes or predatory males. The women of Uzbekistan and Tajikstan abandoned the *paranja*, a long shapeless garment thrown over a woman's head and falling to her feet. They threw away their thick black horsehair veils. 'Off with the veil!', 'Down with the veil!' were the slogans that brought them out of their homes to demonstrate in the streets and to burn their veils ceremonially in public or turn them into clothing for the poor.[10]

To train the women, hundreds of vocational and technical schools and institutes were opened where women studied on an equal footing with men. This opening of higher education to women was what women emancipators had been working for all over the industrialized world. With incredible speed they became members of local government bodies, heads and executives of state enterprises, airwomen, agricultural scientists.

The disruptions of war and revolution and a revulsion against the patriarchal family undermined the institution of marriage. Lasting unions based on affection were difficult and a number of intellectuals, like their counterparts in the West, favoured short affairs. There was, however, widespread opposition within the USSR to purely physical sex without affection. Lenin condemned it as:

> often enough wholly bourgeois, an extension of the good, old bourgeois brothel! Love involves two, and a third, a new life, may come into being. That implies an interest on the part of Society, a duty to the community.[11]

But motherhood was also glorified, for workers to build the economy were in short supply. Large families were encouraged and awards made to women for having numerous children: the Motherhood Medal for 5–6, the Order of the Glory of Motherhood for 7–9 and the title of Mother Heroine for women who bore 10 or more children. There was a general restoration and reacknowledgement of women's total economic role.[12]

But there were gaps and brutal bureaucratic destruction of parts of the old society. Little interest was shown between the wars in peoples in the more remote parts of what had been colonial Tsarist Russia, in the Mongols, the Stone Age Chukchees and Koriaks, although they were included in the Asiatic republics of the Union of Socialist Soviet Republics. Families of wealthy farmers – kulaks – suffered greatly in a mass deportation of those opposed to State takeover of their land and to co-operatives from western grainlands to the cold, arid north east. Active women opponents of the new régime were sent like men to forced labour camps where they did heavy work, sometimes until they dropped in their tracks. Middle-class women whose families were not so displaced were compelled to go out to paid work and lost their servants so that they had to do their own housework like the poor. The most striking fact in the accompanying table was the disappearance of what had been the largest category of women workers at the turn of the century, servants and charwomen. They had represented over half the total female labour force.

Table 6 Proportions of Women in Various Branches of Work in the USSR 1897–1961

Percentage of all Women Working

	1897	1929	1940	1961
Industrial and Building Workers	13	30	40	39
Farm Labourers	25	13	6	10
Servants and Charwomen	55	5	8	7
Education and Public Health Workers	4	22	24	24
Other	3			

Source: *Women & Children in the USSR*, pub. Central Statistical Board of the USSR Council of Ministers, Moscow, 1963, p. 99.

However, the Soviet government leaders, imbued with the history of European revolt including the initiatives of Frenchwomen in 1848 to lighten domestic work, recognized a responsibility for providing care for the children of working mothers. They saw it as less necessary for white-collar than for agricultural and factory workers whose jobs took more energy. Because of the encouragement given to women to have children, it followed that biological female functions were catered for and not ignored as they were among the advanced women workers of the West who were trying to prove their similarity with men in the sphere of work. The number of jobs closed to women in the USSR on the grounds that they were injurious to health has been growing constantly. The Soviet Parliament set up standing commissions on women's work and daily life which propose improvements.

The USSR was aiming at something even more than equal pay and lifting from married women workers the total burden of child care. The government was trying to share as equally as possible skilled work among women and men. Decrees of 1931 gave a long list of skilled occupations in which women were to be given preference to men. On the other hand in medicine it was felt that men were losing too much work to women. An Order of 3 September 1934 provided for the doubling of the number of male medical students because of the excessive number of women students. That year 74 per cent of them were women, and the Soviet government was worried lest in a few years' time there would not be enough male doctors to take the more exhausting posts which were considered unsuitable for women. Their policy made an interesting contrast with that in Britain where the male predominance in medicine was maintained partly by means of allowing women to make up only a small quota of each year's intake of medical students.

Hostile western commentators seized on the very heavy jobs which Soviet women did in the propaganda war against the new Russian government. But they made no effort to compare these with the kinds of work women did in other countries under older economic and social systems. They 'forgot' the women in the British brickyards, the women working underground in mines, labouring under threat of blows in the ricefields of Portugal and Indonesia and the tea estates of India, toiling on the building construction sites in Singapore; above all, they ignored the great toiling mass of middle-European peasantry struggling, sometimes in medieval conditions, to get a living following the 1918 collapse of agricultural prices.[14] Neither did they pay much heed to the kinds and conditions of work of women in their own colonies.

NOTES

1 Guilbert, *Les Fonctions des Femmes dans l'Industrie*, 23: In 1919 there were over 100,000 women employed in mines in Japan, 63 per cent of them underground, but there was a sharp drop in their numbers in the following nine years, see Vallentin, *ILO Yearbook*, vol. 25, Jan–June 1932, 494: For women working underground in Greek mines, see *International Labour Rev.*, vol. vi, no. 5, Nov. 1922, 713. The Greek government began to restrict their employment only after the 1914–18 war.

2 Information given me by Mary Waugh's daughter, Nurse Marion Miller.

3 Sullerot, *L'histoire et sociologie du travail féminin*, 135:40; Thönnessen, *The Emancipation of Women*, 84,89; *ILO Rev.*, vol. iii, Sept. 1921, 97–101: vol. vi, no 3, Sept., 1922, 448–9, Dr Furno on the hardships of Italian working women; Hooks *Women's Occupations through Seven Decades*, 127–31, 149–50, 161; Flexner, *Century of Struggle*, 298–9; Baker, *Technology and Woman's Work*, 196–7; Drake, *Women in Trade Unions*, 68ff; Hamilton, *Mary Macarthur*, 132ff; Hutchins, *Women in Modern Industry* ch., vii; ILO, *The War and Women's Employment*, Studies and Reps., New Ser. 1, 1946, 2–3; Soldon, *Women in British Trade Unions, 1874–1976*, Ch. 4.

4 Gertrude Tuckwell, President of the Women's Trade Union League and of the National Federation of Women Workers, posthumous papers, TUC; S. Webb, *Problems of Modern Industry*, 80.

5 *1915 TUC Rep.*, p. 373; Flexner, op. cit., 253–4.

6 Lewenhak, *Women and Trade Unions*, 161, 172–5.

7 Thönnessen, op. cit., 7–9, 39–40, 56, 66–70, 76–87, 90–7, 108–9: Frolich, *Rosa Luxembourg*, 181–2, 205–8, 214ff: For similar split in socialist party in Russia see Halle, *Woman in Soviet Russia*, 88, 253ff. For split in the USA among women suffragists when the militant party with a large proportion of Quakers refused to help the war effort, see Flexner, op. cit., 294–5.

8 Lenin, 'International Working Woman's Day', *Coll. Works.*, vol. 32, 161–3; 'Soviet Power and the Status of Women', vol. 30, 1203; Halle, op. cit., 80–3, 87–98.

9 ibid., 97, 105ff; the Kerensky government of Feb–Nov. 1917 left laws enforcing women's subordination intact: A. Kollontai, *Communism and the Family*: Sir John Maynard, *The Russian Peasant and other Studies*, 314: Symons, *Russian Agriculture*, 51–2.

10 Halle, *Woman in Soviet Russia*, 113.

11 Halle, *Women in the Soviet East*, 109, 127ff, 153–60.

12 Ibid., 67, 131–6: Halle, *Woman in Soviet Russia*, 161–3: Symons, op. cit., 46–8.

13 Halle, *Women in Soviet Russia*, 292–4, 317–20; *Soviet Weekly*, 4 March 1978, 9; *ILO Yearbook of Labour Statistics*, 1934–5, 180; Sullerot, op. cit., 123–4, 228.

14 John Lehmann, *Down River, A Danubian Study*, 204–6, 266–7; *International Lab. Rev.*, vol. 111, no. 1, Jan. 1921, 141–3.

Chapter 13

WOMEN WORKERS IN INDUSTRIAL COUNTRIES BETWEEN THE WARS

By the 1920s it had become clear that in most industrial countries the proportion of women workers relative to numbers of women in their populations was stagnant or falling. Decreases were apparent in Italy as early as 1881, in Austria from 1891 and in the United States between 1910 and 1920. There was also a decline in Denmark, Norway, Belgium, France, the Netherlands, Sweden, Scotland, Ireland, Hungary, Switzerland, Australia and New Zealand. In England and Wales and Japan there was barely any change in the proportion of women workers in the population between the 1911 and 1921 censuses. Thus, as Antonina Vallentin showed in a very important article in the *1932 ILO Yearbook*, the extraordinary increases in women's employment during the 1914–18 war did not disturb an overall, long-term trend. Because of the continuing population increase more women were coming on to the labour market than could be absorbed. The numbers of jobs available were not keeping pace with the numbers of female job-seekers. Agriculture was one of the areas of declining demand for them. It was being mechanized. But at the same time, young women, like young men, were attracted to the towns. This constant inflow of countrywomen helped to hold down earnings in manufacturing trades, offices and shops. Even so in many countries it was still in the agriculture, forestry and fishing group of trades that most women worked, and for women that meant agriculture, huge numbers of them still as 'unpaid family labour' (see Table 7). The greater the extent of small farming, the greater was the proportion of women in the whole working population. Thus in Austria as a whole at the 1923 census there were 48·2 per cent of women of working age in employment; but in the agricultural provinces, a far higher proportion: 65·7 per cent in Lower Austria; 67·27 per cent in the Tyrol; 71·97 per cent in Carinthia.

The proportion of women who were domestic servants fell during the first two decades of this century in Austria, Germany,

Table 7 Countries in which Women Made up a Third or More of those Occupied in Agriculture, Forestry and Fishing in the early 1930s

Year	Country	Women as % of Total	Nos. of Women Occupied	Nos. of Women Unpaid Family Workers
1934	Estonia	51·12	227,775	164,011
1934	Bulgaria	50·89	1,397,025	1,305,627
1930	Romania	50·71	4,180,900	—*
1933	Germany	49·75	4,648,782	3,469,614
1935	Turkey	47·79	3,096,799	—
1931	Poland	44·33	4,323,080	3,271,200
1930	Finland	42·73	473,339	—
1931	France	41·46	3,193,733	—
1930	Czechoslovakia	40·91	1,096,535	636,555
1931	Yugoslavia	36·58	1,864,593	1,491,401
1934	Austria	34·86	349,741	175,604
1930	Japan	—	6,442,588	—
1931	India	—	28,015,863	—

Source: *ILO 1939 Yearbook of Labour Statistics*, Table 11.
* No figures given.

France and the United States, and very slightly in the Netherlands. But after 1921 because of mounting unemployment, numbers of women in this occupation began to rise. In the United States the bulk of women in this form of work were negroes, or other impoverished ethnic groups. In general a far larger proportion of negro than of white women went out to work for a living, about 42 per cent of negroes against only 20–25 per cent of whites.[2]

In England and Wales a decrease in numbers of female private indoor domestic servants between 1901 and 1921 was arrested because, in order to diminish unemployment among women and, consequently, the run on state insurance payments, between the wars Conservative, Liberal and Labour governments alike pursued a policy of what amounted to compulsory domestic service for women. Unemployed women who refused this work when it was offered to them at Labour Exchanges had their unemployment benefit stopped. The result was that domestic service accounted for nearly a quarter of all women at work in Britain[3] and remained the largest single occupation for women; although taking all kinds

of industries together, the female labour force in them outweighed
that in domestic service in Britain and a number of other countries.
However, Germany, Poland, France, Italy and Japan where
women in industry outnumbered those in domestic service, were
all peasant countries (see Table), with a family labour structure
in which there was less demand for paid domestic help.

**Table 8   A Comparison of the Numbers of Women in Domestic
Service Work and in all Industries in Various Countries in the 1930s
(in 1000s)**

Year	Country	Nos. of Women in Industrial Jobs	Nos. of Women in Domestic Service Jobs
1933	Germany	2,759	1,250
1930	Netherlands	·168	·234
1931	Poland	·519	·399
1930	USA	2,401	3,154
1931	France	2,112	·717
1931	Gt. Britain	2,369	1,906
1936	Italy	1,375	·585
1930	Japan	1,430	·697

Source: *ILO 1939 Yearbook of Labour Statistics*, Table 11

As a result of increased world competition, there was a drastic
drop in the manufacture of cotton and new synthetic materials
in industrial countries, hence there was a parallel drop in the
numbers of women textile workers including weavers, the original
female industrial élite. One cause of the growth in numbers of
women working in manufacturing in spite of this, was the development of light industries. In the United States between the wars,
females made up over 50 per cent of the total labour force in
tobacco and silk and rayon manufactures and about two-thirds
of those in knit-goods, clothing and accessories. They dominated
fresh fruit and vegetable grading and packing, monopolized the
most delicate operations in the manufacture of confectionery and
were on the way to dominating the electric lamp industry. By 1930
women and girls not infrequently accounted for 85–90 per cent of
all employees in US electronic tube factories.[4]

SPEED-UP IN WORK

By the late 1920s many of these industries were adopting a speed-up of operations based on time and motion study. Women workers were badly affected since they were mainly employed on repetitive mass production work. Workpeople of course protested. There were huge strikes in British cotton and woollen textile enterprises, in 1932–3 especially, against each operative having to work more looms. Apart from the extra work involved, increasing productivity per worker simply meant putting more people out of jobs. Unorganized women in the Birmingham electrical firm of Lucas struck specifically against the introduction of the Bedaux system. The firm used one of the same methods to check organized resistance as German feudal landowners. They issued different coloured overalls to each separate 'shop' so that anyone going to consult colleagues in a shop other than her own was immediately spotted. In the British hosiery and tailoring trades, women's interests were sacrificed to those of male workers. The male élite in tailoring chiefly the cutters, who dominated the unions, made agreements with employers which accepted the piece-rate method of payment for women only. In return they were allowed to continue to work on the easier system of payments according to time spent on the job instead of payment by results.[5] Even in 'sweated' homework, a woman had had the satisfaction of making a whole garment. It was small recompense for the hardships endured, but there was some creative satisfaction in the job. Now she blindly carried out one small process over and over again. There was no satisfaction whatever in the job and wages and hours were as bad as before. Girls worked a 60–70 hour week. The American *Survey Graphic* printed the pay slip of an experienced woman garment worker, showing she earned one solitary dollar for a fortnight's work including overtime.[6]

High under-employment of women and a simultaneous rise in living standards led to a rise in numbers of women in service trades – transport, catering and hotel work and entertainment. Prostitution in the United States, particularly, became big business, unwilling girls being trapped into it by crime syndicates, their status bordering on slavery.

HOURS AND SHIFT WORKING

It was because of the fears of unemployment that women still resisted limitations on their hours of work as they had in England in the 1870s (see page 155). In 1921 in New York there was a famous revolt against the ban on women working at night by women proof-readers, linotypists and monotypists. They won exemption from this restriction.[7] Again in Britain the government ignored a 1919 ILO Convention limiting women's shift working. The 1928–31 Labour Government tried to institute the limitation, thinking to end the hardships to women of rising at 3.30 and 4 am for the early morning shift. But they had to give up because of trade union opposition, particularly from the printing trades.[8]

The main opposition to restrictions on night-work for women came not from rank-and-file manual women workers, but, as ever from professional 'career' women and militant feminists organized in the British Open Door Council, the International Council of Women and the International Alliance of Women for Suffrage and Equal Citizenship. Along with employers, they held that equality and special protective labour legislation for women were incompatible and that the Treaty of Montevideo which had proposed equal rights for women and men was being abrogated by restrictions. Consequently the League of Nations more or less asked the International Labour Office to 'examine legislation which effects discrimination, some of which may be detrimental to women's right to work'. The 1919 Convention was revised by the ILO General Conference in 1934. Exemptions from limited hours restrictions were specified including 'women holding responsible positions of management'.[9]

Working people did not want to work shifts but they preferred shift work to unemployment. Many believed it right to share available work among them through the 'marriage bar', for instance, or by raising the school leaving age. They accepted that one income going into a home was enough and were at one with governments and employers on these policies. But work-sharing by a refusal to operate shifts was less popular, for unions were able to negotiate extra payments for what were called 'unsocial hours'. Men, who dominated the unions, wanted the extra money; most women, with their homes and family work, preferred shorter hours. Until the general economic recovery began in the mid-1930s, however, they felt they had little choice but to accept shifts. By then many European countries had started war preparations and acceptance of shifts became a patriotic duty.

STATUTORY PROTECTION OF MATERNITY
In 1936 the League of Nations, following the Treaty of Montevideo and bowing to feminist pressure, resolved on an examination of women's existing political, civil and economic status. In accordance with this decision, the International Labour Organization began a systematic study of all aspects of women's work in contrast to its earlier *ad hoc* enquiries. At the same time, various states were legislating on terms and conditions of women's work. Several introduced new restrictions. Ostensibly, as in the past, these were humanitarian. But in a time of shortage of jobs, women were naturally suspicious that such new measures were intended to give preference to men in jobs. One acid test of a government's intentions was how far it provided maintenance for women whom it prevented from working. In Mexico and Brazil, limitations were put on pregnant women lifting heavy weights but there was no extension of maternity allowances. In Italy, where similar restrictions were introduced, there was also an extension of maternity leave and childbirth allowances. Japan also extended maternity leave and childbirth allowances. In Uruguay mothers with dependent children under 14 years of age were brought under the Pensions Act if they worked in industry, commerce and public utilities; mothers of young children would be less attractive employees if their employers had to contribute to pensions for them. In the United States, however, some states were giving mothers of families – not fathers – support allowances and, in 1935, the federal government began to consider applying this provision nationally. Such measures may have been intended primarily to keep women off the labour market, but they implied recognition of the economic value of motherhood and thereby enhanced women's status.[10]

THE RATE FOR THE JOB
The International Labour Organization in its 1934–5 *Yearbook* summed up a growing concern in many countries about the effect the economic depression was having on wages, especially women's wages. Their reaction was to use legislation to keep up wages

through the establishment of minimum rates and to introduce the 'rate for the job'.

Efforts by male-dominated trade unions, and sometimes by legislation, to establish a legal 'rate for the job' also roused old female suspicions that it was a way of protecting men's right to jobs at the expense of women. The elimination of a lower 'women's rate' was effected by legislation both in Australia and Brazil where a new constitution opened employment in the public services to all those suitably qualified, irrespective of sex or marital condition. Peru and Colombia enacted equal pay for the Upper Amazon region through a Protocol of Friendship.

In some states equal pay in the sense of the 'rate for the job' was linked to minimum wage legislation. This was the method by which it was introduced in Mexico and in the United States, for example. Minimum wage legislation was inaugurated in the USA in 1912, but in the 1920s ran into opposition from employers who argued that labour was a marketable commodity so that compulsion to make them pay a legal minimum wage was infringing their property rights. They also claimed that giving women an equal right to the franchise had made them wholly equal so that they were as well able to bargain over wages as men.

In 1920 the Bureau of Labor instituted a Women's Bureau headed by Mary Anderson to deal with equality and other problems of working women. This step was the more remarkable in view of the fact that a smaller proportion of the United States workforce was female than in other countries with similar free enterprise economies (See Table 4). In an investigation it published in 1928 the Bureau remarked on the peculiar hardness of automobile manufacturers towards paying women 'the rate for the job'.

However, by the 1930s there was growing government concern about the effects of cheap female competition on men's chances of work as mechanization eroded skills and employers brought more and more unskilled women into manufacturing industry. President Franklin D. Roosevelt under pressure from Miss Frances Perkin, Head of the United States Bureau of Labor and Mary Anderson, Head of her department's Women's Bureau, and from Eleanor Roosevelt, laid down 'the rate for the job' in minimum scales worked out for most industries. But owing to employers' opposition it was not until 1936 that the State Supreme Court of

Washington accepted that the minimum wage act was constitutional and not until 1938 that the Fair Labor Standards Act laid down the same minimum rates for both sexes.[11]

What happened when minimum wage legislation was directed to eliminating the lower woman's wage alone was shown in Canada. There only women were felt to need this protection and no minimum wage regulations were applied to men. Coupled with high male unemployment, this meant that by 1933 men were being brought in at wages below the local minima fixed for women. They were doing what women had so often been accused of doing; they were undercutting and so pushing the women out of their jobs. To stop this, first of all the women's minima, which applied in all occupations except farming and domestic service, were cut still lower. Then in 1934 a male minimum wage, or joint equal male and female minima were being introduced. In this way the cuts in the women's rates were being restored.

In the introduction of the 'rate for the job' west Europe, including the United Kingdom, lagged behind. When after the 1914–18 war, the British Government and employers dropped the 'rate for the job' as a purely war-time expedient, militants among the highest-graded women white-collar workers kept the issue alive. By the mid-1930s, men in the same grades of work in the public services became more and more alarmed at the threat of cheaper female labour and began to support their demand to protect themselves. Increased unity developed around their joint campaign waged through their trade unions and professional associations.[12] Women's support for labour organization at the higher levels of work paid off. In the United States the persistent coolness of higher-graded women workers to trade unionism was finally breached when in 1935 the National Labor Relations (Wagner) Act made it respectable.

WOMEN IN GERMANY

In Germany while the post-war government proclaimed women's universal right to work, like the governments of other industrial countries it backed men's claims to a prior right to jobs. Nonetheless it was only in 1925 that mounting mass unemployment stopped the growth in the proportion of women in the workforce. The rise in the numbers of workless made social welfare work of the utmost importance so that the government was able to pursue the pre-war trend of channelling militant women's energies into this voluntary activity and away from politics and trade unionism. It is generally agreed that the development of Fascism in Germany was facilitated by high unemployment. It was higher in terms of absolute numbers than anywhere else in Europe. Between 1929 and 1932 it rose by over 100 per cent in the case of men and over 200 per cent in the case of women. It was the men who suffered most, however, almost 25 per cent being out of work by 1932, whereas only about a twelfth of women workers were known to be seeking jobs (see Table). The hostility of men to women workers was sharpened by the increase in their numbers in white-collar work. Despite falling numbers in 1933 in teaching and the liberal professions, and in banking and commerce, women accounted for nearly a third of all those in these occupations (see Table).[13] The male assertion of superiority which was a cornerstone of the Nazi creed also had its roots in the reaction against women intellectuals' relentless campaign for equality.[14]

Table 9   Women as a Percentage of the Labour Force in Different Occupations in Various Countries in the Early 1930s

Year	Country	Domestic Service	Industry	Teaching & Liberal Professions	Banking & Commerce
1930	Netherlands	96·30	14·18	—	25·22
1931	Poland	96·14	20·45	34·39	36·49
1930	Japan	89·24	25·09	17·22	32·69
1936	Italy	88·50	26·21	31·91	27·96
1930	Chile	87·50	30·74	23·53	18·92
1930	Czechoslovakia	87·10	24·25	22·31	34·79
1931	India	80·79	29·66	8·76	26·89
1931	France	80·20	30·89	35·56	42·93
1933	Australia	78·51	15·94	46·12	24·83
1931	Gt. Britain	72·03	28·08	31·97	30·61
1930	USA	65·50	16·74	51·66	21·40
1933	Germany	18·43	21·14	33·38	32·40
1934	Bulgaria	41·18	17·29	37·50	7·41

Source: *ILO 1939 Yearbook of Labour Statistics*, Table 11.

Once the Nazis took power in 1933, they allotted work between the sexes according to the existing trend not only in Germany, but in other countries affected by high unemployment. They simply made them more precise. There was to be only one wage coming into a household. From 30 June 1933 married women were no longer allowed to work. The right of young married couples to loans to help them set up homes was forfeited if the wife went on working. People were encouraged to inform on any wives who continued to earn even through 'homework' or giving private lessons, in music for example; the penalty for disobeying this rule was a heavy fine. A woman teacher, for instance, lost her job as soon as her engagement was announced, although engagements customarily went on in Germany at that time for several years.

At the same time, however, there was a mobilization of girls. The very young were enrolled in the German Girls' League and teenagers in the Work Service Corps for the service of their country. They learned agricultural and domestic work and Nazi doctrines. There were also schools where adolescents were trained as women *führers*. Unemployed Aryan girls could work in voluntary service up to the age of 25. Bursaries for girls were banned and no more than 20 per cent were permitted to take proper secondary educational qualifications. The rest were directed to domestic and social welfare work, agriculture, colonization and the breaking-in of virgin land.

The entry of women into the professions was reduced by discouraging universities from accepting them as students or by imposing strict quotas. Intellectual work was regarded as disastrous for a woman's character and social standing, that is, the doctrine of 'woman's place is in the home' was stringently applied. Between 1932–3 and 1933–4, the numbers of female students dropped by huge amounts: 35 per cent in economic science, 48 per cent in philosophy and teaching, 57 per cent in law. From 1935 women were forbidden to practise law at all and to apply to be judges. Women doctors could no longer take courses in hospitals and were temporarily prohibited from practising.

But effective reduction of the huge number of unemployed came only when two million young people were enrolled in the forces and war preparations were started. The result was that by 1937 there was a labour shortage. The employment policy for women was then reversed. The ban on loans to young married couples if a wife went on working was lifted. Girls who had previously been diverted from higher education were now invited to study nursing, medicine and chemistry. One of the remarkable aspects of these abrupt changes in Nazi policies towards women workers was the women's acquiesence which was not only meek, but at times hysterically enthusiastic.[15]

Differences in some aspects of the conditions of women's life and work in democratic and Fascist states were a matter of degree rather than of principle. The direction of women to domestic service, for instance, was official and explicit in Nazi Germany, but unofficial in Britain. The 'marriage bar' was a universal and long-standing remedy applied only with greater consistency and thoroughness in Nazi Germany and Italy than elsewhere. British and Irish women leaders of women were perturbed by these similarities. By 1935 they were pointing out publicly that forcing women out of their jobs and into their homes was a Fascist solution pursued in Italy and Germany. The government of the Republic of Ireland began to go the same way as those two countries with its Conditions of Employment Act of 1935.[16]

WOMEN AS PIVOTS OF THE NEW CONSUMER ECONOMY

Commercial marriage persisted, but it was given a new look, girls themselves taking the initiative, not parents. To a generation which has grown up in the affluent, post-Second World War society, in which women have had far more chance of finding security through their own jobs, the desperation to obtain a husband may appear incomprehensible. For shop assistants and clerks between the wars, a husband was the way out of a lifetime spent in low-graded, dreary jobs. They were as anxious to escape as any nineteenth-century French dressmaker or English governess had been. The greater the chance of a pleasant home of one's own, the greater the incentive to marry.[17] The gold-digger was a reality as well as a movie fiction.

However, romance and chivalry became more widespread, encouraged by popular literature, women's magazines and the movies. Love smoothed over the inequalities of women in law. It was often only when marriages broke down or when women were widowed that they learnt the hard economic facts.

Marriage was the main reason there were fewer women than men in the dole queues (see Table 10). The 'marriage bar', relaxed in 1914–18, was re-established with the acquiescence of the huge majority of women. Machines had not yet eased and reduced domestic work to the point where even women who had no families felt they wanted to go out to paid work as well for then they would have little freedom or leisure. Only a small minority felt some vocational pull or had training and education to enable them to obtain professional work so that they earned enough to obtain sufficient domestic help and to take advantage of services to give them time to enjoy themselves.

Because of the growing numbers of men out of work, however, family dependence on women wage-earners increased. There was also a large number of spinsters who had to support themselves because girls' chances of marriage were reduced by the large numbers of men killed in the war. It took a heavy toll of men in non-essential white-collar occupations so girls from the same social strata increasingly sought careers in distribution, clerical work and teaching, just the kinds of work in which the 'marriage bar' was most rigid.

Table 10   Unemployment among Women and Men in Four Major West European Countries in the Early 1930s – in 1000s

Year	Country	No. of men 1000s	% increase or decrease since previous figure	No. of women 1000s	% increase or decrease since previous figure
1929	Germany	2000		367·7	
	Italy	212·6		88·1	
	UK	1015·6		243·7	
	France	5·990		3·720	
1932	Germany	4475·8	+ 123·79	1104·0	+ 200·25
	Italy	758·6	+ 256·82	247·8	+ 181·27
	UK	2344·5	+ 130·85	480·3	+ 97·09
	France	231·0	+3756·43	74·3	+1897·31
1934	Germany	2210·4	− 50·61	394·3	− 64·8
	Italy	781·6	+ 3·03	180·1	− 27·32
	UK	1745·5	− 25·55	341·9	− 28·82
	France	360·8	+ 56·19	93·4	− 25·71

Source: *ILO 1934–35 Yearbook of Labour Statistics*, Table 1.

Non-working, spending family women fulfilled two require-ments. By withdrawing from work on marriage they left job opportunities for other women and men. By accepting conspicuous consumption, 'keeping up with the Joneses', they created the mass market for manufactured goods. This was the circular new economy. It ran because women did *not* work.[18] The proof of it lay in the best example of this new economic order, the United States, one of the countries with a low proportion of women working outside their homes (see Table 11). The colonial settler wife had merged in the new home-maker who did no acknowledged productive work.[19] First public then private transport encouraged the growth of conurbations and removed women in their homes even further from their husbands' work, physically and mentally. They set up clubs, vast networks of them, mainly social so that the division of their interests from those of the working members of their families tended to harden. Yet these largely social women's institutions and those of men suggested the separate Stone Age women's and men's societies. Socially, where rising living standards permitted, women were reasserting themselves.

In spite of high unemployment, speed up, low pay and loneliness, all in all in Britain and the United States women's living standards were higher than ever before. 'One third of a nation' said Franklin Delano Roosevelt in 1936, was 'ill-fed, ill-clothed, ill-housed'. That meant that two-thirds were not. In Britain between 1921 and 1931, there was no absolute drop in numbers of women working but a small increase of about 400,000, thanks to the compulsory domestic service policy. There were not enough jobs to take up the extra numbers coming on to the labour market as population went on rising. For some of those in manufacturing trades, however, there was greater provision of pleasant working conditions. The early nineteenth-century radical belief in the greater efficiency of healthy, happy employees was revived in Britain by Quaker confectionery firms. At Rowntrees of York and Cadbury's of Bournville in Birmingham, managements made considerable and imaginative welfare provisions. They set standards of working conditions of which trade unions did not as yet dream and, at various times, encouraged trade unionism too. Light manufacturing firms spring-ing up on new industrial estates round cities, especially to the north of London, adopted similar standards.

The range of professional work for women slowly widened. They had established their presence in science and medicine in the nineteenth century and small numbers continued to come from the universities. But during the war they also established themselves as professional engineers. The small British Society of Women Engineers, for example, was kept in being. They won a foothold in aviation and the aviation industry and in the growing study of economics. But they were almost all upper- and middle-class women.

However, working-class women who lacked their educational opportunities, and whose work although basic to advanced technological societies, was not acknowledged as nearly so valuable, also won greater attention. The United States clothing unions developed all sorts of publicity and recruiting materials for their polynational members. They organized sewing circles, picnics, drama clubs,[20] these last to such good purpose that they put on a very famous revue, *Pins and Needles*, in which the female lead demanded more than the conventional Hollywood romance:

> Sing me a song of social significance
> There's no other song that will do.
> It must be packed
> With social fact,
> Or I won't love you!

In high technology areas, therefore, there were two worlds of women workers. On the one hand there were the women and girls who sweated for piece-rates on assembly lines, hardly daring to raise their heads, having to ask permission to go to the lavatory and being timed while they were there, their lives one seemingly irreversible hell of work-bench and slum home; there were women beaten up for trade union activities; there were women textile workers concealing not only their marriages, but their pregnancies, so afraid of losing their jobs they dared not ask for the statutory weeks off before and after confinements. They kept working till the last few hours and returned to their looms the following day. Or in the Dundee jute mills where marriage did not debar a woman from work, they had their babies beside their machines or in lavatories.[21] There were women scratching for a living in the Oklahoma dustbowl like those in the Joad family in John Steinbeck's novel, *The Grapes of Wrath*, harried out of their smallholdings by ruthless new landowners. They and their families trekked west to the Californian fruit farms and, if they were lucky, found a place in one of the New Deal Government's camps. London women still left their East End slums to go to the Kentish hopfields to do much the same work as their ancestors had done two hundred years before. But there were also women and girls who worked a prescribed 48-hour week, who had lunch breaks when they left offices and shops to gossip with friends over a sandwich and a glass of milk, who had Saturday afternoons to spend at Coney Island, Luna Park in Paris or the Prater in Vienna; who went dancing and took excursions on river boats, who even had a week, sometimes two weeks annual leave when they went off in hopes of romance and adventure. Most of them were from offices, from white-collar jobs like teaching and library work, nursing, medicine and the higher grades of shop work. But holidays-with-pay beyond the few statutory days off at Christmas and other festivals were being granted to more and more people

Table 11   Women as a Percentage of Total Numbers Occupied and of Different Grades in Various Countries in the Early 1930s

Year	Country	W. % of Total Occupied	% of Workers on own account	% of Salaried Staff	% of Wage Earners	% of Unpaid Family Labour
1931	* France	36·56	44·90	34·79	29·00	32·01
1933	Japan	35·75	—	—	—	—
1933	† Germany	35·54	17·65	30·75	29·06	78·11
1933	India	31·83	12·49	—	46·82	—
1933	Sweden	30·97	16·72	38·97	34·08	—
1931	Gt. Britain	29·77	20·51	32·39	32·39	22·06
1933	Italy	28·60	14·14	31·55	28·86	44·74
1930	USA	22·02	5·23	38·65	20·26	49·15
1933	Australia	21·95	12·3	—	26·87	10·87
1930	Chile	19·92	25·75	17·46	17·46	—

* Slightly under a third of all women working on their own account, some as employers, were in the agriculture, forestry and fishing occupations. They represented over two-thirds within this one trade group.
† Over three quarters of unpaid family women workers worked in agriculture, forestry and fishing occupations. See Table.
Source: *ILO 1939 Yearbook of Labour Statistics*, Table 11.

Table 12 Changes in Average Earnings of Women and Men in Various Countries in 1929 and 1939

Country	Currency	1929				1939			
		Men's Rate	Women's Rate	Cash Difference	W % of M	Men's Rate	Women's Rate	Cash Difference	W % of M
Bulgaria	leva	10·01	5·98	4·03	59·74	8·27	6·58	1·69	79·56
Czechoslovakia	kc	153	83			3·86	2·22	1·64	57·51
Denmark	øre					6·30	3·42	2·88	54·29
France*	fr.	3·83	2·26	1·57	59·01				
Ireland	s. d.					1s. 3·6d.	8·5d.	7·1d.	54·49
Sweden	kr.	1·25	0·74	0·51	59·20	1·43	0·84	0·59	58·74
Switzerland†	fr.	1·48	0·77			1·37	0·75		
UK	s. d.					1s. 5·4d.	9d.	8·4d.	51·72
Australia	s. d.	2s. 3d.	1s. 2¼d.	1s. 0½d.	53·70	2s. 3d.	1s. 2¼d.	11d.	54·31
Colombia‡	peso					1·79	0·87	0·92	48·60
Japan‡	yen	2·64	0·99	1·65	37·50	2·57	0·89	1·68	34·63

* Skilled workers' rates only.
† ?
‡ Day rates.
Source: *ILO 1947–48 Yearbook of Labour Statistics*, Table XIII.

including ordinary shop assistants and factory workers. In Britain at the end of the 1930s, millions of women benefited when the statutory Trade Boards (see p. 32) made paid annual leave mandatory.

By the mid-thirties, the world depression which had caused unemployment and underemployment was being resolved. In Europe one of the chief mitigating factors was the adoption of re-armament programmes which created jobs, not least in textiles and clothing as in the past. More people at work boosted consumer demand and industries and increased workers' confidence. By this time, labour organization was accepted in many countries. Women were establishing themselves as top-level professionals in unions as in other kinds of work. Between them and the rank and file, a new generation of women militants was interposing itself. By 1938–9 they were claiming equality not just as workers, but also as union members. As one aspect of this they began demanding special attention to the problems of women workers, and especially of married women, both in regard to the care and education of their children and in social insurance.[22]

NOTES

1 *ILO Yearbook of Labour Statistics*, vol. 25; Vallentin, 481ff; 1934–5, 177–8; Thibert, *International Lab. Rev.*, vol. 27, 1933, Pt. 11, 625–26; Baker, *Technology and Women's Work*, 109–10, n. 26; Hooks, *Women's Occupations through Seven Decades*, 38 for Table:
Percentage of Women 14 years and over in the labour force

	White	Negro
1910	21·4	57·7
1920	21·2	42·4
1930	22·3	42·5
1940	21·4	37·0

and pp. 137–8.

2 Lewenhak, *Trade Union Organisation Among Women and Girls in the United Kingdom*, 1920–65, Ph. D. Thesis, Univ. of Lond.

3 Thibert, loc. cit., Pt. 1, 447; Vallentin, 496, 1921–6, increases in proportion of French women workers:
car and cycle manufacture from 2·0 to 11·7 per cent
chemicals................from 9·5 to 15·6 per cent. Hooks, 102, 109, 115–16, 133–4: Baker, 195–96; Lewenhak, Tables 4 and 14.

4 *Nat. Un. of General and Municipal Workers' Jour.*, 1932, 143, Rep. of Biennial Conference, Lucy Butcher; TUC, *Bedaux: The TUC Examines*

the Bedaux System of Payment by Results, 1933; The General Fed. of Trade Unions, *Rep. on the Bedaux and Kindred Systems,* March 1932; *ILO Studies and Reports, Ser. C,* No. 13, 1939, *Unemployment: Some International Aspects,* 1920–8; Baker, 115–17, 136, n. 65, 227.

5 Beauchamp, *Women Who Work,* 24ff; *Leicester and Leicestershire Hosiery Workers' Un. Mins. of Executive Committee Meetings,* 9, 18, Jan; 6 Feb.; 7 March 1935; Stewart and Hunter, *The Needle is Threaded,* 197–231.

6 Baker, 153.

7 ibid., 402.

8 *TUC Reps.*: 1928, 147–8: 1936, 138–41: 1946, 34; *Scot. TUC Rep.,* 1935, 71–3, 79–81.

9 *ILO Mins. of the 74th session of the Governing Body, Sessions LXXIV–LXXVII,* 20–2 Feb., 1936, pp. 181–5; *ILO Conventions and Recommendations,* 1919–66, 257–9; *ILO Year Books,* 1932, 173; 1934–5, 184–5; *ILO Industry and Labour Information,* April–June 1933, vol. 46, 70–1; July–Sept., 1935, vol. 47, 250–1; Soldon, *Women in British Trade Unions 1874–1976,* 125–7.

10 *ILO Governing Body, Rep. of 1936 Sessions, xxiv-xxvii,* Mins. of seventy-fourth session, Geneva, 20–2 Feb., 1936, 75; *ILO Yearbook 1934–35,* 190–1.

11 ibid., 192, 194–5; Baker, 398–9, 404, 406; Flexner, *Century of Struggle,* 298–9.

12 ibid., 167–9; Baker, 412–14; Spoor, *White Collar Union,* 466–8; Lewenhak, *Women and Trade Unions,* 224ff; London County Council Staff Ass., *Progress Report, 1909–59,* 93; *1944 Roy. Comm on Equal Pay, TUC General Council Memorandum,* App. vii, 67–84; *Amalgamated Engineering Union Mins. of Evidence,* Sect. xiv 2356, para, 3365 Jack Tanner; *1942 Ann. Rep. Nat. Soc. of Pottery Workers,* 4–5; Humphreys, *Clerical Unions in the Civil Service,* 153, 182–4.

13 Baker, 338–9, 361–2; *ILO Yearbook 1934–35,* 180ff; Lockwood, *The Blackcoated Worker,* 142–51; Sayers Bain, *Trade Union Growth and Recognition,* 68ff, 73 Tab. 18; Hooks, 70, graphs; British Min. of Labour, *Manpower Studies No. 7, Growth of Office Employment;* Sullerot, 144–5, 158–9, 173; Thibert, loc. cit., 621–5.

14 Thibert, loc. cit. 449; Thönnessen, *The Emancipation of Women,* 86, 90–8, 107–14.

15 Sullerot, *L'histoire et sociologie du travail féminin,* 175, 180–2.

16 Irish Women Workers' Un. *Nineteenth Ann. Rep.,* 12–18; *Scot. TUC Rep.,* 168, P. Cairns; *1934 TUC Rep.,* 105, Resolution No. 1.

17 Kathe Leichter, Sec. for the Study of Women's Work in the Office of Workers and Employed Persons, Vienna, *So leben wir ... 1. 320 Industriserbeiterinnen herichten über ihr Leber,* 1932 survey; 95·3 per cent of the women questioned said they would prefer NOT to go out to work; wife's earnings averaged 50–75 per cent of husband's: see also Steiner, *Käthe Leichter, Leben und Werk,* 100–2.

18 Jacques Vittori, ILO *Labour Education*, Trade Union Women's Studies, No. 31, June 1976, 30.

19 Hooks, 191–5; Terkel, *Working*, 48–9: Baker, 101.

20 ibid., 154–6.

21 Lewenhak, *Women and Trade Unions*, 215; Lehmann, *Down River*, 84–5.

22 *1938 Scot. TUC Rep., Organisation of Women Committee Rep.*, 79; *1933 TUC Rep.*, 142, para. 139, Memorandum of Evidence to the Board of Education Consultative Committee on Infant and Nursery Schools; *1940 TUC Rep.*, 354–5.

Chapter 14

THE SECOND WORLD WAR AND POST-WAR LABOUR SHORTAGE

There were a great many similarities in developments in women's work as between the second and first world wars, but there were also some marked differences, particularly in the Fascist Axis countries. One lay in the German Nazi use of concentration camps where millions of people, mainly of the Jewish faith, were killed; another was the Nazis' use of people from subjugated countries as a servile labour force – slave labour. The abundance of this imported labour enabled the big numbers of German women to avoid working even during the war. Towards the end they were being urged – not conscripted – into light work with the assurance that East European women would do the heavy labour. Broadly speaking, German labour policy towards conquered peoples went in two phases. At first Belgians, French, Greeks, Czechs and Dutch were subject to indirect pressure. It must be remembered that there was an established tradition of migrant labour from the Netherlands to Germany. Under the occupation the economies of these countries were run down. Work became scarce but men, women and teen-agers were told there were jobs in Germany to entice them to go of their own accord. Wages in their home countries were kept deliberately low and rations short. By 1942, following the invasion of the USSR, there was an acute labour shortage in German industry so people were forcibly deported to make up for it. Poland in 1940 and the USSR from April 1942 had already been subjected to forcible deportations. In Poland regular Gestapo hunts rounded up all fit men and women first in the west of the country immediately after the fall of Warsaw, and then·elsewhere in November 1942. By 1944 there were about 1,700,000 male Polish slave workers and 270,000 women other than those conscripted into German brothels, and thousands in concentration camps; 400,000 to 500,000 'picked, healthy, strong girls from the Eastern regions' (Russia) were sent to Germany to 'free from their work the very much occupied German peasantry'. Transport conditions were appalling especially for Poles and Russians. The Swiss paper *Der Landbote* described Ukrainian women set to work in fields and stables in Weihenstephan. They worked an 11-hour day. According to the *Münchner Neueste Nachrichten* their diet was almost entirely cabbage and potatoes. These deported slave workers were, however, paid wages, and in many cases they were allowed to send money home, graded in the men's case according to whether they were married or single. The Eastern women had their wages stopped for the first few weeks to pay for their clothing. But they were given no stockings or shoes so 'throughout the winter they were forced to bind pieces of sackcloth and rags round their legs.' They were permitted to leave their camps except during the blackout period but could not enter inns or shops or go to any entertainment. As the Russians pressed westwards from 1944 the treatment of East European deportees was brought up to the standard of that of other nationalities.

Many women deportees from the East and from Luxembourg were employed in private German households as domestics. The employers of those from the East were forbidden to show them any kindness and they were subject to draconian punishments. A 23-year old Polish woman was sentenced to death at Wloclawek for slapping her employer's face, for example.[1]

Japan was fighting in China from 1931 although war was not officially declared until six years later. About 50 million Chinese were made homeless. The men were deported to industrial northeast China and to Japan or conscripted into a Japanese puppet army. The women and children who remained, worked building roads, railways and fortifications. Some on secret installations were said to have been buried alive once the work had been completed. The Japanese enslaved the Filipinos and Javanese as they conquered their territories, keeping them on starvation rations in order to save their dwindling merchant marine the risks and strain of supplying them with food.[2] Both in the Far East and in Europe slavery for both sexes was temporarily resuscitated.

In Italy and in many of the Fascist allied and occupied countries, most women were peasants, labouring under heavy patriarchalism. For them war meant what it had always meant. When men went to fight, they had to carry on the farms. For many the war and its accompanying food shortages ended in illness. They still gathered in the rice and fruit for the big estate owners. But a few expressed their fury at the poverty thrust on them by landlords and government by joining the Resistance Movement.

Among the allied nations, already before the war with more choice of jobs, girls were opting out of domestic service. As in 1914–1918 the war gave them a chance to do this on a mass scale. Along with stay-at-home wives, they went into munitions, engineering and shipbuilding and replaced men in civilian jobs. In Britain, the United States and Russia, women took over men's work to a much greater extent than in Germany. In the United States they did so voluntarily, but elsewhere they were conscripted. Once more to begin with there was little concern over long hours worked in factories until, in Britain, women union leaders protested and pointed to the rising industrial accident rate recorded in factory inspectors' reports. Similarly low pay and poor conditions for women and girls drafted into munitions work were ignored even by their own trade union leaders until 1942.

The immediate concern of trade unions in Britain as in 1914–18, was about the effects of cheap female labour on their male members' pay. As a result, whether or not they admitted women to membership, they stepped up the pre-war policy of demanding the 'rate for the job' for women replacing men and used industrial tribunals to see it enforced. At the same time they made great concessions in waiving apprenticeship agreements in order that women could be trained quickly. The employers, on their side, also followed 1914–18 precedents, taking the chance to speed-up the introduction of technological changes, sub-dividing jobs and imposing on women supervision they did not need in order to avoid equal pay.

There were however, some differences. Unions notably encouraged women to enrol and, to a greater extent than in the First World War, to take over a lot of union work in branches. One of the great trade union events of the war was the decision of the British Amalgamated Engineering Union in 1942 to accept women members instead of leaving the organization of women engineering workers to the two main general unions, the Transport and General Workers' Union and National Union of General and Municipal Workers.

There was a huge improvement in women factory workers' welfare in Britain once Ernest Bevin became Minister of Labour in 1940. He had been one of the most powerful figures in the pre-war Labour Movement, the General Secretary of the Transport and General Workers' Union. He was the more susceptible to pressure from leading women trade unionists. The result was the sudden provision of medical services and day nurseries for women in industries important to the war. For the first time British women workers were aware that notice was being taken of their special needs.

Thus the pre-war movement among active women members for greater recognition in their unions was encouraged. These women were not diverted by official euphoria about women's contribution to the war effort. They threw back at the TUC proposals on women's economic role in the changeover from war to peace because they were patterned on post-1918 conditions. They would not accept that only those who had been working in pre-war occupations other than domestic service had a right to return to their jobs. They asserted the right of every woman, married or not, who had been working during the war to continue working if she wished.[3]

THE POST-WAR LABOUR SHORTAGES IN THE WEST

For about twenty-five years, from 1945 to 1970, the main belligerents in the Second World War and other advanced technological countries suffered from a labour shortage or had 'full employment' which alleviated the harsh competition that had characterized the previous hundred and more years. For the usual short-term post-war boom when war losses were made good was succeeded by an export drive and by continuing war preparations as wars broke out or threatened to do so in various parts of the world. In capitalist advanced-technology countries there was a general expansion of welfare services and education which created more work for women. The result was a consumer boom which created still more jobs.

Another consequence was higher earnings for younger age groups which permitted marriage at a lower age than before the war when people had to save for years to be able to afford to set up homes and start families. The younger marriage age ensured the breakdown of the 'marriage bar'. Attempts to reimpose it after 1945 gradually faded out. Married women who did not return to work while their babies were still small, were seen by the late 1950s to be going out to jobs again once their children reached school-leaving age.[4] The incentive was the rise in the family's standard of living when a wife was earning. It enabled ordinary working people to share in the new consumerism and forget the deprivations of the pre-war years. Aids such as day nurseries and factory health services of wartime standards were not needed to bring married women into jobs. Women became part of the cycle of production in which they themselves manufactured the canned and frozen foods, the labour-saving machines for homes; in which they provided the services that in turn eased their own domestic work-load and enabled others to go out to make luxury articles. Married women workers, in traditional fashion, relied on older women in their families or on paid child-minders to 'mind' their children. Or they worked part-time or did homework which had been disappearing between the wars. By 1943 homework was sufficiently on the increase in Britain to be a matter for discussion at the Trades Union Congress and was still causing concern in the 1970s.[5] It was not only young mothers who wanted to go out to work but middle-aged women and grandmothers.

Most women still gave priority to work in homes and for their families. So the pre-war generation acquiesced in secondary status in paid work. Part-time workers accepted the view that they were casual labour and since jobs were plentiful, fitted in outside work with their domestic jobs and holidays. They helped to create a labour turnover problem.[6] Many, especially of the older women, however, stayed in their jobs despite disadvantages. Unions often did not bother to negotiate for them and, like married women, they were expected to leave first in any cut-back in staff and were not accorded the usual union right of 'last in–first out'.

Women's difficulties in finding child-minders increased because of the growing extent and speed of the break-up of urban communities. Employers were calling for mobility of labour. Ruthless assaults were made on slum housing without thought of the social effects. The decline of patriarchal monogamy which had been proceeding slowly for centuries was suddenly speeded up. Divorce rates in advanced-technology countries soared, partly because of immature marriages. Because of girls claiming greater sexual freedom, the numbers of babies born out of wedlock increased. Women, because of their social and economic inferiority had the worst of these changes. Mothers left to fend for themselves and their children faced greater difficulties than men over housing, jobs and rights to family allowances. Among the unsung heroines of the post-war years were the grandmothers who, in middle age, took on the upbringing of their grandchildren to help their daughters.

Patriarchalism was by no means dead in the high-technology western world. In West Germany, husbands still had a legal right after the Second World War to chastise their wives physically and in Britain and the United States 'battering' of wives still went on. Work outside the home was still dominated by men. Trade union emphasis on pay as opposed to hours and working conditions still prevailed. There was even some regression in standards in comparison with the 1930s in that speed-up and payment-by-results systems were accepted without demur. Everywhere the cry was 'Productivity!' So shifts and overtime were worked and women forced to accept them. Instead of using the strong bargaining position conferred on them by the labour shortage to shorten hours of work, the male-dominated unions more than ever seemed to conspire with employers against women's interests. Productivity bonuses, overtime and shift rates were used as ways round government curbs on pay increases. Employers dependent on female labour were sometimes readier to make concessions to women on hours that would fit in with family work, on pleasant working conditions, or on provisions for the care of children of working mothers than the women's fellow men workers.[7]

Girls were still directed and manipulated into low-graded ancillary work which they found boring. One result of this in capitalist countries was high labour turnover. In manufacturing but especially in the new mass female occupations of office and distributive work,[8] women and girls found the variety which the work itself lacked, by changing their employers. They were not a stable labour force. These kinds of work had displaced domestic service as the greatest single women's occupation. But because of a continuing demand for maids in hospitals and hotels, and for catering workers, high-technology capitalist countries began importing labour on a large scale from countries at an earlier technological level, including considerable numbers of women.[9] Earlier most immigrant workers had been men who left families to carry on subsistence farming and handicrafts, sending money back to them. There was a slightly increased awareness among girls and women of each others' cultures and work as a result.

High labour turnover[10] hindered the development of women's trade unionism. Fear of unemployment had taught people the importance of organization before the war. Now with full employment that fear was increasingly lifted and there was no other education as a substitute for this experience. Numbers of people with whom union organizers had to deal were, however, growing. In Britain, to keep memberships and ensure dues were paid, they found employers usually the bigger public and private corporations, who would virtually endorse the 'closed shop' and deduct union dues along with tax and social security payments before pay was handed to an employee. This device made unions more remote. For many young people payment of union dues was the same as payments to the state. They had no interest and no loyalty either to union or employer. Only when they landed in some sort of trouble did they start to find out the realities of work. Women particularly were woefully ignorant of their rights to compensation payments from employers for injuries at work. Only the most serious were ever reported.

For various reasons, few British women went to trade union schools. After the war especially many wanted rest and an escape from work and unions which were connected with it. Many were still timid. Sometimes their trade unionist husbands were jealous and would not let them attend female, let alone schools for men and women. Although union growth increasingly was coming to depend on the recruitment of women, unions were slow to follow the example of the United States Tailors and Garment Workers and cater imaginatively for female members.[11]

High labour turnover and indifference to trade unions were also encouraged by employment agencies which took advantage of the new boom in the labour market, negotiating ever-higher wages for domestic, catering, office staff and nurses, taking over the functions of trade unions in their competition for the custom of girls and women workers.

From the late 1950s there was growing concern in unions in high-technology countries that technological changes were favouring women and threatening men's jobs, hence the revival of the old male protective device of equal pay.

Electronic computers were really developed during the Second World War. By 1959, two thousand of them were estimated to be in use in the USA. The boom in employment created a boom in banking, since many people had money to save. This, in turn, hastened the introduction of electronics in banking. Firms and public authorities turned to electronics and computers because of difficulties in obtaining enough staff for low-grade, repetitive processes, and because of high labour turnover. Thus the U.S. Bureau of Labor Statistics found one firm in 1954 in which a work-force of 198 at an average salary of $3,700 was replaced by 85 employees at a salary of $4,200, four-fifths of them girls and women. In this way the problem of finding staff was reduced.[12] But the growing demand for labour prevented a rise in numbers of unemployed in spite of the introduction of new technology. There was also a demand for the deftness by now traditionally associated with women, as physical strength was with men, for the new processes of microminiaturization and transistorization.

THE ROOTS OF THE NEW WOMEN'S EMANCIPATION MOVEMENT

In advanced-technology countries, the general view of men was that it was a good idea for wives to earn and increase family income provided that at the same time they took almost total responsibility for home and family work. However, just after the end of the war there were signs that men were beginning to think that they ought to take some share of these jobs. Progress came in the United States where by 1945 the number of married women working outside their homes exceeded the number of the single for the first time in modern history.

When men came out of the Forces, many undertook study under the GI Bill of Rights. Their wives took jobs to support families while fathers combined their studies with looking after children and homes. In the evenings if they wanted to go out together, they employed baby-sitters of their own social class. Husbands of women in domestic or other service work took a greater share in the care of their children than those in any other occupation. Men who were least involved were farmers or farm workers, pro-fessional and managerial workers and generally those in the south. Mothers in clerical and sales occupations were the most likely to have their children cared for away from their homes.

The idea of a husband owning a wife receded and there were a few statements about the value of women's work on farms. Thus a Professor of Agriculture in Minnesota calculated that a good farmer's wife had a value of 69,000 dollars. *The New York Times* of 8 October 1946, quoting him, raised it to 'a flat $100,000, without quibbling' for 'a lady who runs a house, takes care of the children, looks after the chickens, heats the milk and bottle feeds orphan lambs, helps in the garden, makes pies enough so a man can have a piece for breakfast, bakes beans every Saturday ... is willing to make home-made biscuits with reasonable frequency ... and understands that a man wants fried potatoes for supper five nights a week.'[13]

The movement towards a more equitable sharing of paid work and family work grew very slowly. But the Women's Rights lobby was strong enough to gain from President J. F. Kennedy in December 1961 a Status of Women Commission which emphasized the need for facilities for caring for children of working mothers. A Department of Health, Education and Welfare document that year highlighted one of the key problems, that of decision-making by husband and wife in all aspects of domestic work, finance and child care. Special courses were run to bring women into hitherto largely male spheres and men into those left to women. There were small steps towards that interchangeability of work roles present among Stone Age hunter gatherers.

There were two technological developments that helped this sharing of work in homes or at any rate improved the standing even of stay-at-home wives. Increasing mechanization in homes proved women's capacity for working with machines. They made for a slight similarity between the work of a male factory worker and the work of his wife in their home. More important in this respect was the family car which either marriage partner could drive. It not only demonstrated women had a skill equal to that of men, it broke their isolation in homes. They were no longer dependent on sometimes inadequate public transport.

At the same time capitalist advanced-technology countries introduced compulsory secondary education. In spite of a 'vocational' emphasis which strengthened the division of labour between women and men, girls coming out of schools in the 1950s were more knowledgeable and confident than their mothers before the war. There had always been a strong correlation between secondary education and the Women's Emancipation Movement. Secondary education did for post-war girls what the educative experience of war work had done for older women especially in the United States in breaking the 'woman's place is in the home' tradition.

There was a movement towards class as well as sex equality in that upper- and middle-class girls who went to work because of the war did not withdraw from the labour market when the war ended. They continued to take jobs in high-class offices, as air hostesses and to staff the upper and middle grades of white-collar occupations. Their bosses, aware of their social standing, petted and wooed them. Girls found it even harder to reconcile this treatment with their general economic, social and legal inferiority.

Although women were put off trade unionism in many ways, numbers in membership rose. They could be more readily recruited in factories and large offices than in the old domestic service. It was the *proportion* of those joining in several important trade groups that did not increase. Overall for nearly a generation after the war in Britain this proportion barely altered. But the growth in actual numbers, taken together with improved education and wartime experience, prompted women to use unions more and more in their struggle for economic equality. They not only went to union meetings and demanded union support for policies to help them, they ignored special 'women's sections' and stood with increasing success for election in competition with men at local level. Nationally a few were reaching top union jobs, but here numbers did not noticeably increase; sometimes they fell compared with pre-war. This was a growing source of irritation to the most energetic and able.

THE STRUGGLE FOR EQUALITY IN PAY
The rallying-cry of the Women's Movement was 'Equal Pay'. Women who did the same work as men in the public services in Britain won a notable victory when they finally extracted from a Conservative Government in 1954 the phased introduction of the 'rate for the job' over the next seven years.

The mass of women who were not making progress noted that among men, the commonness of a job or skill did not necessarily make their work low-paid. For example, carpenters, postmen or bus crews were not at the bottom of the pay scale. Yet in engineering women workers in Britain, who did work mainly graded as semi-skilled, were still on union-agreed rates below those of unskilled male labourers. And in certain highly-skilled branches of textile manufacture in 'women-only' processes, a women's rate still applied in some places. Low pay was still due to their sex.

In Japan a Labour Standards Act of 1947 introduced equal pay in a very limited way. A Women's and Minors' Bureau was set up, charged with the interpretation of the Act together with the investigation of working premises and co-operation with an Inspectorate. A National Public Services Act a month later provided for the 'equal treatment of both sexes', a principle which was applied in the public services, but not by private employers whose outlook and policies remained those of the big silk enterprises of the late nineteenth century (see pages 168–9). There were now no institutional barriers to girls obtaining the same vocational education and training as boys. Public schools were open to both sexes as in other advanced-technology countries, yet girls' training was unequal. 1971 statistics showed that while there were more girls than boys at the primary and secondary education levels, only 10 per cent of girls received higher education as compared with 18·5 per cent of boys. The proof of the post-war legislation's ineffectiveness was its re-enactment in the form of a Working Women's Welfare Act in 1972. But it carried no penalties for failure to observe it.[14] Nevertheless a step had been taken towards women's economic equality.

Despite the opposition of the governments of some high-technology capitalist countries, the International Labour Organization in 1951 promulgated Convention 100 re-stating that 'equal pay for work of equal value' was the universal standard for the remuneration of women. The Convention became a standard aim for the Women's Rights Movement.[15]

The European Community of the six countries, France, Italy, West Germany and the three Benelux countries instituted the 'rate for the job' in its inaugural Treaty of Rome in 1957. After initial delay in implementing this Article, they gradually went on to adopt the ILO's standard of 'equal pay for equal value'. The trouble was that there was no legal force behind the policy, and women's average wages continued to become ever lower than those of men (see Table 14) proving that either they did not have equal opportunities for obtaining higher-graded work, or their own work was not properly evaluated.[16] When the small British-mandated territory of Israel became an independent state, women there were given the 'rate for the job'. Their labour was needed to build up agriculture and on heavy work like road- and house-building. By the late 1950s the bulk of the English-speaking world, along with some feudal and semi-feudal countries, was lagging behind in women's pay parity.

Pay rates were being determined by job evaluation experts but the resulting agreements tended to preserve the principle of women's lower earnings even when their work was proved to have the same value as that of men.

It was a peculiarity of many high-technology countries that the average women's pay, even when calculated on an hourly basis so that variations in numbers of hours worked should not have made a difference, tended to be lower than that of men. A major reason for the difference was the fact that men worked more over-time and night shifts, or 'unsocial hours' than women and these periods of work carried higher remuneration, whereas employers made efforts to accommodate women workers' hours to their domestic and child care work. Evening shifts, when mothers could more easily count on other members of the family being available to look after children, did not carry higher rates since the recompense to the women lay in fitting hours to suit them. Other reasons for women's lower average pay were the larger numbers of women than of men in lower-paid work including part-time work, and the old determination to keep differentials in favour of men, often using the outdated and specious 'family wage' theory of men as the sole family providers. It was also due to the new tactic of percentage wage increases in place of absolute settlements in which specific amounts of cash were negotiated. There was a ring of equality about negotiating for women the same percentage rise as men workers. But the same percentage of a higher wage of, say, £12, amounts to more in cash terms than of a lower wage of, say, £5. As a result in some countries the cash difference between the average wages of women and those of men has widened so that while women have on average a higher percentage of the men's rates of earnings, the cash discrepancy between their rates and those of men is greater, for example in the Federal Republic of Germany, the United Kingdom, Denmark and Belgium. As the actual cash earnings of women rose, employers and union negotiators could argue women were better off. But the real value of women's earnings, like those of men, was also related to whether or not there was inflation. In four of the five 'third world' countries shown in Table 13, women made considerable progress

Table 13 Average Earnings of Women and Men in Various Countries in 1958 and 1968

Country	Currency	1958				1968			
		Men's Rate	Women's Rate	Cash Difference	W % of M	Men's Rate	Women's Rate	Cash Difference	W % of M
MANUFACTURING INDUSTRY									
Egypt (weekly)	piastres	228	112	116	49·12	305 (1965)	235	70	77·05
El Salvador (hourly)	colones	0·70	0·45	0·25	64·29	0·90	0·70	0·20	77·78
Burma (monthly)	kyats	142·24	90·36	51·88	63·53	154·24 (1966)	136·31	17·93	88·38
Taiwan (daily)	dollars	27·85	19·49	8·36	69·98	58·88 (1966)	32·59	26·29	55·35
Belgium (daily)	fr.	233·4	131·9	101·50	56·51	389·7	246·3	143·40	63·20
UK (hourly)	s. d.	5s. 7d.	3s. 2d.	2s. 1d.	62·00	10s. 0d.	5s. 8d.	4s. 4d.	57·20
ALL WORK OTHER THAN AGRICULTURE									
Denmark (hourly)	øre	570	387	183	67·89	1329	978	351	73·59
France	fr.	192	163·3	28·7	85·05	4·07 (New frs.)	3·52	0·55	86·49
Fed. Rep. of Germany	mark	2·51	1·58	0·93	62·95	5·10	3·54	1·56	69·41
Kenya (monthly)	shillings	139	83	56	59·71	266 (1966)	246	20	92·48

Source: *ILO 1968 Yearbook of Labour Statistics* – Table 18 Manufacturing Industry and Table 19A All Work other than Agriculture.

towards equality in earnings with men with both the cash and percentage differences of women decreasing. The exception was Taiwan where laws to equalize women's status with that of men proved largely ineffective. Of the five west European countries, France matched this performance. But in the United Kingdom, as in Taiwan, women were averaging a lower percentage of men's rates in 1968 than ten years earlier, and the cash difference had widened proportionately more – by over 100 per cent. The ILO reported in 1977 that the earnings gap between women and men in the United States had gone up by 50 per cent between 1955 and 1974.

Averages conceal great differences in individual earnings. But if they hide the growing numbers of women who, by means of pressure of unions, by the late 1960s were making progress towards the 'rate for the job', they also mask the even larger numbers in low-paid work.[17] In most high-technology countries the policy persisted of using women as cheap labour, however great the dependence on them and however great their work skills.

In addition to the lower women's rates of pay, and their concentration in lower-graded jobs, married women were treated unequally over social insurance including unemployment insurance in a number of countries. Their inclusion on similar terms to those for men in both state and private enterprise schemes was still a matter for debate in International Labour Organization publications in the late 1970s.[18]

Women were increasingly aware of the discrepancy between their real economic value and the way they were treated. The realization was especially sharp among the middle class as more of them engaged in paid work and obtained higher education. It could be argued that by the mid-1960s they were among the most exploited women in the world. The men of their class expected a far more elaborate life-style than those of a lower social class but paid domestic help was disappearing. 'Do it yourself' was once more becoming the principle of existence. They would have echoed the woman coal-bearer's remark in 1842 that when she came home from her job she 'had it all to do.' A college education opened the door to intellectual fulfilment but the Establishments in capitalist high-technology countries seemed determined to close it again. It was this that provoked Mrs Betty Friedan into writing *The Feminine Mystique*, published in 1963. In it she castigated the

Table 14 Hourly Average Earnings of Women and Men in Occupations other than Agriculture in EEC Countries, 1967 and 1976

Country	Currency	1967				1976			
		Men's Rate	Women's Rate	Cash Difference	W/M %	Men's Rate	Women's Rate	Cash Difference	W/M %
France	fr.	3·57	2·98	0·59	83·47	11·48*	9·92	1·56	86·41
Fed. Rep. of Germany	mark	4·99	3·46	1·53	69·34	11·08	8·02	3·06	72·38
Belgium	fr.	56·42	37·67	18·75	66·77	173·94	121·84	52·10	70·05
Netherlands	guilder	4·03	2·90	1·13	71·96	11·50	9·36	2·14	81·39
Luxembourg	fr.	66·05	38·09	27·96	57·67	181·03	120·94	60·09	66·81
Denmark	øre	56·42	37·67	18·75	66·77	173·94	121·84	52·10	70·05
UK	pence	46·3	27·6	18·70	59·61	152·2	108·6	43·60	71·35

*Sampling design revised.

Note: comparable figures for Italy and Ireland not supplied to ILO.

Source: *ILO 1977 Yearbook of Labour Statistics*, Table 18.

mass media for 'programming' women with college educations as home-makers, whereas only a satisfying career could save them from boredom and psychological problems.

The degree of animosity shown by women to their governments and employers bears some relation to their prospects of obtaining jobs, and also of their chances of higher-graded jobs. Rebellions are sparked off both by despair, and by high hopes of success and irritation at having a desired aim almost within reach. Women in Italy had much less chance of a salaried, administrative or managerial job than in many other countries; they accounted for two-thirds of all 'wage-earners', a factor behind their strong Women's Rights campaign.[19] Women in the United States on the other hand considerably increased as a proportion of the labour force, from 27·47 per cent in 1950 to 39·75 per cent in 1976, a generation later. But they accounted for only 33·65 per cent of administrative and managerial grades. It was the educated, middle-class North American women who were the most vociferous proponents of the extreme wing of the post-war Women's Movement. But it was ordinary working women, particular trade union members, the economically essential, who gave it its strength. However, what made their progress possible were prosperity and labour shortages.

WOMEN WORKERS IN PEOPLES' DEMOCRACIES

The whole of Eastern Europe lost a considerable proportion of its population as a result of the Nazis' actions. Furthermore as a result of the war there was a considerable surplus of women over men.[20] In all those East European countries in which Socialist governments were established after the war, as in the Soviet Union, the importance of women workers to a considerable extent was due to labour shortage.

In the Soviet Union the movement to educate women and so give them equal opportunities of obtaining high-level jobs was halted by the war. In 1939 after 20 years of work, only 104 out of every 1,000 women had had secondary and higher education.[21] So as part of post-war reconstruction, huge women's educational programmes were instituted. By the early 1960s these were showing results.

Table 15a   Women's Work and Gradings in the Soviet Union in 1939 and 1959

Women	1939	1959
Heads of construction sites, state and collective farms, administrative bodies	176,800	535,000
Scientific workers, teachers at institutions of higher learning, heads of research institutions	34,900	120,200
Engineers and technicians, agronomists, livestock experts, veterinary surgeons and foresters	400,700	1,814,700

By contrast the numbers of women working in agriculture rose much less:

Table 15b

Women	1939	1959
Agricultural workers	20,159,600	19,742,700
Family members working on personal plots	7,868,500	8,950,900
TOTAL	28,028,100	28,693,600

Source: *Women and Children in the USSR*, 94–6 incl. n., 40

The agricultural workers were those on state, collective and co-operative farms. On state farms in 1940, women made up only about a third of all workers. When men left during the 1939–45 war, women took over their work and still represent a higher proportion of the rural workforce than before the war. Another reason for this was that the balance shifted in favour of personal plots after the war and on these women did most of the work. The contempt of townspeople appointed to senior managerial posts on state farms for the rural workforce, and class stratification among the country people themselves were causing tensions in the late 1960s and early seventies. At the same time, in Central Asia, Communist Party officials were still combatting efforts to reintroduce polygamy, child brides, the bride price and marriage by abduction.

As in other countries which were adopting new industrial

technologies, the rural population was declining as a proportion of the country's total population, so a shrinking workforce has been dealing with an increasing acreage on state farms. To raise productivity the Russians introduced shift-working. For instance in the Ilyich's Behests Agricultural Artel in the Smela district of the Ukraine, dairymaids have been working a shift system since 1952. Their earnings have been high enough to make it unnecessary to supplement them by working on their own plots.

In general, however, agricultural wages were the lowest of all in the USSR, in consideration of the produce workers had from personal plots, for their own use or for sale. But by 1968 wages had risen to leave transport and communications in bottom place. Agricultural workers have been treated more and more like factory workers, receiving holidays with pay, cultural and educational facilities, schools, crèches and nurseries. However, seasonal unemployment is a major problem. Russian agricultural workers' jobs end temporarily each autumn with the onset of the severe midcontinental winters and although much work is then done in homes, the old cottage industries have been displaced increasingly by modern manufactures. The sharp drop in employment particularly affects women:

For example, in the Novosibirsk oblast (district) in December 1967, the collective farms could offer employment to only about 67 per cent of their members, leaving 66,000, a large number of them women, without farm employment.

But at harvest time the sudden demand for a greatly increased labour force has been met largely by housewives, nurses, students and school children.[22]

To try to deal with this situation, the Soviet authorities have organized a mobile force of machine operators, tractor drivers and drivers of combine-harvesters who follow the harvests from south to north. Private contractors are now organizing similar gangs, the personnel being mainly male. When the early Soviets were making great efforts to mechanize farming in order to raise food production, they encouraged women to become tractor drivers. But by the 1960s women made up only 6 per cent of all those working on motor or electric transport in farming regions.

What women agricultural workers wanted was the elimination

of long stretches of seasonal unemployment, although they still carried on cottage industries and repair and maintenance work in the winter. Increasing mechanization would give them this. But it was leading to their displacement by men so that they lost work altogether. In this they faced a dilemma common to all advanced-technology countries.

The same situation developed in Romania, Hungary and the German Democratic Republic where the hoe and the rake were only being replaced by machines in 1965.[23] The result of the introduction of agricultural machinery, as in the Soviet Union, was a decline in numbers of women in agriculture, their traditional main occupation.

But even in the 1970s the work was nothing like as completely mechanized as in the USA and Britain. Women agricultural workers' jobs in the Soviet Union were then still likened to those of women 'in underdeveloped countries'. The situation in Poland in 1976 was still medieval in that eighty per cent of farms were still privately owned and the young men were going off to the towns and leaving the women and old people to work them.[24]

The official attitude to domestic work, however, remained more enlightened than in capitalist countries. 'Socialization' of domestic work, that is its performance by paid labour outside homes, was still the aim, whereas in the West moves in this direction were due to haphazard private enterprise, not deliberate state policy. So there was a steady growth in the Soviet Union in numbers of catering establishments, cooked food shops and meals delivery services to homes. More laundries and repair shops were opened. At the same time steps were taken to ease housework through increased output of domestic machines. Mrs Pandit, Pandit Nehru's sister who was Indian ambassador to the USSR, remarked on the striking similarities between the USSR and the USA. The similarities existed also with other countries. By the late 1960s public housing was being built, with domestic machines already installed, in both the Soviet Union and the West.

However, by the 1970s there was some evidence that 'socialization' was not what women wanted. They were demanding more time off paid work to look after homes and children through part-time jobs and a shorter working day. Like women in industrialized capitalist countries they found that going to work outside their homes often meant harder, more monotonous, less pleasant work

than inside their homes. For, the USSR had adopted the same frag-
mented mechanized processes, the same production incentives to
speed up work as the industrialized capitalist countries. Like almost
all countries coming late to industrialization, it opted for the most
up-to-date technology available. Inevitably therefore that produced the same kind of atomized, repetitive work. At the same
time all the help given to women did not really remove the double
load of work. They still carried the primary responsibility for
family and domestic work. The greater equality they had in job
opportunities than women in capitalist countries rested, however,
on the work they did outside homes. If they became more
dependent on their husbands' earnings, they might regress and lose
status. Such Soviet women, dissatisfied despite socialisation, risked
losing the freedom and status which economic independence and
equality conferred, the very things for which Western women were
struggling so hard.

But another and more important similarity existed between the
condition of Soviet and Western women. A recent sociological
survey showed that half the men covered were playing an equal
role with wives in caring for children, and a third or more joined
their wives in cooking, dishwashing and daily housekeeping. In
some Soviet Central Asian republics, newly married men and
young fathers now go to conferences during which they compete
in the performance of household jobs such as cooking and
cleaning.[25]

The great advance for women workers since the Second World
War in both capitalist and socialist advanced-technology countries
was not just in more equal opportunities for jobs, in greater equality
in pay, in greater recognition of the value of paid work outside
their homes. It also included an acknowledgement that the work
they did inside homes had considerable economic value. A debate
is now taking place as to how women were to be directly compensated
for such work.

NOTES

1 *United Nations Organization Rep. No. 8*, 1944, 5–8, 16, 19, 21–4.

2 *International Lab. Rev.*, 1945, 530.

3 ILO *The War and Women's Employment*, Study and Rep., 1946; 1941
and 1943 *TUC Nat. Women's Advisory Committee Reps.*; 1941 *TUC Rep.*,
290–1; *Nat. Un. of General and Municipal Workers' Jour.*, July 1941, 309–10;
British Statistical Digest of the War; Hooks, US Dept. of Labor Women's

Bur., Bklet No. 200, *British Policies and Methods of Employing Women in Wartime*, 1944; Min. of Labour and National Service pamphlet, *The Employment of Women, Suggestions to Employers*, March 1941; Baker, *Technology and Woman's Work*, 199–201, 414, 416; Lewenhak, *Women and Trade Unions*, 235ff.

4 Oppenheimer, *Amer. Jour. of Sociology*, 78(4), 1973, 958; Dahlstrom and Liljestrom, 25 et seq.; Baude and Holmberg, 108–13 in Dahlstrom ed., *The Changing Roles of Men and Women*; *Min. of Lab. Gaz.*, 1952, 267; 1965, 252; 1968, 360–3 etc.; *British Government Social Survey*, Audrey Hunt, *A Survey of Women's Employment*, Rep. SS379; Klein, *Britain's Married Women Workers*, 24–8; Baker, 235.

5 1949 *Ann. Rep., Nat. Un. of Hosiery Workers*, Sect. G; 1956 *TUC Nat. Women's Advisory Committee Rep.*, 25–6; *Nat. Un. of Gen. and Municipal Workers' Jour.*, March 1952, 66–7.

6 *Min. of Lab. Gaz.*, Dec. 1962, 458–9.

7 *Times Business Rev.*, 8 May 1967, 25; Confed. of British Industry pamphlet, *Employing Women*, Sept. 1967; Klein, 119; *1966 Scot, TUC Women's Advisory Committee Rep.*, 16; Baker, 202–4, 208–9, 218, 221–35.

8 *Min. of Lab. Manpower Studies No. 7, Growth of Office Employment.* See also Table.

9 Böhning, *International Lab. Rev.*, vol. 111, March 1975, 254–5.

10 *Min. of Lab. Gaz.*, 1948, 246 etc.

11 Krebs, 185, 192, 196; Vogel, 17; Leijon, 161ff in *ILO Women Workers and Society*; *To Form A More Perfect Union, Rep. of the Nat. Commission on the Observance of International Women's Year*, 45–7, 307–9, 317–18; Werthmeier, *ILO Labour Education*, No. 31 3ff; Baker, 335ff; *Time Magazine*, 4 Sept. 1978, 35, 'Labor Comes to a Crossroads' stated that in 1976 less than 16 per cent of women were in trade unions, a considerable difference from Professor Baker's findings in the mid-1960s.

12 Baker, 212ff.

13 ibid., 102–3, 110–11.

14 Takahashi, *ILO Women Workers and Society*, 111–13, 126–7.

15 The later ILO Convention 111 committed signatories to altering national policy so as to eliminate discrimination because of race, colour, *sex*, religion, political opinion, national extraction or social origin in respect of employment or occupation i.e. sought to take a step towards implementation of Article 55(c) of the United Nations Charter. The British Government refused to ratify on the grounds that this would infringe free collective bargaining between employers and workers' organizations. See HMSO, CMD 783.

16 Sullerot, *ILO Women Workers and Society*, 89ff.

17 *To Form A More Perfect Union*, 65–6, 182–3; Krebs, 188; 1969 *TUC Rep.*, Frank Cousins, 505–7; Pauline Pinder, *Women At Work*, PEP vol. xxxv, Broadsheet 512, May 1969, 593–4, 598.

18 Gelber, 65ff; La Roque, 83ff; Sullerot, *L'histoire et sociologie du travail féminin*, 305ff.

19 *Sunday Times*, 11 Dec. 1977.
20 Symons, *Russian Agriculture*, 135; Berent, *International Lab. Rev.*, vol. 101, No. 2, Feb. 1970, 174, 191; Turchaninov, *ILO Women Workers and Society*, 149–50.
21 *Soviet Weekly*, 4 March 1978, No. 1, 882, Women's International Special issue, 7; Central Statistical Board of the USSR Council of Ministers, *Women and Children in the USSR*, pp. 51–2, shows proportions of women who were literate and who had some secondary or higher education were higher among urban than rural population.
22 Symons, 138, 140, 145 (quoting Zhukovskiy, 1942, 23), 146–8.
23 *Democratic German Rep.*, 19 Nov. 1975, 165–6, reprint of article by Rosi Blaschke in *Neues Deutschland*.
24 Symons, 149–51; *Times*, 3 August 1976; Berent, 177–9.
25 *Women and Children in the USSR*, 16; *Soviet Weekly*, 4 March 1978, 7.

Chapter 15

WOMEN WORKERS IN TRADITIONAL TECHNOLOGIES

Awakening nationalism and revolt against colonial rule all over the world began in the First World War and has been growing ever since, one country after another winning independence. Through nationalism women too started breaking out of their ancient segregation and inferiority, from 1910 in Egypt, 1911 in China, 1912 in India, 1914 in Syria and subsequently in other countries occupied or economically dominated by foreign powers. For women were essential to the success of national independence movements.

CHINA

China was not directly under colonial rule but was affected by what has been called 'economic imperialism', that is exploitation as a market and a source of raw materials by Western powers. The revolution of 1911 swept the feudal dynasty of the Manchus from power. The new government immediately banned foot-binding. The modernization of girls' education began. Girls from well-to-do families went to school and university and were not segregated from boys as they grew older.[1] Neither wives nor daughters had been able to inherit land. However, in 1931 a law gave daughters equal rights of inheritance with sons and made wives legal heirs of their husbands. But it was little observed outside the cities, and in Taiwan, the last refuge of the nationalists, the old exclusion of women persisted after the 1949 revolution.[2]

In 1927 the Communists were expelled from the nationalist party, the Kuomintang. In March of that year, Mao Tse Tung in a *Report on an Investigation of the Peasant Movement* in Hunan spoke of men being dominated by three systems of authority: political, clan and religious. But women in addition were 'also dominated by men'. These were the

four thick ropes binding the Chinese people ... With the increasing bankruptcy of the rural economy in recent years, the basis for men's domination over women has already been undermined. With the rise of the peasant movement, the women in many places have now begun to organize rural women's associations; ... the authority of the husband is getting shakier every day.[3]

In August 1927 war between the Communists and the Kuomintang began. During 1933–4 soviets were established in Kiangsi in the south and 1423 'production and distribution' co-operatives were set up, owned and run by the people, in which the Communist aim of equality for women as citizens and workers was introduced. Following the Long March from Kiangsi in 1934–6, they established themselves in the north-west in Shensi and Yenan. Here foot-binding, which epitomized the Chinese subjugation of women, was still the rule. The Communists ran into strong opposition to their efforts to promote women's equality from men and from tyrannical mothers-in-law who habitually took out on their daughters-in-law their subjugation and servant-like status to which they themselves had been subjected in their youth.

The Communists had to create their own factories for servicing their armies and in these they utilized women's skills, manufacturing shoes and clothing for their troops. Edgar Snow in his classic work, *Red Star Over China*, described them in the main industrial centre behind the Communist lines, Wu Ch'i Chen. Except in the arsenal and uniform factory, most of the workers were young women aged 18 to 30, some of them married to Red Soldiers. They had trade unions with a women's section presided over by Miss Liu Ch'un-hsien, a former mill worker, who like many Chinese Communists had studied at Moscow's Sun Yat-sen University. Workers were more highly paid than army commanders. They worked the factories on a 24-hour shift basis for 8-hour shifts, 6 days a week, Miss Liu Ch'un-hsien told Snow. They had free such medical attention as was available, and compensation for injuries. The women were remunerated on the basis of 'equal pay for equal labour'. They had four months' paid leave before and after childbirth and there was a 'nursery' for their children which was a great step forward by peasant standards although Snow thought it crude and conditions generally Spartan compared with North American standards. But he compared them with those in the non-

Communist south:

> I remembered Shanghai factories where little boy and girl slave workers sat or stood at their tasks twelve or thirteen hours a day, and dropped, in exhausted sleep, to the dirty cotton quilt, their bed, directly beneath the machines. I remembered little girls in silk filatures (spinning factories), and the pale young women in cotton factories sold into jobs as virtual slaves for four or five years, unable to leave the heavily guarded, high-walled premises day or night, without special permission. And I remembered that during 1935 more than 29,000 bodies were picked up from the streets and rivers and canals of Shanghai ...[4]

By giving women the chance to work for cash and by paying them personally, the Chinese Communists, like those in Russia, broke their total dependence on men.[8] But the change was harder to bring about in China than in Russia. Because of the overall lower population density and much later development of feudalism in Russia than in China, the tradition in large areas was for women to take at least an equal share with men in farm work. Whereas in much of China, the custom of women *not* working outside their homes was very old and deeply rooted. Hence the step for them into paid work on an equal basis with men was much harder. However, even in China an undefined co-operation was the basis of survival of the mass of the Chinese people. The Communists made it explicit. Without the co-operation of women as well as men, like the Russian Communists, they could not have won and retained power.[5]

Except in the Communist-controlled areas, husbands' and fathers' authority was to a great extent intact until the 1949 revolution. The Communist government based its policies for women as citizens and workers on their experiences in the areas they ran during the war. They immediately enacted a Marriage Law which promulgated monogamy in order to put an end to concubinage. It also laid down equal rights for both sexes including the right to divorce. Some women, conditioned to the point where oppression had become a convention, opposed the law and many men ignored it.[6]

The Communists in the now traditional pattern of ex-feudal countries distributed land as smallholdings to poor peasants. By the mid-1950s, the peasants were being persuaded to group themselves in semi-socialist Agricultural Producers' Co-operatives. 'With the completion of agricultural co-operation,' wrote Mao in 1955,

> many co-operatives are finding themselves short of labour. It has become necessary to arouse the great mass of women who did not work in the fields before to take their place on the labour front.[7]

In the countryside as well as in all urban and industrial workplaces women and men were to receive equal pay for equal work in production. From 1958 the Agricultural Co-operatives were being grouped in larger Communes as part of the effort to improve output in a still largely peasant economy.[8] To free women from work in their homes as part of this Great Leap Forward, the communes followed the wartime policy of providing communal dining rooms, nurseries and kindergartens. Cutting down on women's work in processing food for families was the best thing the revolution did, one old lady told Felix Greene.[9]

But famine still occurred and girls shared in the very heavy work of bringing new land under cultivation. Girls' lumbering teams came to the forest farms of the Greater Khingan Mountains, an area of intense cold, and to the Laochao River. They not only cut large amounts of timber, some of it with hand axes, for railway sleepers to extend the line into the forest, they shifted a huge amount of stone and sand and built extensive living quarters and 14 kilometres of road. As in the Soviet Union the educational opportunities opened to peasant women enabled some to become agronomists, specialists in animal husbandry, in stock-raising veterinary science and fish farming.

Girls and women also went into conventional heavy industry, a few reaching the most skilled jobs as chiefs of furnace teams and steam locomotive crews.[10] It has been said that the aim of Mao and his supporters at this stage was not the introduction of women into skilled jobs in heavy industry and transport on a mass scale, but the provision of proof by means of examples of women's equal capacity with men for such work in order to undermine men's persistent assumption of superiority.

In towns, jobs were not ready and waiting to be filled and urban employment opportunities grew fitfully. At times there were shortages of jobs for women due in part to the large scale of peasant immigration into urban areas. As a result the official encouragement to women to work outside their homes was not constant but spasmodic. They were taken on as required in the same way as in capitalist countries. Sometimes housework and care of children were acknowledged as useful work and women's role as men's dependants was even stressed.

The jerky progress of women's liberation was a reflection to some extent of political struggles within the Communist Party between the Mao and Liu Shao-chi factions. During the Cultural Revolution of 1966–72 Liu and his supporters were blamed for the 'back-to-the-home' movement for women of the mid-1950s. As part of the cultural revolutionaries' effort to break the still-surviving social hierarchy, a great deal of authority for running industry as well as health services and marketing was devolved from the central government to local communities. One of the results was that women became Chairmen of the Revolutionary Committees of Street Committees, and girl students as well as boys were Red Guards. Thirty students from a Peking girls' school produced a plan for reforming the examination system so that working people would have more say in who should have the chance of a college education. It was substantially accepted after the Cultural Revolution ended.[12]

In China there have recently been signs similar to those in the Soviet Union and in high-technology capitalist countries of a growing consciousness on the part of men of the value of women's work inside homes, for example in poems:

I, too, used to –
   come home from work, sit on the bed,
   And do not a thing but wait to be fed.
When I understood that looking down on women was
part of the reactionary teachings of Confucius
and Mencius, I saw that our women are working as
hard as our men to build socialism and should enjoy
equality in the home. Now if I get home before
my wife I start cooking the meal.[13]

Statistics show that in China the absolute numbers of industrial and white-collar women workers, including those in government and administration, increased during the 1950s, not altogether surprisingly. Within that increase, the percentage of women in the total numbers of these workers also rose, although there were still fewer of them than of men.

Table 16   Women Workers other than Peasants in China, 1952–9

Year	Total No. of Workers (in 1000's)	Total No. of Women Workers (in 1000's)	Women as Per Cent of Total
1952	15,804	1,848	11·7
1953	18,256	2,132	11·7
1955	19,076	2,473	13·0
1956	24,230	3,266	13·5
1958	45,323	7,000	15·4
1959	44,156	8,286	18·8

Source: Chen Chu-yuan, *Scientific and Engineering Manpower in China*, p. 145. He used the State Statistical Bureau's *Ten Great Years*, pp. 180 and 182 for 1952–8 and *China News Service*, 22 Feb. 1960, p. 11 for 1959.

Now Chang Ching, Mao's widow and great exponent of women's equality has been disgraced. She was criticized among other things for her efforts to import Western feminist plays. One aspect of the Cultural Revolution was a surge forward in women's equality. The Cultural Revolution itself is in disgrace and it remains to be seen how far the initial Communist movement to establish women's economic parity with men will grow.

WOMEN WORKERS IN INDIA SINCE THE 1939–45 WAR

India after the Second World War to a great extent presented a mirror image of west European countries during the early Industrial Revolution. Between 1961 and 1971 the proportion of women in the Indian labour force declined by 14·18 per cent, from nearly a third to slightly less than a sixth of the total (see Table 17). Simultaneously women's share of agricultural work had been rising ever since 1931 as their share of industrial and service work dropped, because more women hired themselves out as agricultural and other labourers. They were women from rural families whose holdings were too small and poor to support them, from families impoverished by the breakdown of the joint or extended family system, villagers and others working at home handicrafts, all hit by the rising cost of living since the 1939–45 war. But agricultural skills are common and often family workers held down rates of pay to labourers. A Minimum Wage Act of 1948 is still not applied to agricultural labour in some states. In any case at the 1971 census it was found that 92·1 per cent of women workers in rural areas were illiterate and could not assert their rights.[14]

Slavery persisted in British India, Burma and Assam. Britain signed the 1926 International Slavery agreement for abolition only in 1957, despite their fine record in helping to end the enslavement of Africans and their efforts to liberate slaves in Arab countries. Indian families from poverty-stricken villages were enticed to work on Assam tea estates with promises of a better life. Women and girls were employed as pickers because of their delicate touch. They found themselves confined to the plantations, paid only a small wage and having to produce their own food off small plots in much the same way as West Indian negro slaves. In the late 1920s cases were reported by a British Trades Union Congress delegation of their being kept at work by the threat of the whip. Nevertheless independent strikes on the isolated plantations were rife at this time. Attempts to help tea workers were discouraged by the British authorities for they caused trouble with local chiefs who helped to supply plantation labour.[15]

From the eighteenth century because of foreign occupation, particularly British, Indian handicrafts were declining. The gains of Lancashire and Scottish women cotton power loom weavers and of the jute workers in Dundee were made partly at the expense of Indian women and men who lost work as a result of their competition. Some jute and textile factories were set up in India and women, men and children were being brought in to staff them, as they were the tea plantations. But by the twentieth century technological changes were putting them out of work. Handicrafts were turned into 'sweated' homework. Women in both urban slums and villages today stitch garments cut out for them by a man, and make paper bags, packets of incense and tobacco. Despairing of a livelihood in the country, they are driven to the towns by hunger, leaving their share-cropper husbands. They find jobs as domestic servants who are outside the protection of the Minimum Wage Act. According to the 1974 *Report of the Committee on the Status of Women in India*, most of the women domestic workers in Calcutta were lone mothers who took on daily charring work and who usually have daughters aged from eight years old to help them. Local bodies maintain lists of sweepers and drain and latrine coolies whom they take on as casual labour when wanted. These women claim that because of their sex they have little chance of permanent posts. A study group of the Indian National Commission on Labour confirmed there was a reluctance to employ them even on this work. In any case the spread of modern sanitation is gradually doing away with such jobs, one instance of modern technology reducing the demand for unskilled labour which has been mainly made up of girls and women.

There are a few survivals of women's ancient economic independence. In the hills, for example, women have retained a monopoly of the craft of hand-weaving and still bring their wares to market themselves, for instance at Imphal in Manipur. The decline in women's share of marketing has more than offset the slight rise in numbers of women in the medical and teaching professions and in white-collar work.

Despite the outcry about women working underground in European mines, women went on doing this work in India until 1939. Their withdrawal was stopped by the Second World War and they continued to work underground until Independence in 1950. The attitudes of Indian women underground mine-workers were the same as those in Britain over a century earlier. They did not like the work, but they preferred it to the alternative of unemployment. They were not slave labour but worked on a sub-contracting system very like that in a number of nineteenth-century British coal mines.

Work in cotton, woollen and jute mills was also very similar to that in nineteenth- and early twentieth-century Britain with systems of fines and deductions, for example, of two days' wages for one day's absence.[16] Ester Boserup has pointed out, however, that in the late 1960s against the general depression of women there have been cases of female agricultural labourers obtaining equal pay. She instanced the prosperous Punjab where there was a labour shortage because women from farmers' families did not customarily work, and where there was also little low-caste or tribal labour for hire. In Central India, where earnings of tribal women and men for weeding and transplanting were also sometimes the same, the reason was quite the reverse; there labour was plentiful and men competing with women for jobs had to accept low rates.[17]

Legal welfare provisions in work were put forward as the main reason for the growing disinclination to employ women. Employers told the Indian Committee on the Status of Women in 1974 that they did not want to employ women because they did not want to have to pay maternity benefit and observe government restrictions on women's hours of work, on the weights they were permitted to carry and other limiting conditions. But the decline in numbers of women workers in occupations other than agriculture had begun before these government restrictions were introduced. So long as the extended family system lasted, numbers of women requiring to take extended maternity leave were low. In addition, for fear of losing their jobs, women made no claims. Thus claims from those in factories and mines decreased between 1961 and 1971.

From the beginning of this century there have been progressively fewer females than males in the population. One reason for this is the dowry system (see page 83). There is evidence that infanticide of girls is still practised. What is certain is that the

Table 17   Trends in the Occupational Distribution of Female Workers in India, and of the Proportion of the Female Population at Work and of the Proportion of Women in the Total Labour Force, 1911–71

Year	Agri- culture	Industry	Service	Female Workers as % of Total Female Popu- lation	Female Workers as % of Total Labour Force	Females per 1000 Males in the Popu- lation
1911	73·9	14·7	11·4	33·73	34·44	964
1921	25·5	13·5	11·0	33·73	34·02	955
1931	72·3	13·7	14·0	27·63	31·17	950
1951	76·8	11·2	12·1	23·30	28·98	946
1961	79·6	11·6	8·8	27·96	31·53	941
1971	80·1	10·5	9·4	11·86	17·35	930

1941 omitted as sample too small to be valid (2%).
Source: *Report of the Committee on the status of Women in India*, Government of India, Dept. of Social Welfare, Ministry of Education and Social Welfare, New Delhi, December 1974.

neglect suffered by girls from the moment of their first appearance in the world is accepted as one of the reasons for the surplus of males over females.[18] As a popular Indian saying puts it: 'Bringing up a daughter is like manuring and watering a plant in someone else's courtyard.' Yet a girl's value is still reckoned in terms of her capacity to work. 'It is her labour power that people call wealth!' as one mother put it in a survey shown by the Indian delegation at the 1974 United Nations Conference on Population and Economic Development.

NATIONAL INDEPENDENCE AND CLASS PRIVILEGE

Besides nationalism the ancient privilege arising from caste, class or family connections enabled some women to overcome the disability of their sex and achieve high status. Immediately after independence was gained a few middle- and upper-class women in India and the Arab countries reached leading professional jobs. Because of the masses of poor women and men they had behind them, there was no problem about finding servants who released them from the work of caring for children and homes just as in the case of Europe two hundred years before. And just as there had then been generous European husbands, so in the twentieth century there were Hindu men who made generous marriage settlements on their wives. For instance, it was because of advantages of caste and wealth that Mrs Pandit, sister of Pandit Nehru, Prime Minister of India after Independence, started as Health Minister for Uttar Pradesh and then in 1947–50 became the first Indian ambassador to the Soviet Union. In 1950–3 she was High Commissioner in Britain and then India's ambassador to the United Nations. Mr Nehru's daughter, Mrs Gandhi, became Prime Minister of India. In Sri Lanka, Mrs Bandaranaike, widow of the Prime Minister, took over from him. While such women had the advantage of literacy, few of them had any higher education because, when they were young, their countries had little to offer them.

Similarly lack of education was outweighed by wealth in the Near East. In the United Arab Emirates there are rich women who are highly successful in running businesses, farms and fleets of taxis, although they still wear veils and are illiterate.

However, in other Moslem countries, women's progress in obtaining top jobs has been linked to their growing access to education. Thus in Egypt in 1962, Hakmet Abuteid, one of the educated élite, became Minister of Social Affairs in President Nasser's government, the first woman to gain Cabinet rank. The sister of King Hassan of Morocco, Princess Lalla Aisha, supported by a brilliant woman cultural attachée, was Ambassador to Britain during 1965–9, while Madame Halima Embarek Warzazi was a United Nations delegate, one of many such women from the Arab states. In the Sudan the posts of Chairman of the Members' Committee of the Peoples' Assembly (a sort of combination of the Speaker in the British House of Commons and the Chief Whip) and the Deputy Minister of Social Affairs have both been filled by women. In 1969, Lebanon appointed its first woman judge, Mrs Chidiac. In Jordan as a result of relatively high educational standards for women, by the early 1970s they made up 30 per cent of the labour force outside homes. Some are prominent in the professions and in government work. Among the Palestinians, after Israel had been established, fathers tended to invest in daughters' education instead of land or other property. Palestine has been exporting, as workers to other Arab states, educated women and girls who have become one of the main forces making for women's emancipation in the Middle East. In two of the poorest

Table 18   Literacy and Education among Women and Girls in the Middle East, Early 1970s

Country	Percentage of Illiterate Women	Percentage of Illiterate Men	Country	Women as % of University Students
Libya	96	62	Kuwait*	60
Algeria	91	70	Egypt	28
Iraq	86	71	Iraq	24
Jordan	85	50	Tunisia	23
Egypt	80	60	Algeria	20
Syria	75	59	Syria	19
Lebanon	20	13	Saudi Arabia	7

Source: J. S. Szyliowiz, *Education and Modernisation in the Middle East* (Cornell Univ. Press 1973) except Syria – Tabitha Petran, Journalist, and Libya, R. Mead & A. George, 'The Women of Libya', Middle East International, July 1973, from Minority Rights Group Rep., No. 27 revised edn.
* Most Kuwaiti men go abroad to University.

countries, Tunisia and South Yemen, women now have equal rights with men not only in work but in their homes. In Tunisia this was largely the work of one man, President Bourguiba, who referred to the veil as 'that odious rag'. In South Yemen it followed from the establishment of independence and a Marxist government in 1967, which pursued the Socialist pattern of bringing girls and women into work outside their homes, again because of a shortage of trained labour and a desperate need to build up the economy. Drives were mounted to eliminate illiteracy and a specialist school for women set up to speed the development of fishery and agricultural co-operatives. There women learn to drive and repair tractors, trucks and fishing boats, to do carpentry, masonry, building and mechanical work. This type of female education is virtually unknown in other Arab states and in capitalist countries with the exception of Israel. Girls have appeared unveiled as television announcers, starting with the more liberated Palestinians and Egyptians. Miss Tamader Tawfik became secretary-general of the Union of Egyptian Radio and Television and is now, at 57 years of age, president of Egyptian Television. Miss Safia el Mohandis in 1976 succeeded her husband when he retired as head of Egyptian Radio. By 1976 65 per cent of the 8,500 Egyptian radio and television staff were women.

In Bahrain economic forces have been the direct cause of the breakdown of barriers against respectable urban girls going out to work. With low wages and a steeply rising cost of living, men wanted wives old enough and well-trained enough to be able to earn.

But not working is still a mark of high social status in some Arab states, as in the boast, 'No Kuwaiti woman does menial work'. She does not have to because there are enough poor Indian, Egyptian and Palestinian women who are imported even for lesser professional work. The ancient matriarchy still echoed in the 1970s in the provision that any Kuwaiti girl who at 18 had not found a husband was given a government pension. Women had no vote. Yet there was compulsory primary schooling and, since most men went abroad for their university studies, 60 per cent of university students were women.

CONTINUING ILL-TREATMENT OF WOMEN
Alongside women's progress in economic emancipation, cruel-

ties persist, however. Moslem husbands, not only Arabs but also South East Asians may divorce wives at will, a system that has been called 'a staggered form of polygamy' – variety without the expense of the upkeep of more than one wife at a time. Among the Berbers of Morocco, maternity remains a real form of work, a girl marrying a man to provide him with legitimate heirs and once the job is over, returning to her kin, to repeat the process with another man perhaps six times in her life. Again the men do not have the expense of a wife's upkeep beyond the time when she is actually of use to them and the children are cared for by their female blood relatives, an interesting sidelight on the breakdown of matriarchal power.[19]

In some places husbands retained the right to kill their wives until the present day. Among the Maria Gonds of Bastar in India, sudden death may be the fate of a wife who provides an evening meal unsatisfactory to her husband. In Arab villages, because of the importance of a bride's virginity, father or brothers may kill girls who indulge in no more than flirtation. The practice is known as the 'honour murder' and there is little deterrent in law. Outright slavery, involving women, men and children, and therefore the slave trade, still exists. The slave-wife persists so that traditional marriage remains a nightmare for girls. An Algerian doctor in a radio talk in 1964 stated that 175 suicides or attempted suicides had recently been brought to the hospital where he worked in Algiers, all the cases being educated girls who went back to their uneducated families and, disappointed that the treatment accorded them had not improved, decided to take their own lives rather than submit to traditional arranged marriages. An article in *People*, organ of the International Planned Parenthood Association, in 1975, noted of Algerian wives:

> If a man abuses his authority, the woman will become his slave in the strictest economic sense of the word. If he is good, she will have to give thanks every day of her life for the good fortune that has placed her in the hands of such a good master ...

In the 1960s the French sociologist, Germaine Tillion, reported that where young European girls dreamed of husbands and homes, poor girls in Algiers and Constantine set out to obtain jobs that would give them economic independence so that they would never have to marry. The practice of cliterectomy is still widespread (see pages 81–2). While modern mothers are trying to spare their daughters this ordeal, older women keep the practice alive and a certain kudos is given to it so that little girls may plead with distressed parents to have it performed on them, not realizing what is in store for them.[20]

WOMEN'S SELF-DEFENCE

In the Philippines women lost all property rights under the Spanish occupation. Spanish customs did not, however, go very deep into the central wild, hilly areas of the islands, but were mainly imposed in the more easily accessible coastal areas. In 1892 the United States took over the territory and returned it to the Filippinos themselves in 1946. The new independent government immediately gave women and men equal constitutional rights. They returned to the old custom whereby a woman keeps as her own the property she brings with her on marriage. If she dies childless it reverts to her kinship group or her parents. Women's work contribution is recognized and divisions of wealth and class are more important than those of sex. But the Roman Catholic influence persists in that there is no legal divorce, only separation.[21] In Mexico and in South American countries with their feudal Spanish and Portuguese legacies, women have found it hard to make headway against *machismo* (aggressive masculine superiority) and patriarchalism. Debt bondage still being rife there as it is in India, men still bind their female relatives and children to work for creditors whom they cannot repay.[22] But Women's Rights Movements have started, one of the earliest in Peru. And in Bolivia the left-wing Revolutionary Front had as its vice-president in 1978 Domitila Chungara, a miner's wife, who has written a book to publicize the miners' plight.[23]

It was because in the twentieth century full feudalism had not evolved in many areas in Africa south of the Sahara that women there sometimes opposed colonialism on their own initiative. The women still had their own societies linked all over the continent through their markets. Their manufacturing skills were still acknowledged.

European colonial rule was more recent here than in India and, as in China, was mainly used to exploit resources indirectly through concessions obtained almost always from native men whom the

Europeans maintained in power or put in power sometimes against the wishes of the people. The Europeans in the twentieth century no more understood the economic importance of African women, nor that men sometimes wielded power on their behalf or derived power from their mothers and sisters and at least consulted them, than their ancestors had done in the fifteenth.

The cocoa, cotton, palm oil and other commodities which had been staples of the African barter trade were now sold to Europeans who gave help both in growing these cash crops and in developing family farming – help that is to men, but not to the traditional farmers, the women, who were the custodians of ancient methods and used a slow working rhythm. Their aim was subsistence rather than profit. They were said to be less open to new technological ideas than men. But men too have not readily agreed to give up a farming system in which women do most of the work for one in which they have to do a great deal more. Their resistance to the 'sales talk' of government agents has been overcome by the cash paid to them for surpluses they grow under more modern cultivation methods. Their independent cash income broke the economic power and importance of the women who became poorer as the men grew richer. It is interesting to note that this was the reverse of the Russian and Chinese Communist policies by which the depressed women were given cash incomes.

Women sometimes tried to take up the cultivation of cash crops but the European authorities discouraged them. In Uganda, for example, they began cultivating cotton. But in 1923 the British Director of Agriculture decreed that this 'could not be left to women and old people.' A decade later a majority of the men were growing not only cotton but also coffee, and were importing hired labour from other less advanced tribes to do most of the work for them just as in India. European policies of instructing only men and ignoring women had particularly unfortunate results when the scale of emigration to other regions increased.[25] Women left to carry on traditional farming and crafts remained illiterate to a greater extent than men. In a society in which literacy does not count for much but other skills count for a good deal, lack of it does not greatly undermine status. Such was the case among the women of Buddhist Burma, Java and Bali, as we have seen pages 86–8). But in the new European-style economy which was being imposed on tribal Africa, making a livelihood increasingly depended on literacy and those who lacked it, that is the women rather than the men, were at the greatest disadvantage.

In non-Moslem parts of Nigeria, women's societies were invoked to organize resistance on three occasions in the 1920s: the Dancing Women of 1925, the Spirit Movement in 1927 and the Aba Riots in 1929. These last began in Owerri Province in the heart of the Nigerian Ibo country when the British attempted to assess what they considered to be the people's taxable wealth. Everything was lumped together on the British model as pertaining to males, including the women, children and domestic animals.

Despite the assurances of the British Resident at Port Harcourt that the women, 'the trees that bear fruit', were not to be taxed, the women remained suspicious and the mobilization spread and spread. About ten thousand women converged on Aba, an important trading centre and 'proceeded to attack and loot the European trading stores and Barclay's Bank, and to break into the prison and release the prisoners'. Similar attacks were made on factories and other buildings at railway stations and trading centres. On two occasions when the women attacked police and troops, they were met with fire from rifles and a Lewis gun. A total of 50 were killed and 50 wounded. They forced the British to give them assurances that their property rights were safe and to abandon the idea of assessing the women's livestock and property for tax purposes.

The British were by no means the harshest of the colonial powers in Africa. But after the Second World War they faced similar trouble in 1955 in the British Cameroons among the Kom, Bafut and Nsaw women when, to prevent soil erosion, they ordered the women to make their soil beds for planting crops horizontal to the hill slopes instead of in the traditional vertical fashion. In this instance they were trying to introduce better cultivation methods to the women. But the women were unco-operative. An inexperienced and impatient British official uprooted their crops and the revolt began.[26]

Where African women south of the Sahara still had great economic importance, they used their traditional societies to establish their rights once independence was gained. For example the women of Guinea-Bissau successfully pressurized President Sekou-Touré into passing measures they wanted.[27]

The old colonial powers, which include Russia and China, have a sense of guilt towards their former colonies, or they want to maintain advantageous economic links with them. Hence the result has sometimes been an acceptance of tyrannical male rulers, and sometimes even outright support for them against popular feeling. 'Aid' is sometimes accompanied by acquiescence even a romanticizing of brutality, of 'machismo', and has weakened women's efforts to improve their economic status.

But the really great tragedy resulting from colonialism and economic imperialism has been encouragement to abandon a subsistence economy in which people managed to survive, for the growing of cash crops which leave them dependent on imported food. Consequently they are open to pressures from advanced-technology countries not necessarily in their best interests, especially not those of women whose economic independence suffers more than that of men.

NOTES

1 Nehru, *The Discovery of India*, 27–9; Nayer in B. E. Ward ed., *Women in the New Asia*, 208–11, see also 496–7; *Rep. of the Status of Women Committee of India*, Dec. 1974, 238–9; Minority Rights Group *Rep. No. 27, Arab Women* (revised ed.), 6–8; Snow, *Red Star Over China*, 25–39.

2 Davin, *Woman-Work*, 8–16, 34–5, 116 n. 1; Han Suyin, *Destination Chungking*, 24–5.

3 Mao Tse Tung, *Quotations* ('The Little Red Book'), 294–5 from 'Rep. of an Investigation of the Peasant Movement in Hunan, March 1927', in *Selected Works*, vol. i, 44–6.

4 E. Snow, op. cit., 286, 289–91; D. Davin, op. cit., 40–3, 57, 74–7; The *ratio* of women's to men's earnings before the Revolution seems to have been similar to that in the West. In Shanghai and Hankow their average maxima was just under 50 per cent that of men: in Wusih, Soochow and Wuchan it was a good deal above 50 per cent as were the minima in Shanghai, Hankow, Wusih and Soochow: child labour was very much cheaper than that of adults. See *International Lab. Rev.*, vol. 23, 1931, 854.

5 Felix Greene, *The Wall Has Two Sides*, 118; Dumont, *ILO Women Workers and Society*, 45.

6 Davin, 84ff; Snow, *China's Long Revolution*, 46–7.

7 Mao Tse Tung, *Quotations*, 298 from 'The Socialist Upsurge in the Countryside'.

8 Joan Robinson, *Economic Management in China*, 11.

9 Greene, 115, 124, 161 (personal history of Mrs Chang).

10 *China Pictorial*, e.g. 1976, No. 2, 20, 5; No. 3, 12–15, 24–7, 30–5, etc.

11 Davin, 178–9.

12 ibid., 168–72; Robinson, 35–6; Gittings, *A Chinese View of China*, 152–3, 156, 165–72.

13 Wei Yung Sheng in *China Reconstructs*, Feb. 1975, vol. xxiv; Greene, 167.

14 *Economist*, 12 Aug. 1978, 'Where Serfs Are Taking On The Sahibs'; *Rep. of the Committee on the Status of Women in India*, 1974, 150, paras. 5.7–5.10; Table vii, p. 159.

15 Purcell and Hallsworth, *TUC Rep. on Labour Conditions in India*, 34–5; P. Fraser, MD, *Slavery on British Territory*, booklet, 28–9.

16 *Rep. of the Committee on the Status of Women in India*, 149–51, paras. 5.6, 5.10–5.12; 153, paras. 5.24–5.27; 178, paras. 5.115–5.126; 181, paras. 5.130, 5.134; 188–91, paras. 5.158–5.161, 5.167, 5.174–5.175; 199, paras. 5.196–5.199; J. Nehru, op. cit., 360; A. A. Purcell and J. Hallsworth, op. cit., 25; *ILO Rev.*, vol. liii, nos. 1–2, Jan.–Feb. 1946, Indian Labour Welfare; Coal Mining in the State of Hyderabad, 103–5; *ILO Coal Mines Committee Rep.*, Geneva 1947, 2nd session.

17 Boserup, *Woman's Role in Economic Development*, 75.

18 *Rep. of the Committee on the Status of Women in India*, 10, Table 1; 191–3, paras. 5.177, 5.179, 5.182, 5.184; 199–200, paras. 5.199–5.205; 201; 238–9; Masumdar, 'About Women in Patrilocal Societies in South Asia', in A. Appadorai ed., *The Status of Women in South Asia*, 56, 61–2; K. S. Bhatnagar, *Dikpatura, Village Survey, Census of India*, 1961, Pt vi, Monographs, No. 4, Madhya Pradesh, 61–2, 65.

19 *Minority Rights Group Rep.*, No. 27, (revised ed.), 4–7, 9, 11–16. Anthony McDermott, T. Petran: *TV World*, June 1978.

20 Majumdar, 51; Tillion, *Algeria; The Realities*, 38 n. 1, 58; Greenidge, *Slavery*, 34, 36–43, 46, 54 quoting Emanuel La Gravière; British Anti-Slavery Society, *Slavery Today*, 9 Jan. 1975, 1, 'Cruel Ring' punishment of a Yemeni slave wife who tried to run away; also pp. 2–3; *The Sunday Telegraph*, 17, 24 March 1963; Boserup, 45–6, 'the legal ban on slavery introduced by European colonial powers provided an incentive for men to marry girls whom otherwise they might have kept as slaves'; *Minority Rights Group Rep.*, No. 27, 10, quoting *People*, vol. 2, No. 1, 1975; 14, 17, n. 17, quoting Fadela M. Rabat, *La Femme Algérienne*; *Slavery Today*, 9 Jan. 1975; 1, reprint of article by Anne Balfour-Fraser from *The Baptist Times*; Patrick Montgomery, *The Contemporary Review*, vol. 223, Aug. 1973; he points out that Jomo Kenyatta in *Facing Mount Kenya* defended the less severe forms of female circumcision as important to Kikuyu nationalism.

21 Fox in Ward ed., *Women in the New Asia*, 343–4, 351.

22 Greenidge, 75ff; ILO Inter-Agency Rep., *Towards Full Employment*, 1970, 67.

23 *The Guardian*, 15 June 1978, 7.

24 Boserup, 19, 54–5, 60–1; Tothill ed., *Agriculture in the Sudan*, 245; de Schlippe, *Shifting Cultivation in Africa*, 145; Aventurin in *ILO Women Workers and Society*, 36; Guy Standing, *International Lab. Rev.*, vol. 114,

No. 3, Nov.–Dec. 1976, 28; A. I. Richards, 'Mother-Right Among the Central Bantu', in *Essays Presented to C. G. Seligmann*, eds. Evans-Pritchard, Firth, Malinowski, Schapera, 279; Kaberry, *Women of the Grassfields*, 137–8.
25 Leith Ross, *African Women*, 22ff, quoting Marjorie Perham, *Native Administration in Nigeria*.
26 Ritzenthaler, 'Anlu: A Women's Uprising in the British Cameroons', *African Studies*, No. 1, 1960, 151ff.
27 Mrs Krishna Swami, Commonwealth Secretariat, London.

Chapter 16

WOMEN'S LIBERATION AND THE NEW
TECHNOLOGICAL REVOLUTION

The world picture of women workers in the late 1960s and early 1970s was that in most countries they were of considerable importance in the labour force. The message of the accompanying Table 19 giving a few examples of the proportions of women occupied in various broad categories of work, is that with the technologies most of the world is currently using, most countries could not do without female labour. In respect of women workers, the world may be divided up roughly into three: countries in which women account for about half of those occupied in non-domestic work, countries in which women account for about a third of those so occupied and those in which they account for less than a quarter. Within these overall categories, there are considerable differences in kinds of work done by women. There are what might be called the 'clerical-service countries' as opposed to agricultural and manufacturing countries, that is places where women make up much higher proportions of the labour force in these forms of work. The 'service' category comprises medical, teaching and even, in some cases, sporting services as well as the more obvious hotel, catering, shop and domestic service. In general terms of the five categories of work shown in Table 19 in the 1960s and 1970s, manufacturing was least important and the conglomerate 'service' work the most important.

Not only in agriculture, forestry and fishing but also in manufacturing industry and commerce, socialist and African and Asian countries had larger proportions of women in their workforces than some of the leading capitalist countries. On the other hand, India and the Arab countries generally supplied examples of the smallest proportion of women workers. But it is not clear how far this is because their work in agriculture and handicrafts for their families was simply ignored as in the cases of Algeria and Mexico.[1]

On the question of work gradings, high-technology capitalist countries are not at the top in respect of administrative and managerial grades, but come out on top in respect of the lower-graded wage-earners. Countries that are sparsely populated like Finland have high proportions of women among their administrators and managers. But so have countries like Brazil and Argentina which have still not shaken off a feudal past. For in these, class is more important than sex and the high numbers of women in these categories is partly due to the fact that large numbers of poor *men* are not obtaining higher education and so lack the chances of top jobs.[2]

Countries with the most complex modern technologies co-exist with places in Africa, South America and Oceania and pockets elsewhere, where women carry on hunting, gathering, hoe-farming and marketing their produce – places where they have maintained their economic importance and, with it, a good deal of independence. But in many cases their independence and status have been undermined by the commercialization of the bride price, by the dowry system, by the growth of wife slavery and sometimes by polygamy on a scale which leaves them very insecure. The work of large numbers of women in feudal Hindu, Buddhist and Moslem areas still consists of hard physical labour for their families in agriculture, handicrafts and trades and the vast majority of them are unequivocally in the power of some man.

THE POPULATION 'EXPLOSION'

The renewed women's rights movement of the mid-twentieth century began in highly propitious circumstances when labour was short. But there were anxieties by the late 1960s about a population 'explosion' and its relationship to food and power resources, as the 1974 United Nations Conference on Population and Economic Development showed. At that time, France, Austria, part of European Russia, Burma and many African countries considered that they were under-populated. Under-population, not over-population concerned two Latin American countries, Bolivia and Chile. In the spreading shanty towns around some Latin American and African cities, population growth is checked by a high infantile mortality rate and short life expectancy. The mere movement of peasant women in search of work into towns does not, as has been suggested, reduce the birth rate.[3] It does this only among the better-educated urban women who have regular jobs and hence expecta-

Table 19 Women as a Percentage of the Total Workforce in Various Occupations in Different Countries, 1966–76

In some of the countries in which they were of most importance:

Country	Agriculture, Forestry and Fishing	Country	Manufacturing Industry	Country
Romania	57·26	Thailand	50·20	Czechoslovakia
Poland	52·84	Philippines	46·86	Sweden
Fed. Rep. of Germany	52·71	Czechoslovakia	44·87	USA
USSR	52·37	German Dem. Rep.	42·99	Canada
Tanzania	51·12	Indonesia	42·62	Switzerland
Thailand	49·73	USSR	39·72	Hungary
Japan	49·14	Rep. of Korea	38·13	Australia
German Dem. Rep.	44·90			France
		Japan	36·51	
Czechoslovakia	44·23	Ghana	35·15	UK
New Caledonia	42·86	Greenland	35·00	Poland
Rep. of Korea	42·64	Iran	34·44	Greenland
Ghana	42·40	USA	30·37	Israel
				· New Caledonia

In some of the countries in which they were of least importance apparently:

Iran	2·24	Kuwait	1·25	India
Egypt	3·91	Egypt	3·06	Algeria
Cuba	4·94	Algeria	4·11	Indonesia
Mexico	6·32	Rep. of SA	7·14	Kuwait
Argentina	6·61	Libya	9·09	Egypt
Spain	10·60	India	12·87	Syria
				Ghana

*Countries with a large hotel trade.

Source: *ILO 1977 Yearbook of Labour Statistics*, Tables 2a and 2b.

Clerical Work	Country	Service Work	Country	Commerce
83·04	Greenland	90·91	Ghana	87·53
79·07	New Caledonia	80·00	USSR	73·54
78·89	Jamaica	79·37*	Brazil	71·63
			Poland	70·44
74·94	Sweden	77·88		
			Czechoslovakia	69·86
66·85	Poland	76·05		
			German Dem. Rep.	68·05
66·85	Czechoslovakia	73·43		
63·86	Brazil	71·63	Philippines	61·41
62·50	Hungary	70·49	Thailand	56·12
			Fed. Rep. of Germany	55·94
60·31	France	70·20*		
60·27	Switzerland	69·76*	Switzerland	55·13
60·00	UK	69·32	UK	53·63
54·59	USA	61·59	Sweden	51·69
50·00				

Clerical Work	Country	Service Work	Country	Commerce
4·02	Zambia	9·33	Iran	0·77
5·00	Syria	12·50	Algeria	2·19
10·15	Egypt	13·47	Morocco	4·48
10·15	Iran	15·34	Tunisia	5·94
10·31	Algeria	15·38	Egypt	6·16
12·63	India	16·66	India	6·14
15·91	Greece	20·99	Tanzania	10·00

tions of higher living standards and of greater security. Among the poor, children as potential workers still seem to carry the best hope of warding off destitution and of help in sickness, just as they did in west Europe in former days. The problem has been the uneven distribution of wealth both within countries and internationally. The conference, as many countries pointed out, was not just about population, but also economic development.

THE WOMEN'S MOVEMENT WORLD-WIDE

It was pressure from women in the capitalist countries particularly that prompted the United Nations to designate 1975 as International Women's Year to encourage member countries to introduce measures to help women to equality as citizens and workers. It was a moment of high hopes for women. Some countries for the first time began to apply the United Nations Charter principle of equal rights for all, irrespective of race, religion or sex.

The affluent capitalist states have dominated the mass media so that the publicizing and promotion of Women's Liberation has tended to be in terms of the issues uppermost in the thoughts of the most literate women in these countries. On the one hand only a small minority of such women are living below subsistence level and, on the other, only a small minority of women in non-industrialized world have bras to burn. Priorities are different. The Women's Movement in capitalist high-technology countries has been slow to realize that there is something to be learnt from women in much earlier cultures who have gained high-graded jobs and official government posts more easily than they have done. In some the lesson of the last 8000 years is still visible – that women's social status is dependent primarily not upon their working but upon their economic independence and freedom, just as in the case of men. When women turned to enslaving others, when they themselves became objects of commerce through the bride price or dowry systems, when men took from them the most highly regarded of their manufacturing jobs, and their marketing functions, they lost, to a great extent, acknowledgement of the value of the vast amount of work they continued to do.

In heavily urbanized countries, the crux of the whole inferior status of women was less the work they did outside their homes than the work they did inside. It was here that the traces of the old slavery, of being in the possession of a male, lingered. Two forces were establishing a value for this kind of women's work. One was the law.[4] The other was men's acceptance of a share of responsibility for domestic and child-care work. They are thus not only easing women's work, they are undermining the employers' argument that one reason for not giving women higher-graded jobs is because of their extra absenteeism due to their family responsibilities.[5] The trend has been encouraged by anthropologists who have questioned the desirability of a total dependence of a child on its mother. They have pointed out that children grow up better in countries with communities intact which show concern for them and take an interest in their upbringing.[6]

Women in acquiescing in their total responsibility for their children have become, in advanced-technology countries, the victims of their own mass media which some of them help to operate. The role fitted in with their search for an easier as well as a more secure life.

There have nevertheless been some unlooked-for developments in women's work in capitalist high-technology countries. Women in general had never given up gardening, including the growing of herbs and vegetables, and poultry-keeping and continued these occupations in suburban gardens. Some of the middle class in the 1970s turned to old handicrafts, going to pottery, weaving, upholstery and carpentry classes. An Act in Britain in 1976 against discrimination on grounds of sex, was followed by the appearance of a few women in the building trade. Similarly in the United States by 1978 about 1700 women had gone of their own free choice to work underground in the now mechanized coal mines of Pennsylvania, but here they had the motive of high pay.[7] One after another current male monopolies are being breached.

Following International Women's Year, women in advanced-technology capitalist countries have realized that legislation in itself accomplishes little. It merely creates the possibility of change. Girls in such countries have still to fight their way into higher education and higher-graded jobs. Women must still fight equal pay claims in the courts and the courts have not always been sympathetic.[8]

WOMEN WORKERS AND THE WORLD ECONOMIC CRISIS
By 1975, however, the great employment boom which had built up virtually ever since re-armament began in the mid-1930s, was collapsing. Unemployment was growing in all high-technology

Table 20   Grades of Women Workers in Various Countries, 1960s and 1970s

Women as a Proportion of all those Economically Active			Women as a Proportion of all Employers and those Working on their Own Account			Women as of all

In some of the countries in which they were of most importance

Country	Year	Per Cent	Country	Year	Per Cent	Country
USSR	1970	50·45	Romania	1966	57·87	Fed. Rep. of Germany
Tanzania	1967	47·79	Poland	1974	55·29	Japan
Bulgaria	1975	46·81	Ghana	1970	53·04	Norway
German Dem. Rep.	1971	46·27	Tanzania	1967	52·88	USA
Poland	1974	46·17	Czecho-slovakia	1970	46·88	Belgium
Finland	1976	45·46	Finland	1976	39·31	Netherlands
Romania	1966	45·23	Bulgaria	1975	30·00	Israel
Czecho-slovakia	1970	44·58	Japan	1976	29·76	Greece
Ghana	1970	44·18	Hungary	1976	29·36	Australia
Hungary	1976	43·72	Belgium	1976	24·69	Italy
USA	1976	39·75	Indonesia	1971	24·37	New Caledonia
Thailand	1976	38·44	Thailand	1976	24·12	Ghana
Japan	1976	37·37	USA	1976	22·45	Switzerland
UK	1971	36·52	Fed. Rep. of Germany	1975	20·72	Thailand
Yugoslavia	1971	36·03	Chile	1970	20·45	Yugoslavia
			UK	1971	20·13	Hungary Finland

Source: *ILO 1977 Yearbook of Labour Statistics*, Tables 2a and 2b.

a Proportion Wage-Earners			Women as a Proportion of all Salaried Workers			Women as a Proportion of all Administrative and Managerial Grades	
Year	Per Cent	Country	Year	Per Cent	Country	Year	Per Cent
1975	85·29	USSR	1970	49·18	USSR	1970	63·57
1976	79·96	Finland	1976	46·67	Poland	1974	47·28
1976	79·71	Bulgaria	1975	46·08	Brazil	1974	46·75
1976	79·25	Czecho-slovakia	1970	43·81	Argentine	1974	46·63
1976	77·21	Denmark	1975	42·91	Sweden	1974	46·27
1971	75·40	Hungary	1976	42·79	Israel	1976	43·82
1976	75·00	Poland	1974	41·94	Romania	1966	43·40
1971	69·02	USA	1976	40·73	Chile	1970	42·98
1971	68·75	Norway	1976	39·87	Australia	1971	42·27
1976	66·72	UK	1971	38·05	Czecho-slovakia	1970	41·59
1976	66·67	Israel	1976	35·32	Greenland	1970	40.00
1970	66·67	Switzerland	1970	35·00	Canada	1970	39·86
1970	66·42	Belgium	1976	33·44	Rep. of SA	1970	38·18
1976	65·94	Australia	1971	32·81	France	1970	37·21
1971	65·41	Japan	1971	32·41	USA	1976	33·65
1976	60·75	Thailand	1976	31·80	UK	1971	30·88
1976	60·00						

countries. The United States had over-extended itself economically. In the gathering slump in 1973 the Arab oil-exporting states
suddenly acted together to raise the world price of their staple
export, thus setting an example to every country dependent on
exporting much-wanted raw materials.

Into this situation was thrown a new bomb-shell, the micro-
electronic revolution, the development mainly in the United States
and Japan of a minute computer at cheap mass-production rates
which would take over precisely those forms of work which had
provided the great post-war boom in jobs for women in high-
technology countries, that is in clerical work, including much of
banking, insurance and distribution, the very means by which they
had escaped from domestic service. (See Table 19.) The amount
of work they are likely to gain in producing these silicon chips
as an extension of their skill in transistorization is not likely to
compensate for the jobs they will lose. Moreover men will lose
work too. Meanwhile rivalry for work between the industrial West
and the Third World is growing largely because Western manufacturers are turning to cheaper land, services and labour in non-
industrialized countries.

The manufacture of silicon chips creates problems for eastern
women. Just as in the first of the modern Industrial Revolutions
country girls as well as those from the poorest and most desperate
social groups are being enticed into this work and kept docile by
Western mass media methods. The job, however, is by its very nature
temporary, since after 3–4 years of micro-miniaturization they start
to develop eye-trouble and have to leave, their lives disrupted.[9]

People opting to remain passive will have the micro-chip revolution thrust on them. They will then look bleakly forward to a future
in which a small labour force manufactures everything that the
owners and controllers of the technology think necessary. The state
of technology is now such that applied thoughtfully and selectively
it could go a long way to freeing every single human being from
want and a life spent in gruelling toil. But the criterion is too often
not 'to achieve levels of human welfare compatible with the dignity
of man ...', let alone woman, but rather the accumulation of
immense private profit and political advantage.

Moreover the application of technology is bounded by the
natural resources it consumes and its destruction of the natural
environment. Nobody can eat silicon chips, nor keep warm by

feeding commercial and governmental information into computers. The crying need of many millions of people is for food.

The volume of protest about what high technology is doing to our planet has been growing ever since the end of the Second World War and the advent of nuclear power. Some part of the uprising of Paris students in May 1968 queried industrialism itself.[10]

New questions have arisen about who is to determine the value of work and of products, and why the price to be paid for improved health and welfare must so often be urban slums and unemployment. There has been a tendency, even among some of the economists writing for the International Labour Organisation, to define work as 'work' only if it consists of the production of up-to-date manufactured goods or services and is easily quantifiable through their own data processing machines. In order to sustain modern industry which produces much less of necessities such as shelter, clothing and food, but more luxuries and non-essentials, a greatly increased agricultural production is extracted from a diminishing number of people. Those displaced have to find other means of supporting themselves and of earning enough to buy food, clothing and shelter they formerly produced themselves. Hunting and gathering peoples, the Brazilian Indians, Australian aborigines, African Pygmies and the San people have not rated at all against the interests of those searching for land off which to live themselves by farming or exploiting deposits of raw materials. Among hoe farmers, some economists have labelled people 'idle' not only if they are at their places of work but not actually working, but because their products are of an unacceptably low value to the high-technology countries these economists represented.[11] In a world that is short of food and necessities, they have ignored the invaluable work of masses of people – the majority of whom in some areas are women – in feeding, clothing and providing shelter for themselves and their families. They are dismissed as 'unpaid family labour'. This is to preserve the basis of the under-valuation of women's work. In view of the importance of women in farm work, the denigration of the peasant is to a large extent the denigration of women.[12] The economic experts from high-technology countries have not yet advanced to 'the study of economics as if people matter'.[13]

There is, however, a third option. No one wants to return to the drudgery and the insanitary living conditions of the past. But

Table 21 Attitudes of Various Countries to Population (United Nations Conference on Population and Economic Development, Bucharest, August 1974)

Countries that Considered they were under-populated		Countries that Considered they were over-populated		Uncommitted countries
Industrialized	Semi-Industrialized	Non-Industrialized	Semi-Industrialized	Industrialized	Non-Industrialized
	Austria	Angola	Portugal	Britain	Nepal	Ethiopia
	Bolivia	N. Yemen		USA	Barbados	Australia
	Chile	Lesotho		Japan	Malaysia	Khmer Repub.
	Albania	Botswana			Dominican Repub.	Equatorial Guinea
	Byelo-Russia	Niger			Guinea-Bissau	Syria
	Romania	Burma			Kenya	
	France*	Zambia			Madagascar	
	China*	Chad			Thailand	
		Nigeria			Bangladesh	
		Mauretania			S. Yemen	
		Congo				

*At the Conference, China and the Vatican both pressed the view that over-population was not a problem. China and France subsequently changed to a concern over their overpopulation. Chinese attitudes to population since the Revolution seem to have fluctuated, cf. Felix Greene, *The Wall Has Two Sides*, 302 with E Snow, *China's Long Revolution*, 45–9.

those who have challenged advanced technology propose instead 'intermediate technology', work that is more labour intensive, foreshadowed perhaps by the farming and small-scale industry of kibbutz and Chinese commune, a technology in which mechanization is not despised but is pursued with due regard to the limited resources of the world and in consultation with populations. Such a technology permits that contact with the natural world and its beauty which is the heritage of everyone.[14]

The majority of the world's women still work in the villages of Africa, Asia and South America and on the farms of central and Eastern Europe. For the majority of them intermediate technology would represent a tremendous advance.

There can be no freedom without economic independence and economic security. The principle holds good for women and children as for men. The human race has reached a point where a crucial choice must be made over technologies. The balance between population and resources, as well as between technology and resources can only be achieved by acknowledging women's importance as workers and individuals. Their work has helped to raise living standards in the past. Through their daily work now, and through their work in the councils of their peoples and of the world, women at all levels of technology from Stone Age to electronic are needed as much as men to devise the harmony and balance the world so badly needs. Indeed, without their participation as equals, no equilibrium is possible.

NOTES

1 *Rep. on the ILO, Economic Commission for Africa, World Young Women's Christian Assocn. and Swedish International Development Authority Workshop on Participation of Women in Handicrafts and Small Industries*, Zambia, 9–10 Dec. 1975; see Jasleen Dhamija, ILO Expert in Handicrafts Development, p. 78; Dhamija, 178–9; Elizaga, 139; Dumont, 46 in *ILO Women Workers and Society*; Cuha, *International Lab. Rev.*, vol. 109, no. 3, March 1974, 238–9.

2 Elizaga 140; but on p. 142 he states that the better off the family, the less likely a girl is to do paid work. Unless figures supplied to the ILO are wrong or some unusual job classification is used, well over 40 per cent of administrative- and managerial-grade workers are women in Brazil, the Argentine and Chile. See Table 20.

3 Concepcion, *International Lab. Rev.*, vol. 109, Nos. 5–6, May–June 1974, 503ff.

4 *Matrimonial Proceedings and Divorce Act*, 29 May 1970, ch. 45, sect. 5(1); sect. 37. *To Form a More Perfect Union*, 228–31. Of 46 States in the USA with 'some form of no-fault divorce, only nine recognize the "contribution of the home-maker" as a factor to be considered in economic arrangements in divorce. Pt. vi, Appendix, 341–8; *F Magazine*, Claude Servan-Schreiber ed., Dec. 1978, 40–1; *ILO Plan of Action on Equality of Opportunity and Treatment for Women Workers*.

5 Myrdal, 'Foreword', *The Changing Roles of Men and Women*, ed. Dahlstrom.

6 Rochelle P. Wortis in *The Women's Movement*, 32ff, Helen Wortis and Clara Rabinowitz eds.

7 *Women's Realm*, 10 June 1978, reprint of article in *McCall's Magazine*, 1977.

8 e.g. *Tribune*, 22 July 1977, Judge Kilner-Brown; *Equal Opportunities Commission Reps.* for cases fought in courts; *F Magazine*, Sept. 1978, 40–1; *To Form A More Perfect Union*, 190–1; Felice Morgenstern, *Women Workers and the Courts*, 53–62.

9 Grossmann, *South East Asia Chronicle and Pacific Rev.*, Sept. 1979.

10 Carpentier and Cazamian, *International Lab. Rev.*, Winter 1977, 68–71; Tchobanian, *International Lab. Rev.*, vol. 111, No. 3, March 1975, 199.

11 J. Mouly and E. Costa, *Employment Policies in Developing Countries*, 31; '. . . in developing countries many people attending their places of work may still be said to be under-employed either if they are idle for much of the time or *if, though they are continuously occupied, the product of their activity is of unacceptably low value.*'; and p. 64, 'Data from some Asian countries, notably Japan and India, suggest that comparing traditional with capital-intensive production the profits per unit of capital employed are not less and per unit of output are slightly higher in the former than in the latter.' i.e. in subsistence economies; Ahooja-Patel, *ILO Lab. Education*, No. 31, June 1976,

12 Elizaga, 129, 139; Standing, *International Lab. Rev.*, vol. 114, No. 3, Nov.–Dec. 1976, 28; Aventurin, *ILO Women Workers and Society*, 36.

13 E. F. Schumacher, *Small is Beautiful*, sub-title; International Labour Office Bull., *Women at Work*, No. 1, Autumn 1977, 23, summary of priorities agreed at the Conference of Ministers held in Lomé, Togo, 1972.

14 Studs Terkel, *Working*, Aunt Katherine Haynes, aged 77, who had been accustomed to working an 18-hour day, on the beauties of the North American fall, 48–9; Dhamija, *ILO Women Workers and Society*, 179.

Index

Abduction of women, 68
Abortion, 30–1
Ackermann, Jessie, quoted, 156–7
Africa, 19, 26, 51–3, 67–8, 77, 79,
   81–2, 95, 98, 115, 124–6, 137,
   260–2
Ainu, 19, 60, 66
Albania, 98
American Federation of Labor,
   186, 188
Amerindians, North: Alaska, 26;
   Chippewas, 40; Arizona, Plains,
   Seri, Omaha, New Mexico,
   Mayas, 47–8; Cherokee, 53;
   Navajo, Cheyenne, Virginia,
   Plains, Pueblos, Iroquois, 65–6;
   73, 95, 139, 144, 173–4
Amerindians, South: Botocudos,
   Pantagonians, 48; Yokaia, 49; 73;
   Caribs, 54; 73; 137; Brazilians,
   173–4, 260, 267
Andaman women, 48
Animals, domestication of, 44–6, 63
Animal husbandry, 106
Arabs, 107, 256–9, 274
Argentina, 267
Aristotle, quoted, 100
Artisans, see Crafts
Artists, women, 134
Asia: Turkoman, Kirghiz, Giliak of
   Sakhalin, Kamchatkans, Kal-
   mucks, 46, 48; 67, 72, 78–9, 81–4,
   95, 99, 110, 201–2, 257–9
Aspasia, 93
Assam, 124
Australia: Aboriginals, 19, 26, 41–2,
   48, 59, 61–2, 64–6, 96; Euro-
   peans, 156–7

Axes, 20

Baking, 94
Balkans, 84
Bantu, 51–3, 59–60, 66
Barbers, 96, 115
Bark cloth, 24–5
Bede, the Venerable, quoted, 114
Belt Cave, Caucasus, 49
Benin, 83
Berbers, 259
Birth, 77
Blindness, 131
Blood groups of peoples, 19
Bondwomen, 91–2, 110–11
Brewing, 54–5, 94, 107, 158; see also
   Innkeepers
Bricks, 96
Bride price, 63–4, 67–8, 73–4,
   79–80, 83, 267
Britain, 148ff, 172–3, 176–8, 184,
   188–90, 209–11, 213, 216, 218,
   234, 253, 261–2
Buddhism, 85, 88, 118, 267
Building, 47ff, 88, 235, 258, 271
Burmese, 86–8, 100, 124
By-industries, 131–2

Caedmon, 114
Cameroons, 51, 98, 124, 262
Camp followers, 111
Canals, 88
Cannibalism, 36
Capitalist farmers, women, 144–5
Caravans, 126
Carrying goods, methods of, 121
Cash crops, 138–9, 145, 261
Cato the elder, quoted, 79